I0722078

JAPANESE PRINTS IN TRANSITION

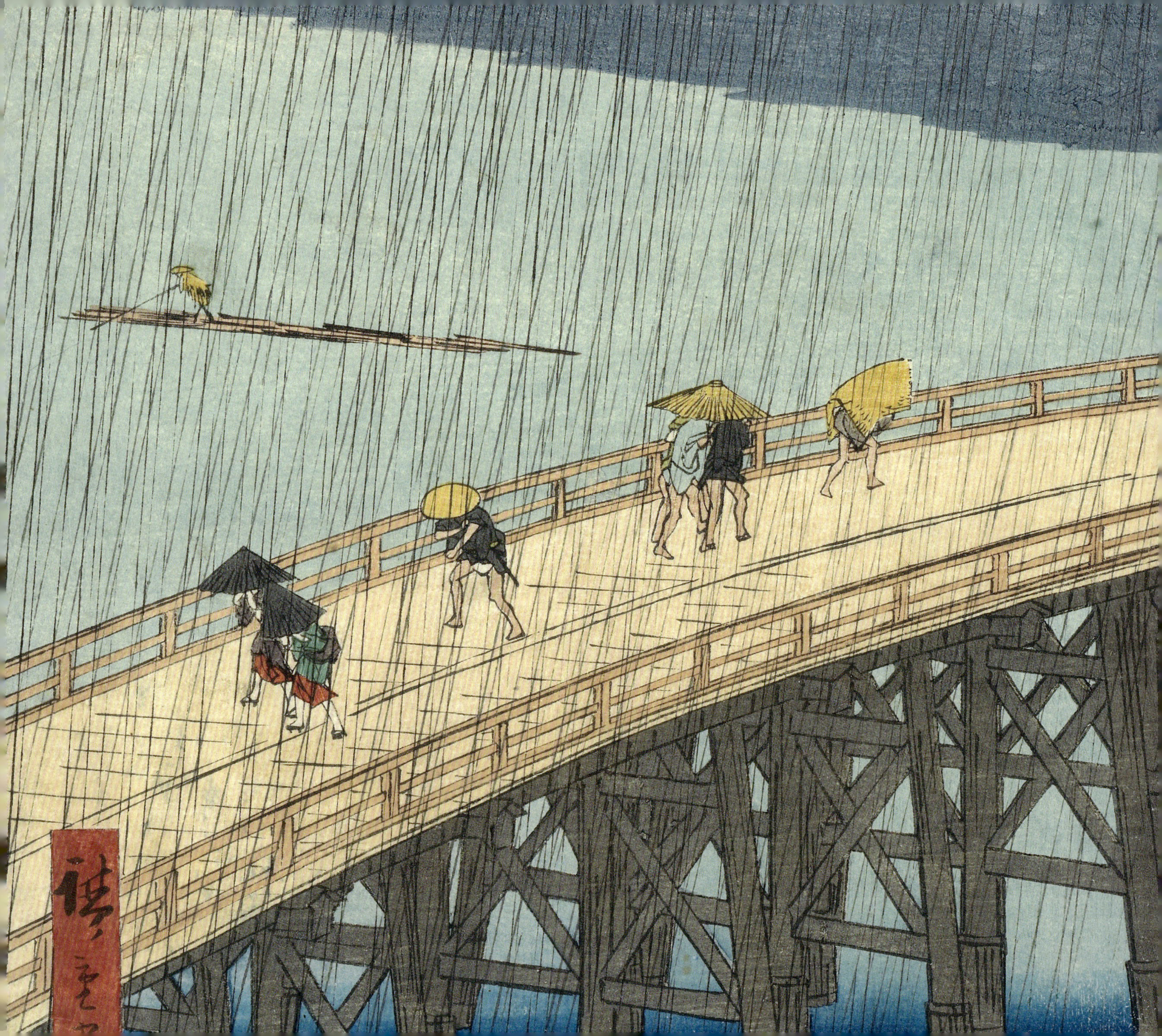

JAPANESE PRINTS IN TRANSITION
From the Floating World to the Modern World

Edited by KARIN BREUER

with an essay by RHIANNON PAGET

Fine Arts Museums of San Francisco and Cameron + Company

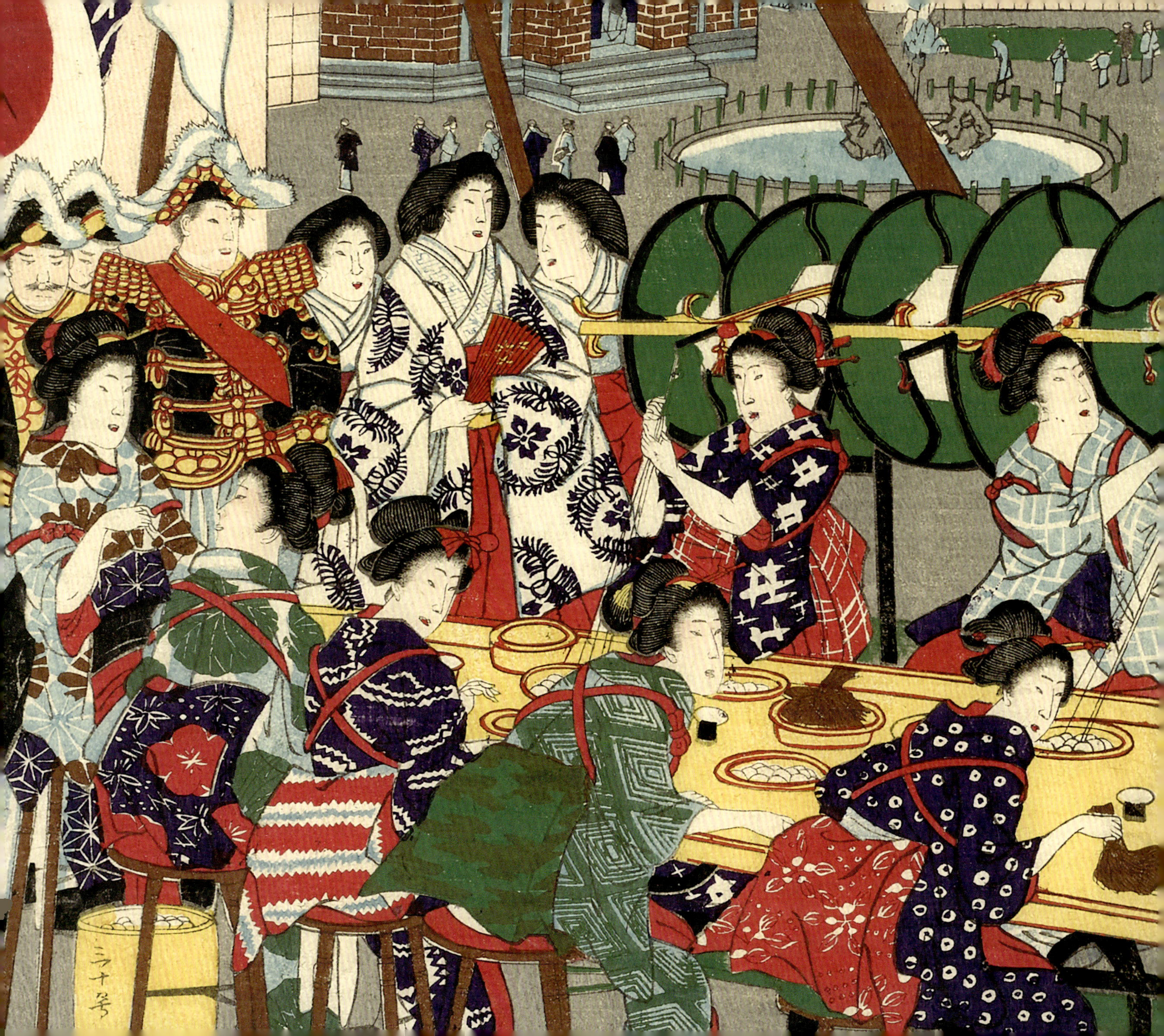

三十号

CONTENTS

DIRECTOR'S FOREWORD

Thomas P. Campbell

Director and CEO, Fine Arts Museums of San Francisco

ON MARCH 17, 1860, a delegation of Japanese dignitaries arrived in San Francisco aboard the *Kanrin Maru* and, later that month, another arrived aboard the USS *Powhatan*. The objective of the diplomatic mission was to bring the first Japanese embassy to the United States and to ratify the Treaty of Amity and Commerce between the two nations. After being entertained over the course of several days in the city, the delegation set sail for their East Coast destination of Washington, DC, where the treaty was signed.

Today, a monument commemorating the arrival of the *Kanrin Maru* stands on the north side of Lincoln Park, near the Legion of Honor. Erected in 1960, it stands in recognition of the efforts by Japan to engage with the West following Commodore Perry's 1853 arrival in the port of Yokohama, demanding that Japan end its two-centuries-old isolationist policy and open its ports to American trade.

The contact with the West that followed Perry's visit triggered social, political, and cultural changes in Japan that were reflected in the imagery of color woodcuts, the popular art form enjoyed by the Japanese for more than two centuries. The delicately colored images of Kabuki actors, courtesans, and scenic views, known as "ukiyo-e," gave way to a wealth of new subjects for artists to capture, including foreign customs and fashion, landscapes transformed by railroads and telegraph lines, and a modernized military led by an emperor determined to elevate Japan's status as a regional power.

This volume, expertly organized by curator Karin Breuer entirely from the Museums' permanent collection, captures this transformation in a chronological survey of prints that begins with color woodcuts of the late Edo period of shogunate rule, when they were eagerly consumed by a wide audience. The book's trajectory follows Japan's history after the overthrow of the shogun and restoration of the monarchy with examples of prints that chronicled current events — including samurai uprisings, popular Kabuki dramas, and sensational crimes. Many prints served as propaganda, celebrating imperial rule, depicting Emperor Meiji, and often the empress, outfitted in elegant Victorian attire overseeing the modernization of the military, industry, and education in the capital city, Tokyo, which itself had been transformed with new Western-style brick buildings, gas streetlights, and railway stations. Also included are color woodcuts designed by the eccentric artist Yoshitoshi, whose career spanned the late Edo period to the first two decades of the Meiji period, and whose representation in the Museums' collection is particularly strong. In a kind of postscript, this volume provides an opportunity to consider the prints — inspired by ukiyo-e — of contemporary artist Masami Teraoka. His subjects poke fun at the impacts of global fast-food culture on traditional Japanese society.

For her excellent essay in this publication, we are grateful to Japanese-art scholar Rhiannon Paget, curator of Asian art at the John and Mable Ringling Museum of Art in Sarasota, Florida. Paget enlightens readers on the development of subjects used in the production of color woodcuts in eighteenth- and nineteenth-century Japan. Through her scholarship and research, she provides explanations of the imagery in individual prints and how they were understood when first made, providing a better appreciation for today's readers and museum visitors.

We also thank the donors who helped make this project possible, including significant support from Carrick and Andy McLaughlin, and generous support from Paul A. Violich, and we acknowledge with gratitude the additional support provided by Alexandria and Dwight Ashdown and Sandra and Paul Bessières for helping us tell this fascinating story.

INTRODUCTION

Japanese Prints in the Achenbach Foundation for Graphic Arts

Karin Breuer

Curator in Charge, Achenbach Foundation for Graphic Arts, Fine Arts Museums of San Francisco

JAPANESE PRINTS constitute one of the notable collections within the Achenbach Foundation for Graphic Arts. Now numbering more than three thousand works, the collection consists primarily of ukiyo-e color woodcuts deriving from the late eighteenth century through the end of the nineteenth century. It also contains a number of *Yokohama-e* ("Yokohoma pictures," post-1859 images depicting non-Japanese foreigners in the port city), and prints from the Meiji era (1868–1912). Thanks to acquisitions made by Achenbach curator E. Gunter Troche in the early 1960s, Japanese prints of the first half of the twentieth century by artists of the *sōsaku hanga*, or "creative print" movement, are also included.

The collection began at the de Young in the early part of the twentieth century, when that museum welcomed Asian art into its holdings. Katherine M. Ball, one of the founders of the Japanese Society of America, and Carlotta Mabury, a San Francisco–based collector of Asian art and textiles, actively donated color woodcuts from their personal collections. The great traditional names of Japanese ukiyo-e, such as Kitagawa Utamaro, Katsushika Hokusai, and Utagawa Hiroshige, among others, were the focus of Mabury's and Ball's collecting efforts when they were forming their respective extensive holdings in the early 1900s. Many of the prints they donated to the de Young are identifiable by their distinctive collector's ink stamps, small stylized marks designed to resemble Japanese emblems.

Through the efforts of the Society for Asian Art, a museum-support council founded in 1958, the collection grew at the de Young museum until 1964, when it was transferred to the Achenbach Foundation at the Legion of Honor.[1]

The Achenbach's Japanese print holdings, many of which had been acquired by Moore S. Achenbach, and its collection of modern Japanese prints, primarily acquired by curator Troche, was three thousand works strong but not fully understood and, as a result, was seldom exhibited. This was remedied in 1984 when the Achenbach received a National Endowment for the Arts grant to allow Roger Keyes, a renowned Japanese print scholar, to catalogue the collection. In addition to creating a fully researched (pre-computer era) inventory of the prints, Keyes can also be credited with introducing a more expansive understanding of the entire history of Japanese printmaking — beyond ukiyo-e — to Achenbach curators and interested audiences. Via his scholarship, teaching, and encouragement, whole areas of Japanese prints such as *surimono* (privately printed, often luxurious prints made for poetry groups); erotic prints, known as *shunga*; Osaka actor portraits; and late nineteenth-century Meiji prints were added to the collection.

Another reason the collection was seldom shown was the requirement that Japanese prints be exhibited infrequently to preserve their color and prevent fading. A survey assessing the print color and condition of all the prints was conducted simultaneously with the 1984–1985 cataloguing project by distinguished paper conservator Keiko Keyes. Her survey data continues to enable curators to select judiciously from among the collection holdings for their exhibitions. In the late 1980s, Roger Keyes organized two important exhibitions in the Achenbach gallery at the Legion of Honor: *Break with the Past: The Japanese Creative Print Movement 1910–1960* (1988) and *Rage, Power, and Fulfillment: The Male Journey in Japanese Prints* (1989). In the 1995 exhibition and publication *Treasures of the Achenbach Foundation for Graphic Arts*, Japanese prints were identified as a special collection within the Achenbach, and a small, representative group was highlighted. Another fifteen years passed before the aspects of the collection were seen again in the 2010 exhibition *Japanesque: The Japanese Print in the Era of Impressionism*. In that presentation, Japanese prints were paired with the European and American prints that had been inspired by them. This publication, an overview of the transition from ukiyo-e to Meiji-era prints, provides yet another rare opportunity to enjoy selections from the Achenbach's holdings of Japanese color woodcuts.

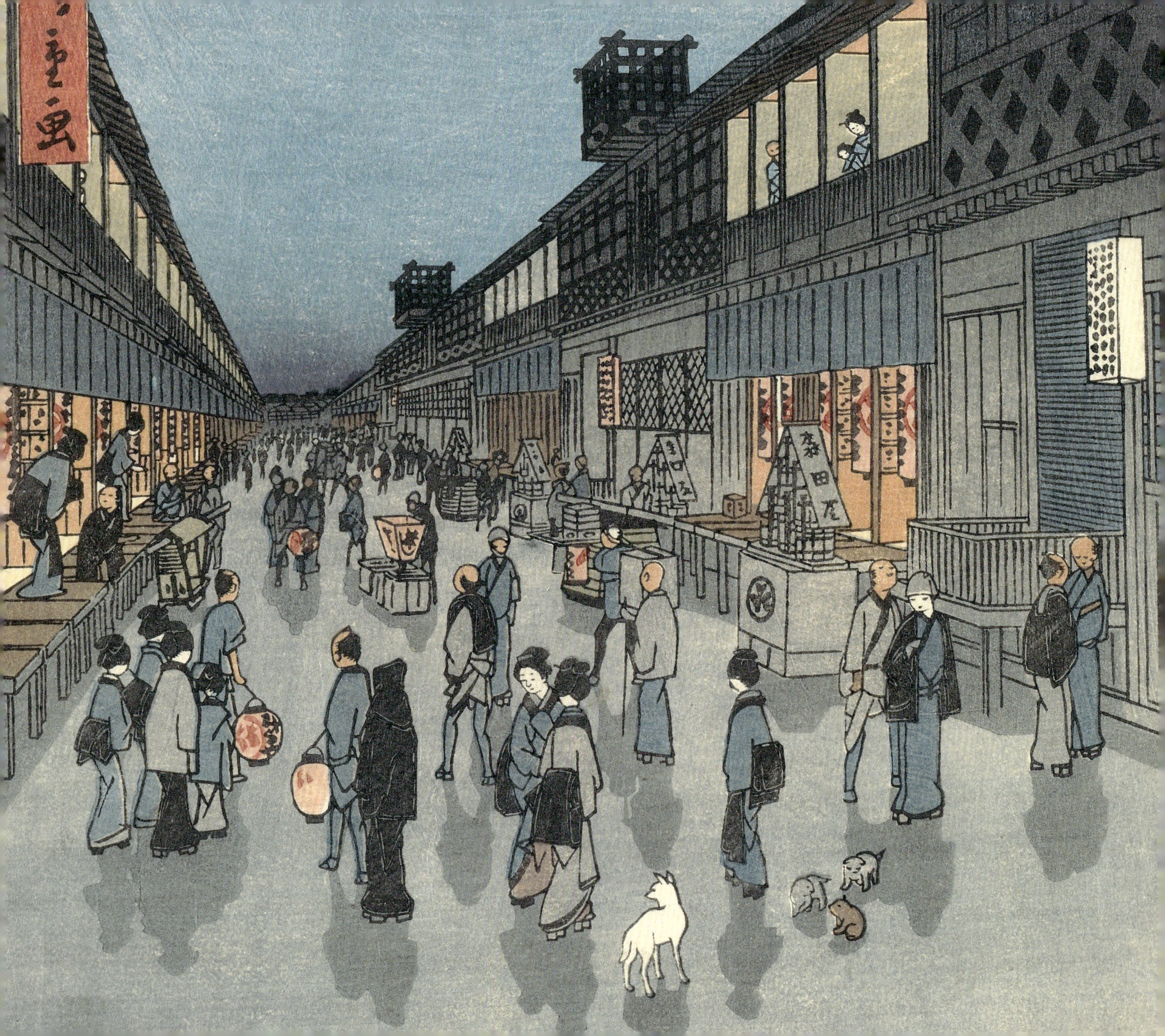
廣重画

JAPANESE PRINTS IN TRANSITION

From the Floating World to the Modern World

Rhiannon Paget

ONCEPTUALLY RICH and technically refined, the woodblock print flourished in Japan between the mid-Edo period (1615–1868) and early Meiji era (1868–1912), mainly in the city of Edo, now known as Tokyo. When the first shogun, Tokugawa Ieyasu, came to power in 1603, he established the provincial fishing village of Edo as the seat of his government. All Europeans, except for the Dutch, who were trusted not to proselytize the locals, were expelled from the country, and Japan's borders were closed. Foreign trade was restricted to the Netherlands, China, Korea, and the Ryūkyū Kingdom (present-day Okinawa). By the first decades of the 1700s, Edo's population had reached one million people, making it the largest city in the world at that time. In the name of maintaining order, the shogunate adopted neo-Confucianism as its state ideology and stratified society into four classes: warriors and nobility at the top, followed by farmers, artisans, and, at the bottom, merchants.

Despite its low status, the merchant class flourished economically, and as producers, consumers, and subjects of the arts, it would profoundly shape the culture of the Edo period. By the second half of the seventeenth century, people all over Japan had access to woodblock-printed books, from travel guides to erotic fiction, that took the Edo metropolis as their source material. New genres of painting featured fashionably dressed prostitutes, Kabuki actors, and scenes of urban merrymaking—the "floating world," or *ukiyo* (fig. 1). Originally a Buddhist term referring to the transitory realm of desire and suffering, *ukiyo* began to be applied to the fleeting pleasures and diversions of urban commoners.[1] Around the 1680s, publishers began to issue a new kind of product: pictures that were sold as single-sheet prints. Designed by pioneering artists Hishikawa Moronobu (d. 1694) and Sugimura Jihei (active ca. 1680–1704), these printed pictures heralded the dawn of ukiyo-e, or "pictures of the floating world" (fig. 2).[2]

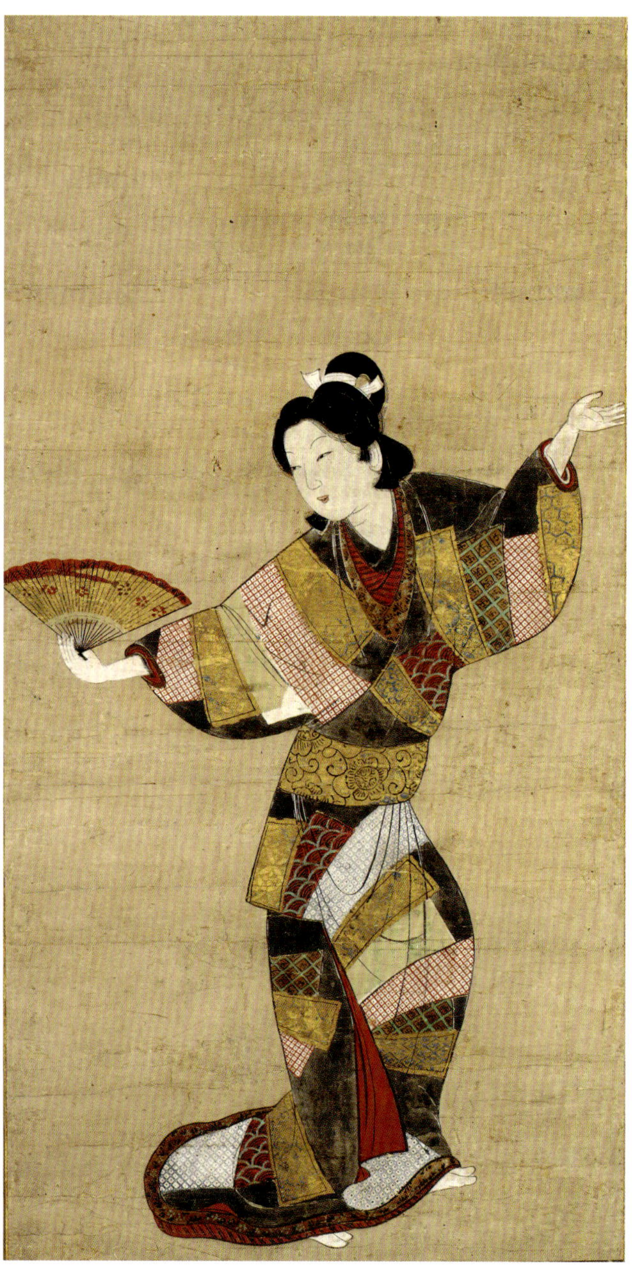

Ukiyo-e were produced by a team of artisans working under the direction of a publisher. The publisher would commission an artist to draw a design, which the block carver and printer would translate into the print medium. Initially, prints were colored by hand (pl. 1). Designs with up to five printed colors, called *benizuri-e*, after the red saf-flower dye that dominated their palette, appeared on the market around the 1740s (fig. 3). Suzuki Harunobu (1725–1770) refined this method around 1765 to create full-color prints, known as *nishiki-e*, or "brocade pictures," for his elite patrons (pl. 7).[3] Aligning the colors was accomplished by using registration marks, which ensured the paper was positioned consistently on the printing blocks. Being mass-produced, prints were relatively affordable and were popular as souvenirs of Edo.

KABUKI STARS

Although regarded by the authorities as outcasts, Kabuki actors were the celebrities of their day, adored by fans across the social spectrum. Their fame was fueled by portraits sold in vast quantities as affordable mementos, or surrogates, of the theater experience.

Kabuki has origins in the risqué performances of cross-dressing female dance troupes in the early seventeenth century. Their shows were so riotously popular that in 1629, authorities banned women from the stage. Boys began performing female roles, but in 1652 they too were outlawed over concerns that they were being offered for sexual ser-vices. Henceforth, all males on the stage were required to shave off their forelocks, signifying that they had come of age, which was supposed to diminish their allure in the eyes of adult men. Actors specializing in female roles were (and still are) called *onnagata*; they can often be identified in prints by the headscarves they are wearing to cover their shaved pates.

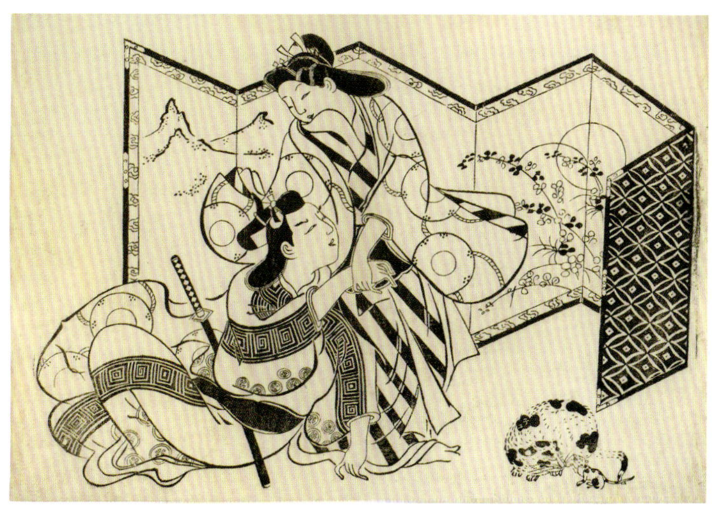

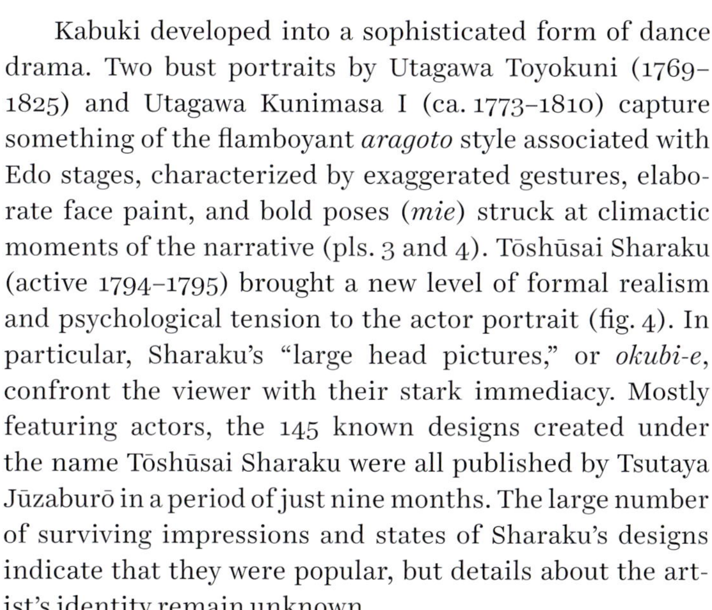

Kabuki developed into a sophisticated form of dance drama. Two bust portraits by Utagawa Toyokuni (1769–1825) and Utagawa Kunimasa I (ca. 1773–1810) capture something of the flamboyant *aragoto* style associated with Edo stages, characterized by exaggerated gestures, elaborate face paint, and bold poses (*mie*) struck at climactic moments of the narrative (pls. 3 and 4). Tōshūsai Sharaku (active 1794–1795) brought a new level of formal realism and psychological tension to the actor portrait (fig. 4). In particular, Sharaku's "large head pictures," or *okubi-e*, confront the viewer with their stark immediacy. Mostly featuring actors, the 145 known designs created under the name Tōshūsai Sharaku were all published by Tsutaya Jūzaburō in a period of just nine months. The large number of surviving impressions and states of Sharaku's designs indicate that they were popular, but details about the artist's identity remain unknown.

The public also savored glimpses of their favorite stars offstage, which offered access to actors' private lives. In *The Courtesan Takao Entertaining the Actors Sawamura Gennosuke and Iwai Kiyotarō at the Miuraya,* Kitagawa Tsukimaro (active ca. 1800–1818) depicted the elite prostitute Takao (at center left) celebrating a gift of luxurious new bedding, visible in the background, with actors Sawamura Gennosuke (center) and Iwai Kiyotarō (right) (pl. 13).

The death of a beloved actor could plunge Kabuki fandom into mourning. An unsigned print shows female devotees of all ages and ranks, as well as a cat, weeping before a memorial portrait of Ichikawa Danjūrō VIII, a handsome actor who specialized in romantic male roles (pl. 6). The image is one of possibly three hundred *shini-e*, or "death prints," released following Danjūrō's suicide in 1854 at the age of thirty-one, a response that has been called "Japan's first mass-media event."[4]

BEAUTIES

Bijinga, or pictures of beautiful people, encompassed images of desirable young people, mostly female. A principal source of *bijinga* imagery was the Yoshiwara, Edo's licensed brothel district. Located in a walled plot two miles outside the city, it was nonetheless a magnet for intellectuals, the warrior elite, and the new rich (pl. 28).[5] Many prostitutes had been sold as children into indentured servitude by poor rural families. Printmakers, emphasizing the luxury and refinement of this world, helped paint a beguiling picture belying the Yoshiwara's grim realities. Stepping out in maximalist splendor, the prostitute depicted in Kikukawa Eizan's (1787–1867) *Yosooi of the Matsubaya* wears eight layers of robes, a heavily brocaded obi tied at the front, and a coiffure radiating tortoiseshell hairpins. Her child attendant appears in matching attire (pl. 19). The expense of maintaining a sumptuous wardrobe and other accoutrements of the profession made it difficult for prostitutes to pay off their debts.

Ordinary women, like the waitresses Osen and Orise in the prints of Harunobu and Kitagawa Utamaro (ca. 1754–1806), were also popular subjects of *bijinga* (pls. 8 and 12). Osen, shown teasing a cat in the lap of a handsome customer, was a renowned beauty employed at the Kagiya teahouse at Edo's Kasamori shrine, and a favorite of Harunobu's. He does not name her, but she can be identified by the crest on her kimono.

Playful references to classical traditions underlie many pictures of beauties. Harunobu's series *Eight Parlor Views* (1766) transposes the "Eight Views of Xiao and Xiang," a theme from Chinese poetry and painting, onto the activities of contemporary women (see pl. 7). The series was commissioned by the shogunal retainer Ōkubo Jinshirō for members of his poetry club, who would have appreciated the literary allusion. Similarly, the six Tama Rivers invoked in two groups of prints by Utamaro are the subject of a classical Japanese poem (pls. 11 and 15).

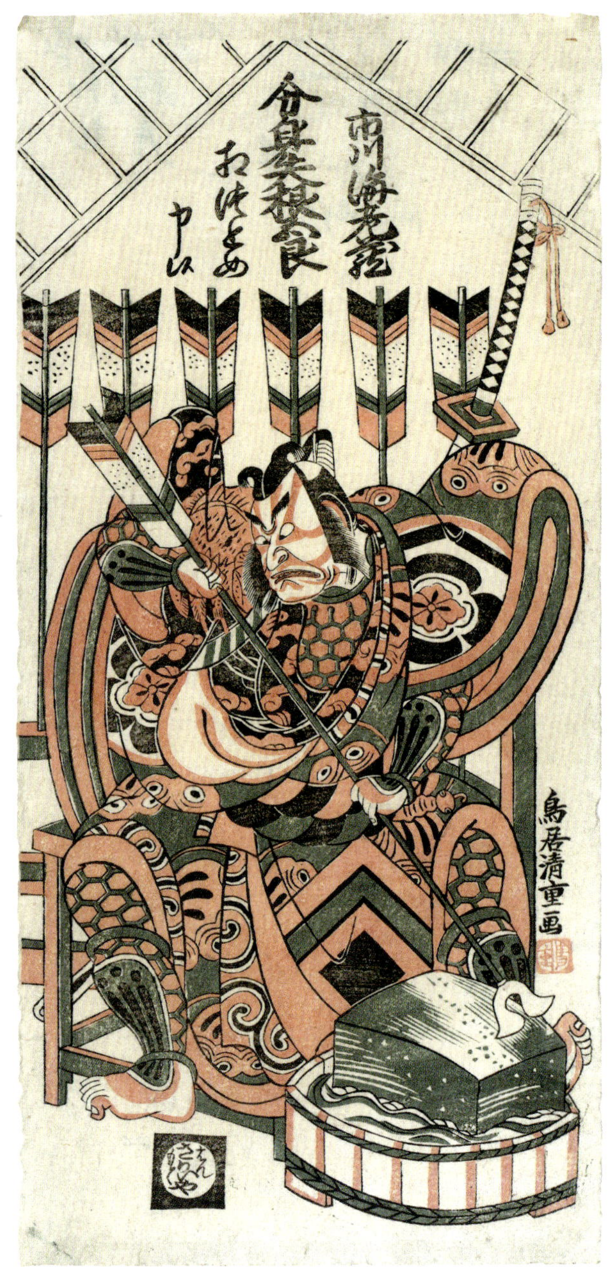

FIG. 3 | **Torii Kiyoshige (Japanese, active 1720–1760).** *Actor Ichikawa Ebizō II as Bunshin Yanone Gorō*, 1754. Published by Sakaiya Kurobei. Woodblock print (*benizuri-e*), ink and limited color on paper, 12 7/16 × 5 11/16 in. (31.6 × 14.5 cm). Museum of Fine Arts, Boston, William S. and John T. Spaulding Collection, 21.5669

THE VIEW FROM EDO

Landscape began to emerge as an independent subject of prints during the late eighteenth century, reflecting a growing interest in travel for leisure among commoners, as well as locals' affection for Edo. For publishers, landscape prints probably represented a safe investment; unlike actor prints, they did not become outdated quickly, nor did they attract the attention of censors.[6] One step in the development of landscape prints were *uki-e*, or "floating pictures," which, like Utagawa Toyoharu's (1735–1814) view of the Ryōgoku Bridge, employed Western-style perspective and low horizon lines (pl. 22).

Katsushika Hokusai's (1760–1849) series *Thirty-Six Views of Mount Fuji* (1830–1833), featuring views of Japan's sacred peak, established landscape as a major genre in ukiyo-e. Weaving together the realistic with the fantastical, Hokusai's images seem to hum with unseen, animistic energies. The series of prints makes advantageous use of the synthetic pigment Prussian Blue, which had recently

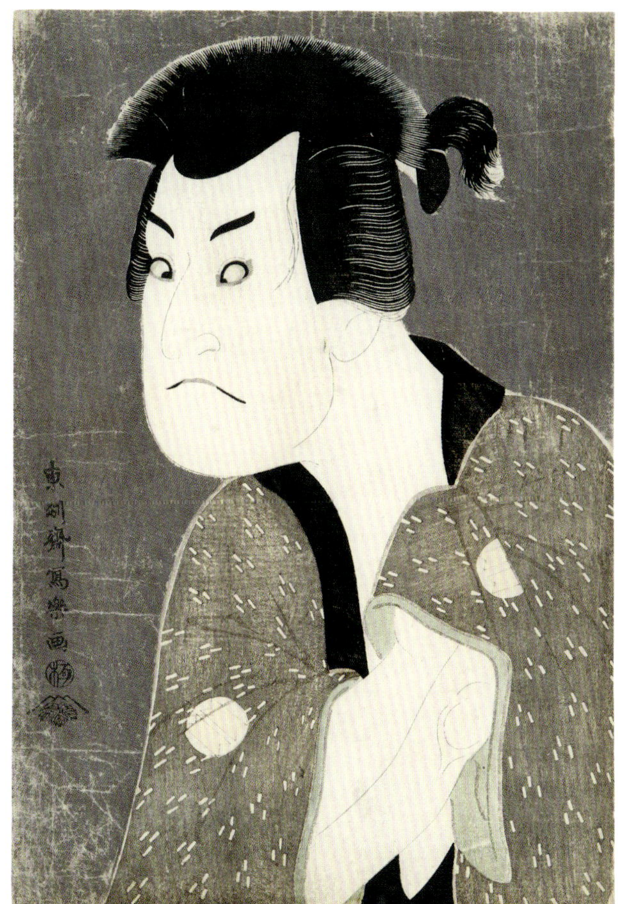

FIG. 4 | **Tōshūsai Sharaku (Japanese, active 1794–1795).** *The Actor Sakata Hangorō III as Fujikawa Mizuemon in the Play "Hana ayame Bunroku Soga," Miyako Theater*, from an untitled series of half-length portraits of actors, 1794. Color woodcut with mica background, "lacquer," and traces of hand-coloring, 14 11/16 × 9 7/8 in. (37.3 × 25.1 cm). Fine Arts Museums of San Francisco, Museum purchase, Achenbach Foundation for Graphic Arts Endowment Fund, 1967.22.10

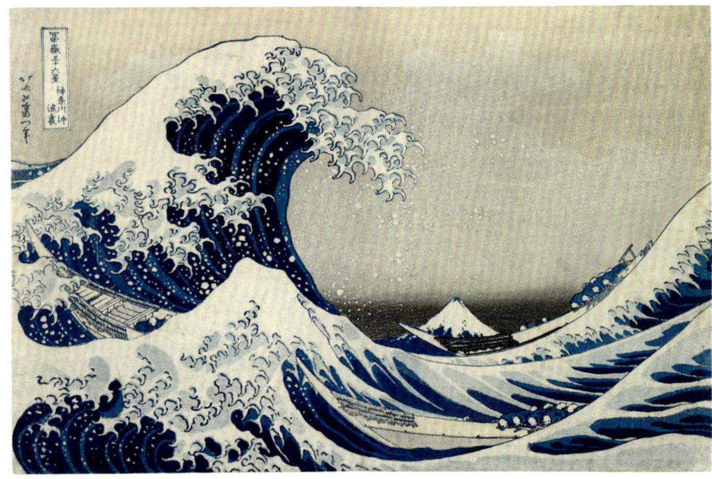 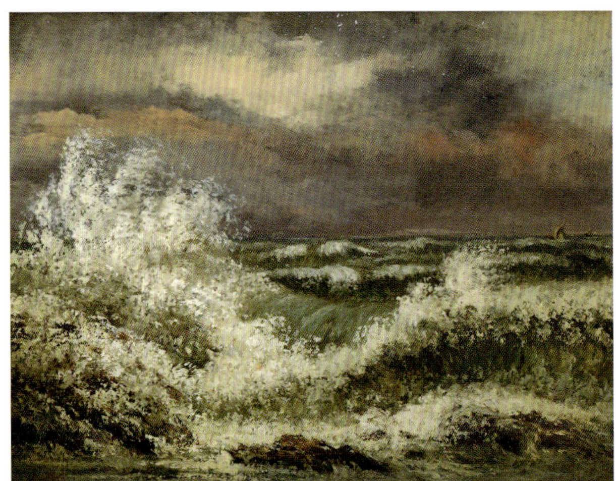

become more affordable (pls. 23–25). The *Thirty-Six Views* series includes several of Hokusai's most powerful and best-known designs, including *Under the Wave off Kanagawa (The Great Wave)* (fig. 5 and pl. 25), whose influence transcended the artist's own time and culture (fig. 6).

Utagawa Hiroshige's (1797–1858) *The Fifty-Three Stations of the Tōkaidō* (1832–1833) depicts scenery around the fifty-three post stations along the Eastern Sea Road connecting Edo and the imperial capital, Kyoto (pl. 27).[7] Hiroshige adapted book illustrations and the work of his peers to draft the designs. His refined and lyrical compositions launched Hiroshige as a rival to Hokusai in the field of landscape prints. His series *One Hundred Views of Famous Places in Edo* (1856–1858) features sites of pride for Edo residents and of interest to travelers: shrines and temples, entertainment districts, and scenic spots (pls. 31–35).[8] Departing from the quiet, picturesque views for which he was known, Hiroshige used a vertical format for the series and an exaggerated perspective for a more dynamic effect. The Japanese title of the series, *Meisho Edo hyakkei*, invokes the classical term *meisho*, or "famous places," which traditionally referred to sites, mostly around Kyoto, that acquired cultural significance through canonical texts of history and literature. By applying this term to Edo's quotidian landscape, the artist expresses his warm regard for the city.

WARRIORS, MYTHS, AND LEGENDS

Prints of swashbuckling warriors and battles from history, and scenes from mythology and literature, called *musha-e*, became popular in the eighteenth century. The designs by Hiroshige and Utagawa Kunikiyo II (1850–1887) depict scenes from the final act of a theatrical version of *The Treasury of Loyal Retainers*, or *Chūshingura*, based on a 1701–1703 incident in which forty-seven samurai avenged the death of their lord, who was sentenced to die by suicide for attempting to assassinate a court official. The prints show the samurai approaching the walls of their enemy's compound and capturing him (pls. 38 and 39). The drama concludes with the samurai delivering the enemy's head to their master's grave before killing themselves.

The foremost artist of *musha-e* was Utagawa Kuniyoshi (1798–1861), whose designs weave together history and fantasy with macabre humor. In *At the Bottom of the Sea in Daimotsu Bay*, a subject drawn from the Genpei War (1180–1185), the ghosts of Commander Taira no Tomomori's forces plot to attack Minamoto no Yoshitsune's ship from their watery grave. A formation of crabs bearing the faces of Taira warriors on their carapaces scuttles out of the frame. The mollusk-encrusted anchor of the Taira ship, which the commander used as a weight to drown himself as victory slipped from his grasp, lies diagonally across the composition (pl. 40).

YOSHITOSHI: LAST OF THE UKIYO-E MASTERS

Active before and after the tumultuous Meiji Restoration (1868), Kuniyoshi's student Tsukioka Yoshitoshi (1839–1892) shared his teacher's affinity for the strange and violent. The series *Twenty-Eight Famous Murders with Verse*, produced in collaboration with his confrere Utagawa Yoshiiku (1833–1904), brought Yoshitoshi notoriety as a creator of *chimidoro-e* ("blood-splattered pictures") (pl. 46). To simulate the appearance of congealing blood, the printer mixed red pigments with animal glue and alum.[9] Yoshitoshi became a founding artist of the new genre of "newspaper pictures," or *shinbun-e*, which capitalized on the rising popularity of daily newspapers following the easing of Edo-period censorship laws. *Shinbun-e* prints were concerned mainly with tabloid-style content, including encounters with the supernatural (pl. 44).

Yoshitoshi's designs became more aesthetically and psychologically nuanced in his later career. In *Fujiwara no Yasumasa Playing a Flute by Moonlight*, an infamous bandit stalks a flute-playing nobleman, but he becomes enchanted by the strange music and is unable to attack (pl. 48). The composition is believed to have been commissioned by

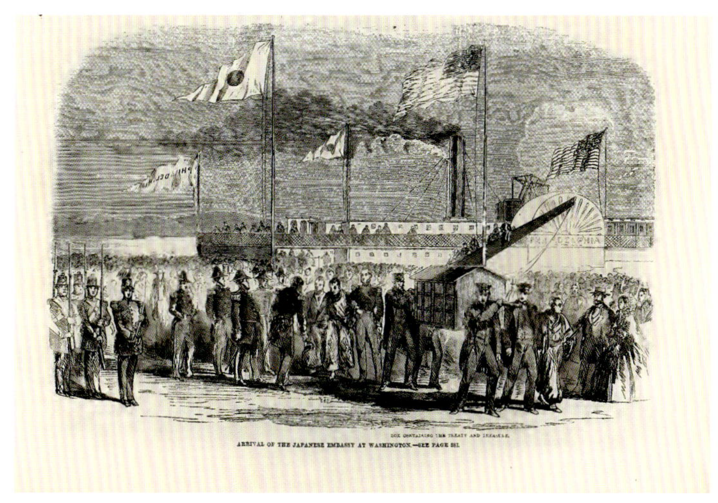

FIG. 5 | **Katsushika Hokusai (Japanese, 1760–1849).** *Under the Wave off Kanagawa (The Great Wave),* from the series *Thirty-Six Views of Mount Fuji,* ca. 1830–1832. Color woodcut, 9 13⁄16 × 14 1⁄2 in. (25 × 36.9 cm). Fine Arts Museums of San Francisco, Museum purchase, Achenbach Foundation for Graphic Arts Endowment Fund, 1969.32.6

FIG. 6 | **Gustave Courbet (French, 1819–1877).** *The Wave,* ca. 1869. Oil on canvas, 23 × 31 in. (58.4 × 78.7 cm). Fine Arts Museums of San Francisco, Museum purchase, Grover A. Magnin Bequest Fund and Roscoe and Margaret Oakes Income Fund, 2006.58

FIG. 7 | **Unidentified artist.** *Box Containing the Treaty and Treasury: Arrival of the Japanese Embassy at Washington.* Wood engraving. *London Illustrated News,* Supplement, June 10, 1860, 585

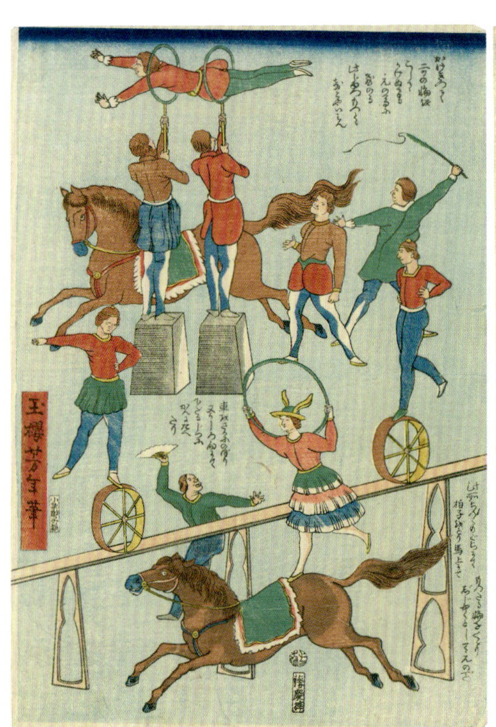
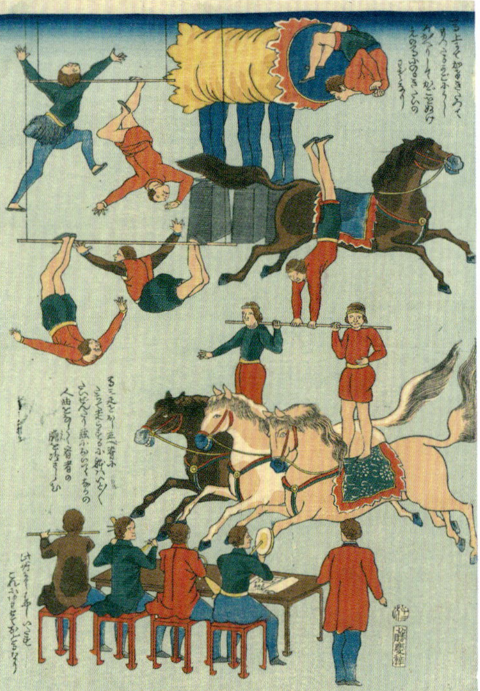
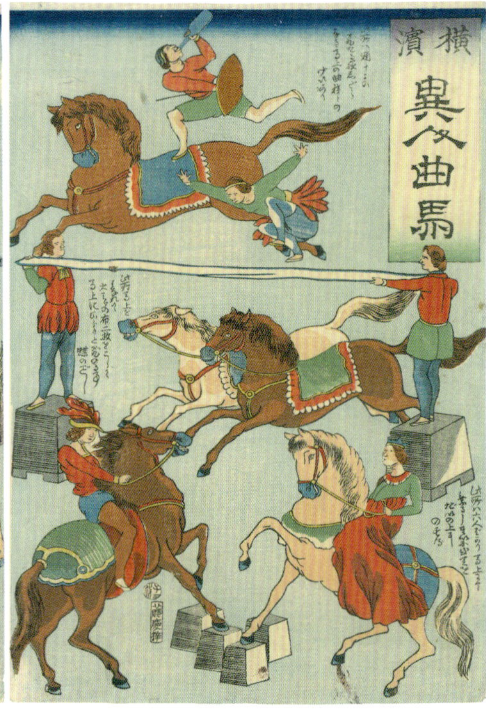

FIG. 8 | **Tsukioka Yoshitoshi (Japanese, 1839–1892).** *Foreign Circus at Yokohama*, 1864. Published by Fujioka Keijirō. Woodblock print, ink and color on paper, 14 ¾ × 29 ¹³⁄₁₆ in. (37.5 × 75.8 cm). The John and Mable Ringling Museum of Art, Sarasota, Florida, Museum purchase, 2020, 2020.17

the publisher Akiyama Buemon after he saw Yoshitoshi's painting on the same subject at a government-sponsored exhibition in 1882.[10] Continuing his partnership with Akiyama, Yoshitoshi embarked on *One Hundred Aspects of the Moon* (1885–1892). The series, using the moon as its leitmotif, draws together stories from history, literature, folklore, and popular culture with haunting lyricism (pls. 42 and 43).

SIGHT UNSEEN: ARTISTS ENCOUNTER THE WEST AND WESTERNERS

Commodore Matthew Perry's "gunboat diplomacy" of 1853–1854 brought the Tokugawa shogunate's 220-year-long isolationist policy to an end. The ominous arrival of Perry's fleet of so-called "black ships" (*kurofune*) in Uraga Harbor, at the mouth of Edo Bay, was a display of military and technological superiority that the authorities could not ignore (pl. 49). In 1858, Japan and the United States signed the United States–Japan Treaty of Amity and Commerce, which favored the foreigners in terms of tariffs and extraterritorial rights. Similar treaties followed with Great Britain, the Netherlands, France, and Russia, who with the United States became known locally as the "Five Nations" (pl. 50). Foreigners began pouring into Japan.

The fascination with these newcomers was reflected in a new type of print, *Yokohama-e*, or "Yokohama pictures," named after one of several Japanese ports newly opened for international trade. More than eight hundred prints were issued between 1860 and 1872, designed mostly by students of Kuniyoshi, Kunisada, and Hiroshige.[11] Supplementing limited eyewitness information with images from Western publications, artists attempted to portray the physical attributes and peculiar dress of the new arrivals, who were mostly confined to Yokohama's foreign settlement, and how they lived and amused themselves (pls. 53–55).[12] The

use of tone and chiaroscuro, for example, to give draped elements the illusion of three-dimensional form, is copied from Western engravings and underscores the exotic character of their subjects.

Utagawa Yoshikazu's (active 1850–1870) *Interior of an American Steamship* (pl. 56) reflects the public's interest in foreign technology. Inevitably, details were sometimes lost in translation—Yoshikazu's "steam train" is actually copied from a wood engraving depicting the shogunal embassy staff posing in front of a paddle steamer in Washington, DC, published in a June 1860 issue of the *London Illustrated News* (fig. 7). Utagawa Yoshitora's (active 1850–1880) prints of America and France imagined what magical lands the foreigners had left behind (pls. 57–59). Evidently captivated by images of a hot-air balloon ascending, Yoshitora made this motif central to his futuristic vision of the United States.[13] Some prints claimed instructive purposes: Yoshiiku's *An Englishman and a Russian Woman* contains common Japanese words with their English equivalents transcribed into syllabary for easy pronunciation. Rice is rendered as "raisu," dog as "doggu," and, somewhat awkwardly, salt as "sheruto" (pl. 55).

The arrival of the first Western circus, the troupe of Richard Risley Carlisle, or Professor Risley, as he called himself, in Japan in 1864 presented printmakers with an exciting new inventory of subject matter (fig. 8 and pls. 60 and 61). Artists emphasized the beauty, skill, and daring of the equestrian acts, which were billed as being from "Western India" to appeal to Yokohama's émigré community.[14]

AN UNSETTLED TRANSITION

The Tokugawa shogunate fell in 1867 and was replaced by a new regime centered on the imperial court and the young emperor Mutsuhito (1852–1912), known as the Meiji emperor, the following year. The imperial court moved from Kyoto to Edo, which was renamed Tokyo, and integrated into the Meiji government. However, concerns that the shogunate would attempt to wrest back control of the country erupted almost immediately into war, with samurai from the feudal domains of Satsuma and Chōshū uniting with members of the imperial court against the Tokugawa loyalists. The latter were defeated at Sannō Shrine in the Battle of Ueno in May 1868 (pl. 62). Earlier prohibitions on depicting current events resulted in a delay in publishing images of these battles for several years.

Civil war broke out again with the Satsuma Rebellion of 1877, led by Takamori Saigō (1828–1877), who had been a ringleader in conflicts against the Tokugawa loyalists a decade earlier. In 1873, disgusted by the Meiji government's decision not to invade Korea, over Korea's refusal to recognize the sovereignty of the new emperor, Saigō withdrew from government duties and established his own militia in Kagoshima. The Meiji government, fearing an uprising, dispatched troops to raid Saigō's base. Kagoshima locals joined the rebellion against the government forces (pl. 64). Saigō was probably killed in battle, and tales of his glorious defeat blossomed in the public imagination. Saigō became the subject of hero-worship among young admirers, and his exploits were glorified onstage (pl. 63). In order to contain his dangerous legacy, the Meiji government opted to issue a posthumous pardon in 1889.

THE EMPEROR SETS THE STYLE

Imperial advisors set about fashioning the Meiji emperor as a modern ruler, military leader, and divine father around whom the nation could coalesce. He made public appearances and sat for six official portraits, overturning a centuries-long taboo against depicting the reigning emperor. In 1872, he chopped off his topknot and began wearing a suit modelled on a Western military uniform.

Dozens of woodblock prints were issued that reinforced the imperial court's official messaging. Many feature the emperor at military reviews, which were staged regularly as demonstrations of the country's discipline and might (pls. 67 and 68). Yōshū Chikanobu (1838–1912) carved out a niche depicting the imperial household on outings and at home. His image of the emperor, Empress Shōken, and crown prince portrays the monarch as the stern but benevolent head of a modern nuclear family (fig. 9). (In reality, the empress shared her conjugal duties with five concubines, one of whom would give birth to the emperor's only surviving son, the crown prince, and rarely appeared in public with her husband.)[15]

Chikanobu and his peers found the empress to be a compelling subject for prints in her own right. They portray her as an exemplar of modern womanhood — educated and publicly engaged without challenging her traditional roles as a dutiful wife and mother. She advocated for the education of women so that they might be better equipped to raise the next generation of leaders. A print by Toyohara Kunichika (1835–1900) imagines her leading students at the Peeress's School in the recital of a poem she wrote, which became the school song (pl. 72).[16] After she adopted Western dress in 1886, artists depicted the empress and her ladies-in-waiting as icons of fashion, dressing them in gowns copied from Western fashion plates published in magazines.[17] The gowns' brocaded patterns, however, remind the viewer that they were woven from homegrown silk in Japanese mills.

MODERNIZATION AND WESTERNIZATION

The Meiji government launched a series of reforms encapsulated by the dual slogans "civilization and enlightenment" (*bunmei kaikai*) and "rich country, strong army" (*fukoku kyōhei*) aimed at "catching up" to the West and overturning the unequal treaties of the 1850s. These included adopting a

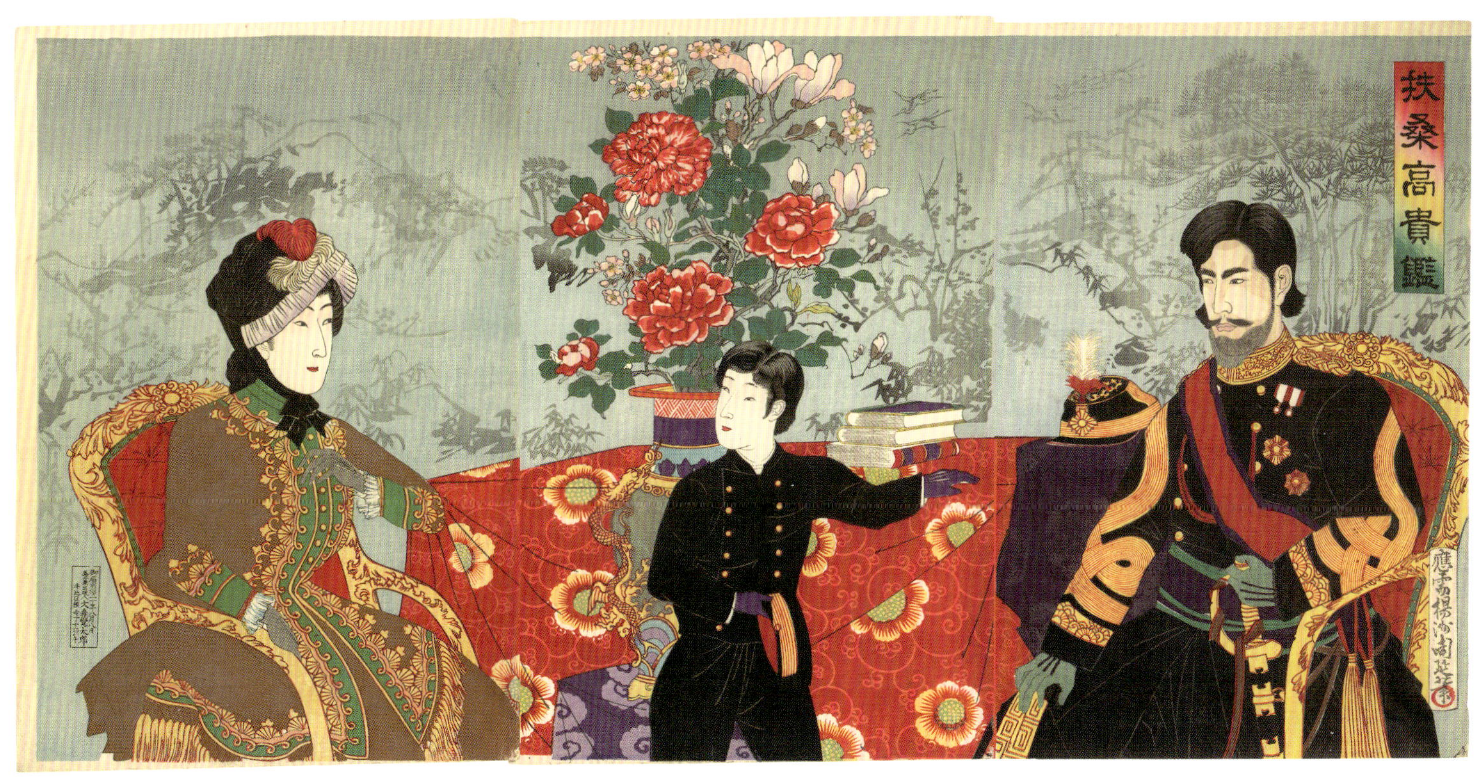

FIG. 9 | **Yōshū Chikanobu (Japanese, 1838–1912).** *A Mirror of Japan's Nobility*, 1887. Published by Fukase Kamejirō. Woodblock print, ink, and color on paper, 14 ¾ × 29 ⅝ in. (37.5 × 75.2 cm). The Metropolitan Museum of Art, New York, Gift of Lincoln Kirstein, 1959, JP3241a–c

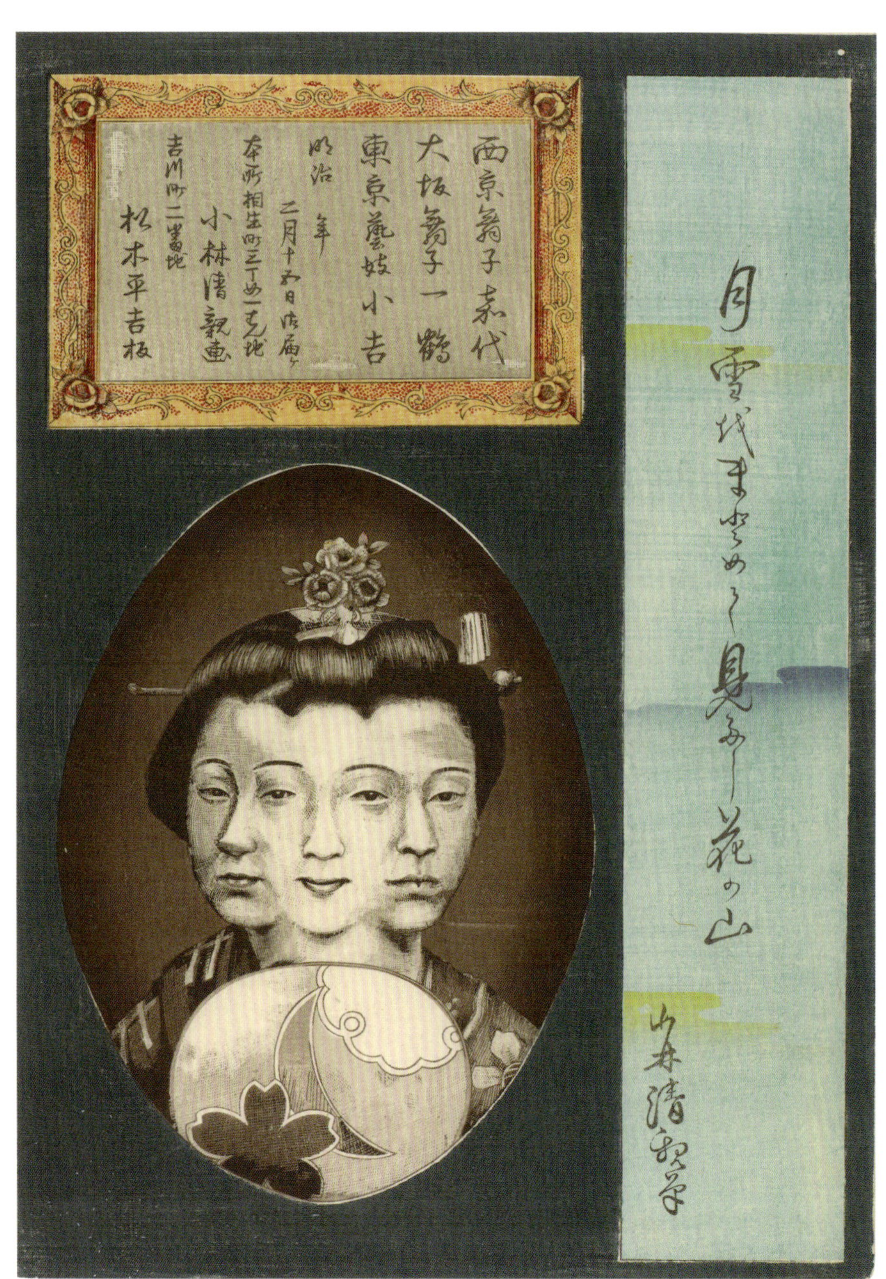

FIG. 10 | **Kobayashi Kiyochika (Japanese, 1847–1915).** *Three Geisha: Kayo of Osaka, Hitotsuru of Kyoto, and Kokichi of Tokyo*, ca. 1878. Published by Matsuki Heikichi. Woodblock print, ink, and color on paper with metallic pigments, 14 ¼ × 9 ¾ in. (36.2 × 24.7 cm). Arthur M. Sackler Gallery, Smithsonian Institution, Washington, DC, Robert O. Muller Collection, S2003.8.1157

constitution and modern parliamentary system, introducing a national education system, and opening universities and hospitals. Japan invested in key industries such as mining, silk production, and shipbuilding, and laid hundreds of miles of railroad tracks, commissioned warships, and established a military supported by national conscription.

Woodblock prints show the landscape transformed by brick buildings, gas streetlights, trains, steam-powered ships, hitherto-unseen wheeled vehicles like horse-drawn carriages and rickshaws (or *jinrikisha*), and figures dressed in combinations of Japanese and Western dress. The construction of Japan's first railway line, which connected Yokohama to Tokyo, resulted in a burst of new print designs around 1870–1874 (pls. 75–78). Printed liberally with new red and purple dyes, these images emanate cheerful confidence in the new age.[18]

Meanwhile, actor prints reflected how modernity was performed onstage. Onoe Kikugorō V (1844–1903), an actor and one of the chief instigators behind efforts within the theater world to propel Kabuki into the new age, commissioned the playwright Kawatake Mokuami to write experimental scripts referencing current events. A print by Kunichika commemorates a scene from a production allegedly inspired by a "magic lantern" (*gentō*) presentation of slides featuring copperplate engravings based on photographs of the catastrophic eruption of Mount Bandai in Fukushima prefecture in 1888 (pl. 73).[19] Another print by Kunisada III depicts Kikugorō V and his castmates in the roles of puppets of "foreign ladies," an "Englishman" on stilts, and two dancing skeletons, from a play inspired by an English marionette show that played to packed theaters in Tokyo in 1894 (pl. 74).[20]

In 1876, Kobayashi Kiyochika (1847–1915) began creating designs that simulate the realism and formal qualities of Western-style painting, printing technologies, and photography — as if to demonstrate that the woodblock print could meet modern demands for objective representations of the world (fig. 10 and pls. 82 and 83). His naturalistic treatment of light and color brings a sense of melancholy lyricism to the modernizing landscape. Kiyochika's pursuit of verisimilitude didn't preclude creative license — his racing locomotive is an American model rather than the British type in use (pl. 83).

Since ancient times, China had been the political and cultural center of East Asia. Western imperialism and internal strife in the nineteenth century, however, threatened the Qing dynasty's (1644–1911) hold over its empire and regional standing. Meanwhile, the Russian empire was advancing perilously eastward. The first Sino-Japanese War (1894–1895) and the Russo-Japanese War (1904–1905) were two conflicts fought between Japan and its neighbors over control of the Korean peninsula and parts of Manchuria, as well as important tests of its progress as a modern military power.

By the 1890s, woodblock prints were meeting competition from photography and lithography, which were cheaper and more efficient to produce. However, long exposure times, heavy equipment, the necessity for a photographer to be at the right place at the right time to get their shot, and the fact that historical events didn't always align with the narratives preferred by the Meiji government, were major drawbacks of photography. The vibrant colors and dramatic (and frequently fantastical) imagery possible with woodblock printing gave it an advantage over newer reprographic technologies. Panoramic battle scenes spanning up to nine sheets of vivid, saturated color were wildly popular, driving a brief revival of the woodblock print industry (fig. 11).[21]

In contrast to the stirring accounts of the heroism and camaraderie of Japan's troops, artists created dehumanizing and frequently racist depictions of the Chinese and Russian combatants and their suffering (pls. 84 and 87). Meanwhile, images of Japan's Red Cross field hospitals and their compassionate treatment of wounded Russians reflected the nation's desire to see itself, and be recognized, as a "civilized" nation (pl. 88). Kiyochika emerged as the most prolific, and arguably most gifted, artist of the genre.[22] Like most of his competitors, he did not travel to the front, but he nonetheless excelled at producing darkly beautiful images of battlefields, such as *Our Elite Forces Occupying the Pescadores Islands of Taiwan* (pl. 87). The design was originally published in December 1894 — well before Japan invaded Taiwan — but was reissued with a title linking it to the Taiwan campaign.[23] Shrewd publishers frequently repurposed designs to meet the demands of their market.

MASAMI TERAOKA: UKIYO-E POP

As a popular visual medium, ukiyo-e was superseded by magazines and picture postcards that employed modern reprographic technologies. Nonetheless, ukiyo-e casts a long shadow — one that reaches into the twenty-first century. In Japan, the collaborative production model, themes, and sensibilities of ukiyo-e were revived in the twentieth century as *shin hanga*, or "new prints," for the Western market and collectors. In the West, artists have responded to various aspects of Japanese prints — the exotic world they depicted, the flattening of space and form, and the bold divisions of color — with their paintings, prints, sculptures, and virtually every category of applied design. The role ukiyo-e played in the emergence of Japonisme has been documented extensively.

In the late 1970s and early 1980s, a decade after moving to Los Angeles to study art, Japanese-born Masami Teraoka (b. 1936) found in ukiyo-e a visual language with which to explore contemporary social issues such as globalization, sexuality, and the HIV/AIDS epidemic, as well as his personal negotiation of culture that is markedly different to that of his native Japan. These ponderings play out in absurd and sometimes raunchy situations. One prostitute's libido is awakened by ice cream, while another hesitates before a McDonald's hamburger. "Should I just bite into it?" she asks, as her tattooed blond companion gets tangled up in her noodles (pl. 89). Elsewhere, in a clear reference to Hiroshige's design for Yotsuya (pl. 34), the burger lies discarded by the feet of a woman wearing towering geta sandals (pl. 90). Teraoka's skillful emulation of the various formal, aesthetic, and stylistic elements of nineteenth-century ukiyo-e — cartouches, seal marks, calligraphic script, graduated shading, parted lips, and fluttering hems — are the result of his careful study of his personal collection of ukiyo-e. Teraoka's practice of appropriation to create and amplify new meaning perpetuates a robust tradition in art, while his choice of source material suggests how ukiyo-e continues to resonate with artists and art audiences today.

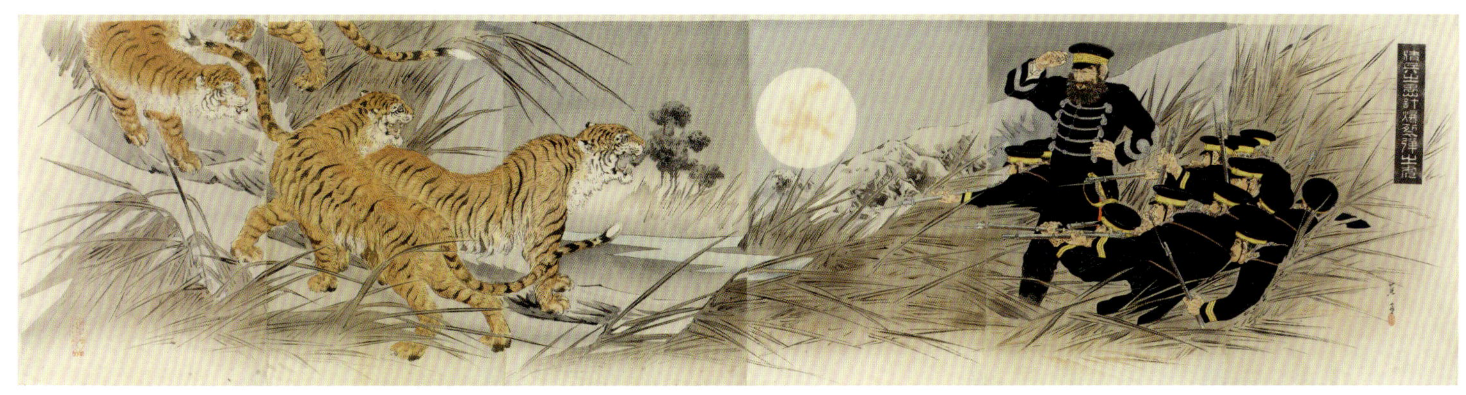

FIG. 11 | **Mishima Shōsō (Japanese, 1856– 1928).** *The Qing Army's Foolish Plan of Using Tigers as Weapons*, 1895. Published by Fukuda Hatsujirō. Woodblock print, ink and color on paper hexaptych, 10¼ × 57½ in. (26.1 × 146.1 cm). Saint Louis Art Museum, Gift of Mr. and Mrs. Charles A. Lowenhaupt, 19:2007a–f

PLATES

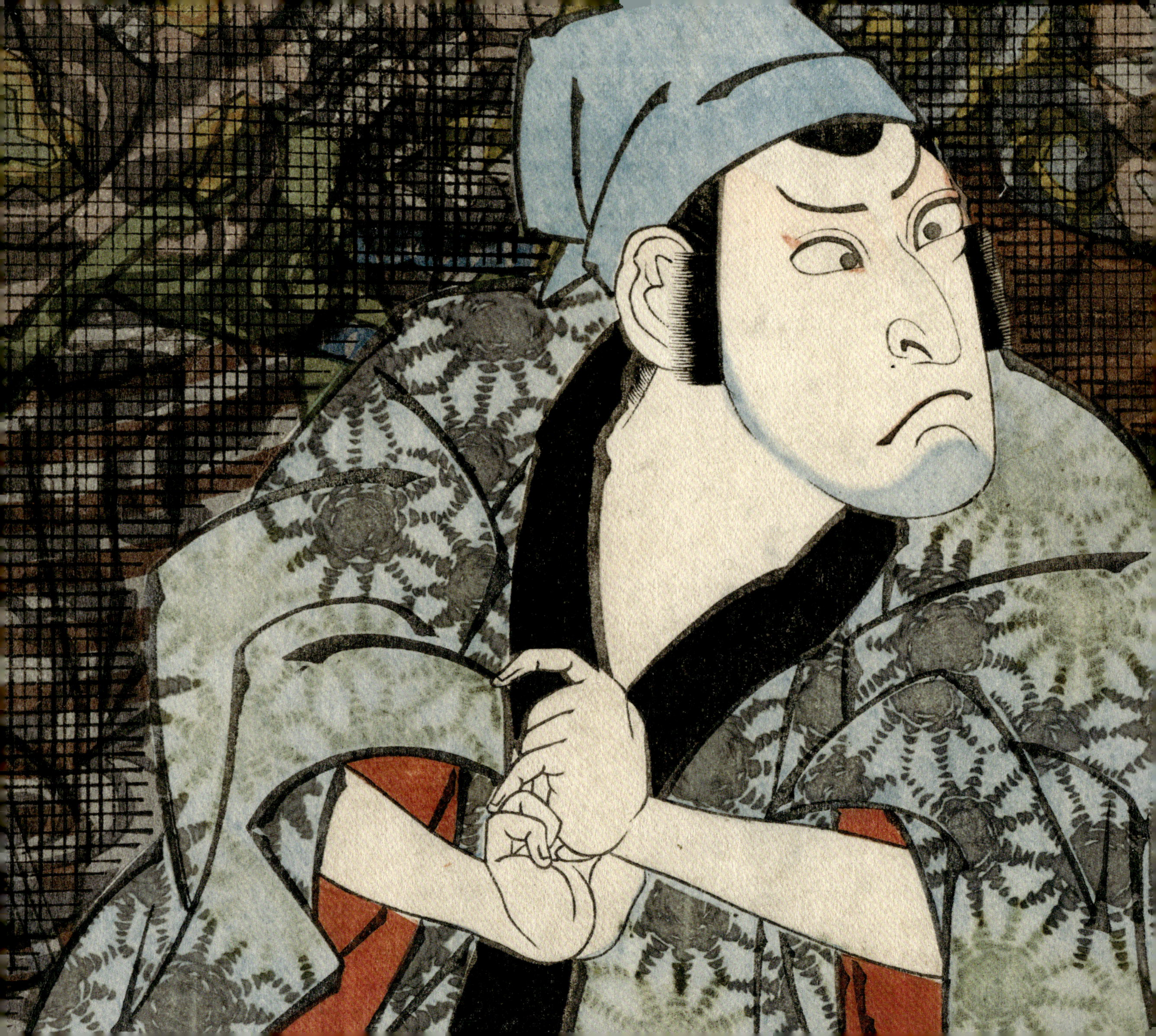

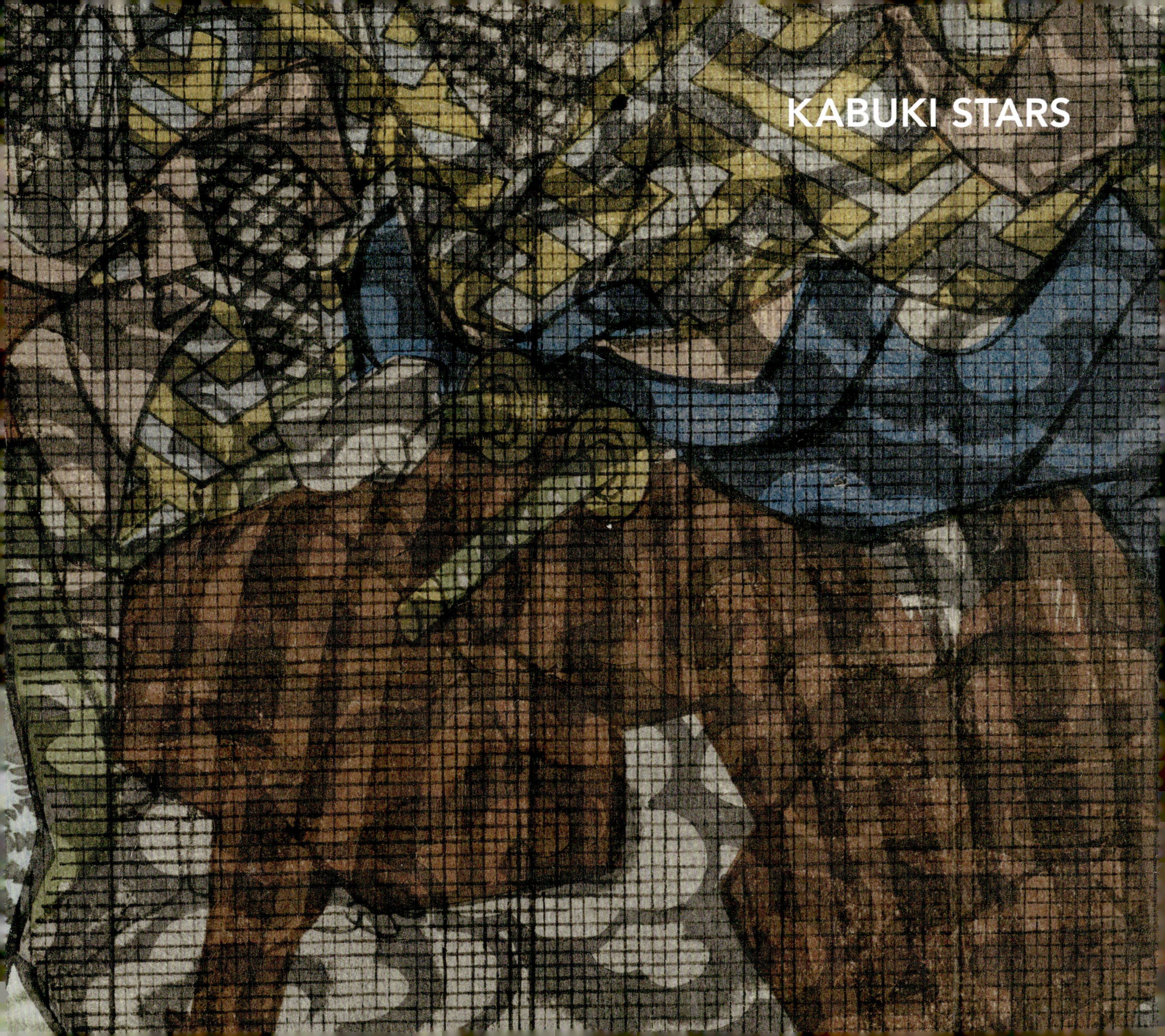
KABUKI STARS

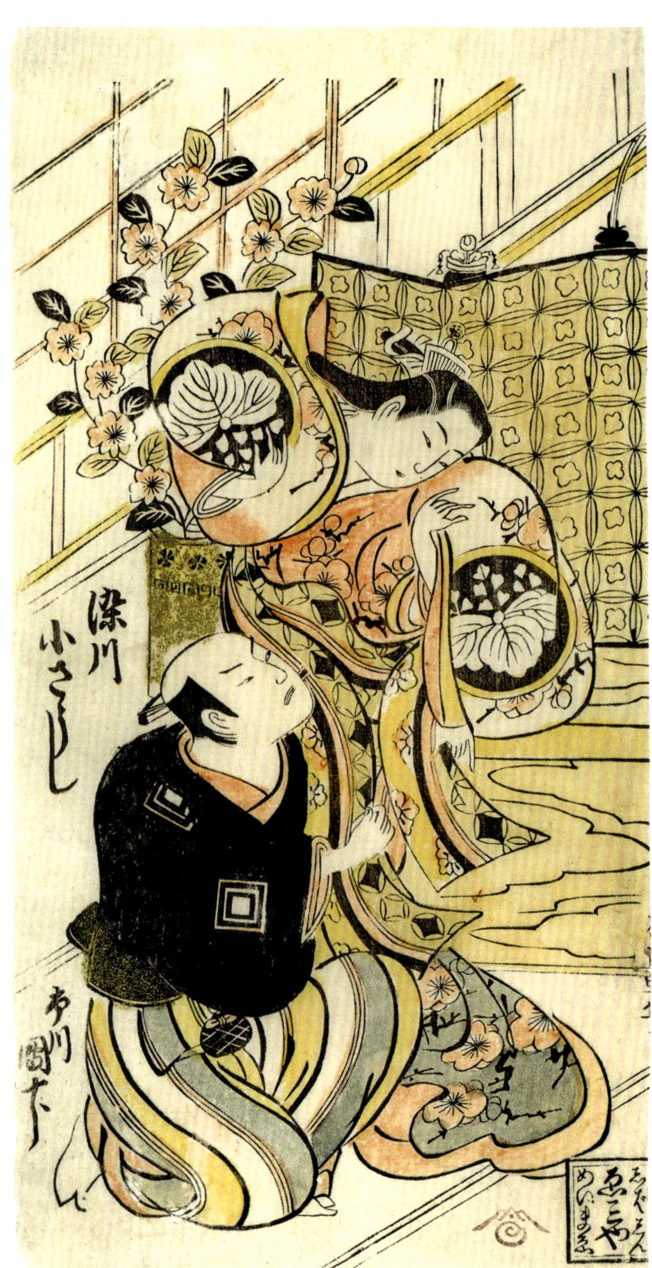

1

Torii Kiyoshige (active 1724–1764)
Somekawa Kozōshi and Ichikawa Danjūrō II as a Merchant
Trying to Seduce a Young Girl, ca. 1720–1729

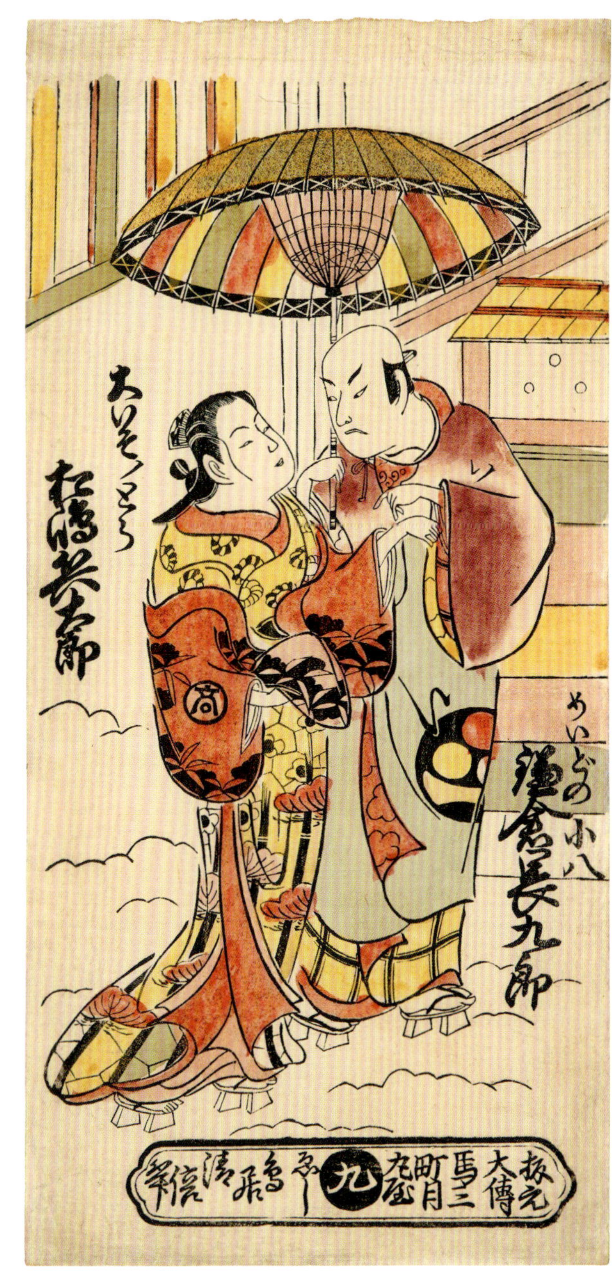

2

Torii Kiyomasu II (1706–1763)

*The Actors Matsushima Heitarō and Kamakura Chōkurō as
Oiso no Tora and Meido no Kohachi*, 1725

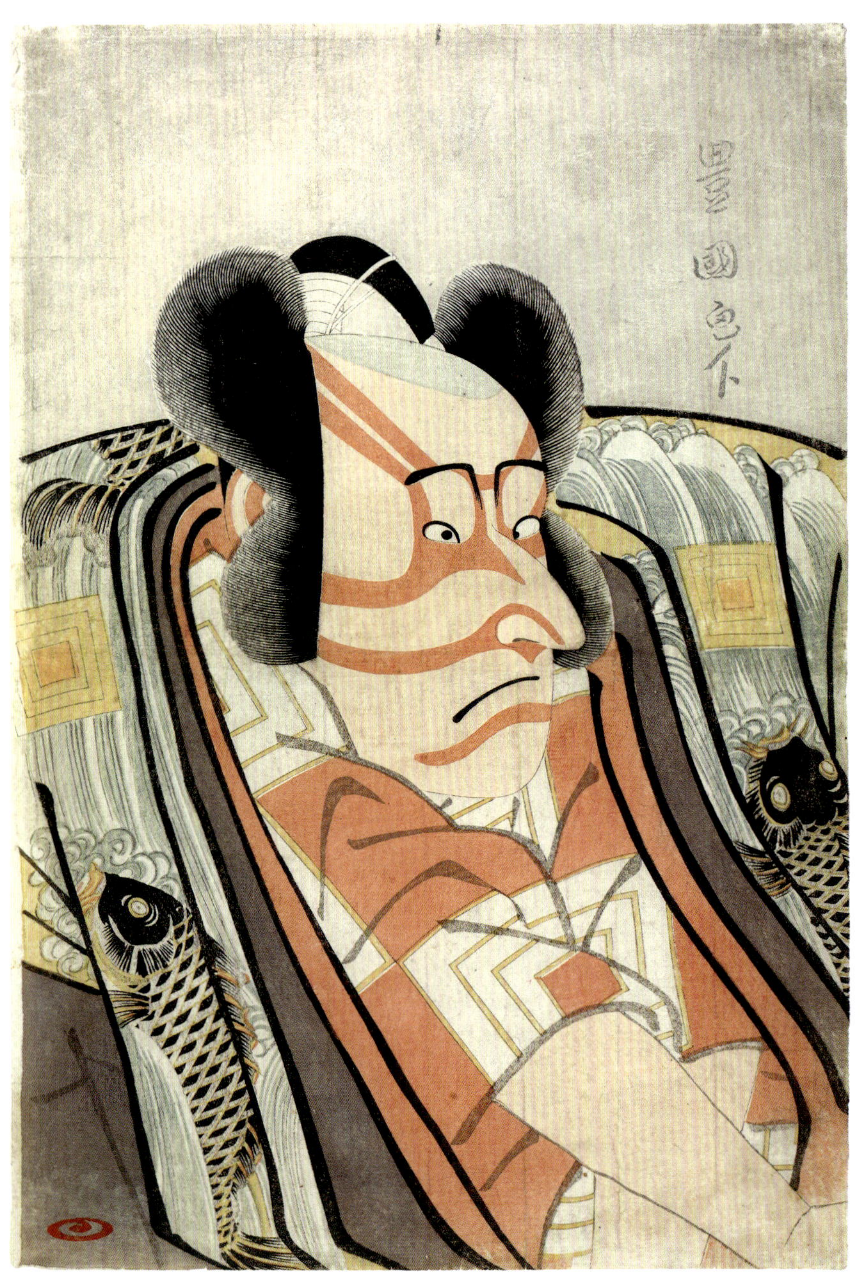

3

Utagawa Toyokuni (1769–1825)
The Actor Ichikawa Danjūrō VI as a Nobleman,
from an untitled series of half-length portraits
of actors, 1796

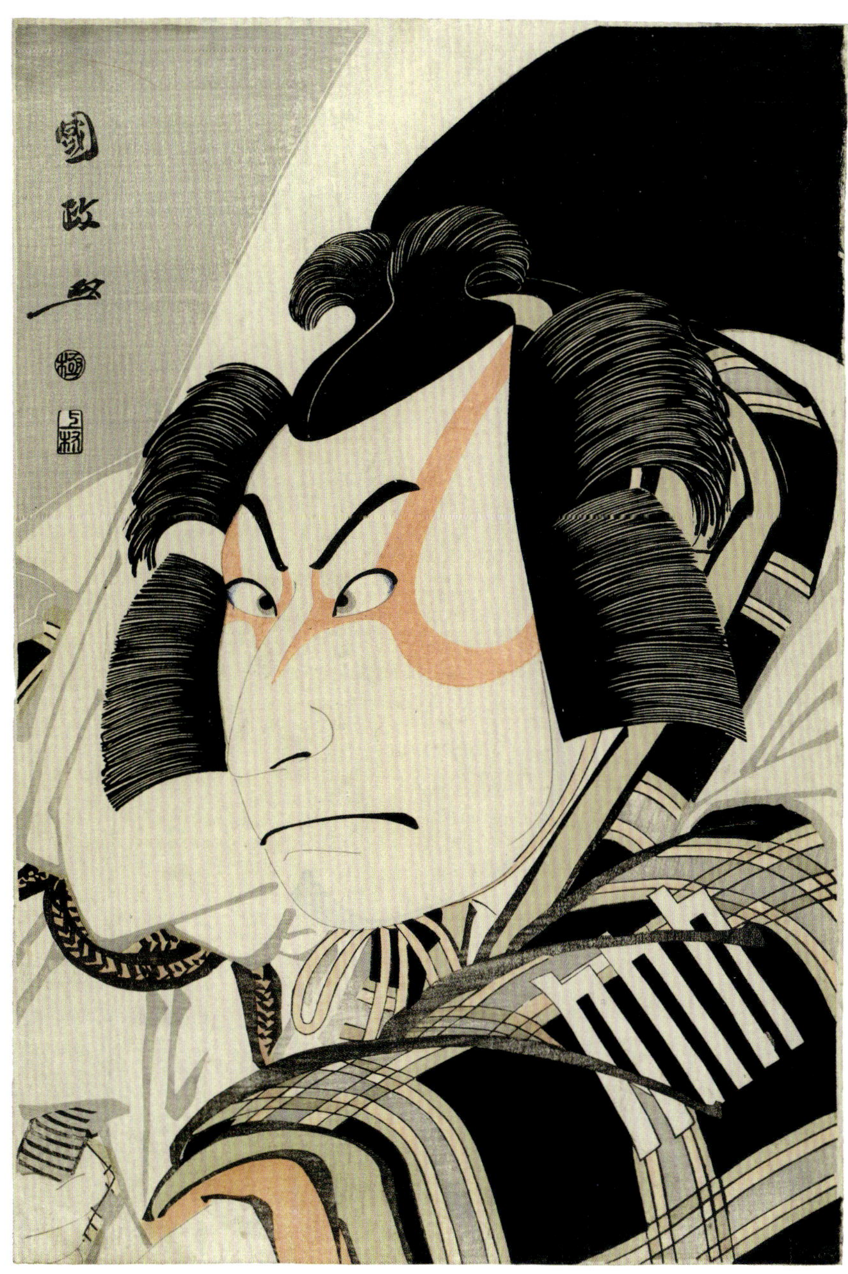

4

Utagawa Kunimasa I (ca. 1773–1810)

The Actor Nakamura Nakazō II as Matsuomaru
in the "Carriage-Stopping" Scene in the Play
"Sugawara's Secret" at the Miyako Theater, 1796

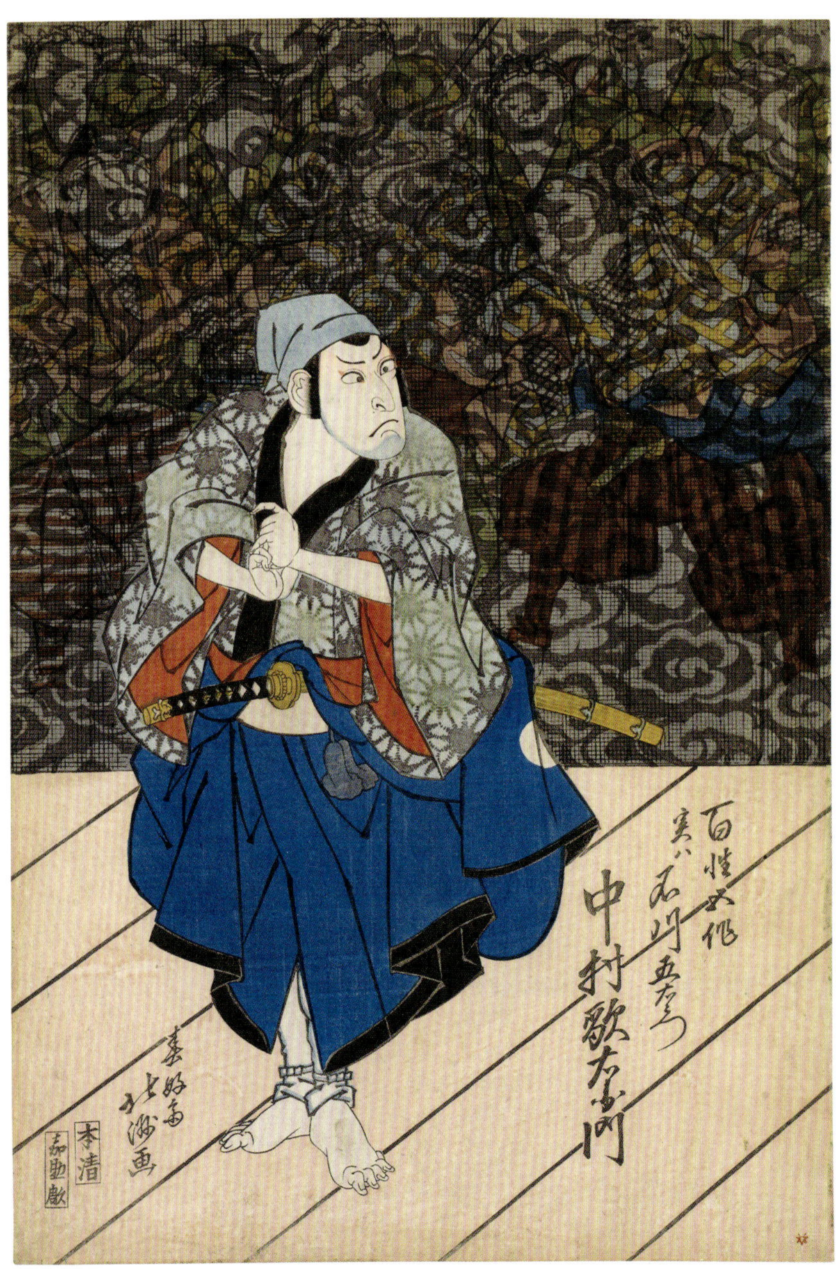

5

Shunkōsai Hokushū (active 1808–1832)
The Actor Nakamura Utaemon III as Ishikawa Goemon, Disguised as the Farmer Gosaku, 1830

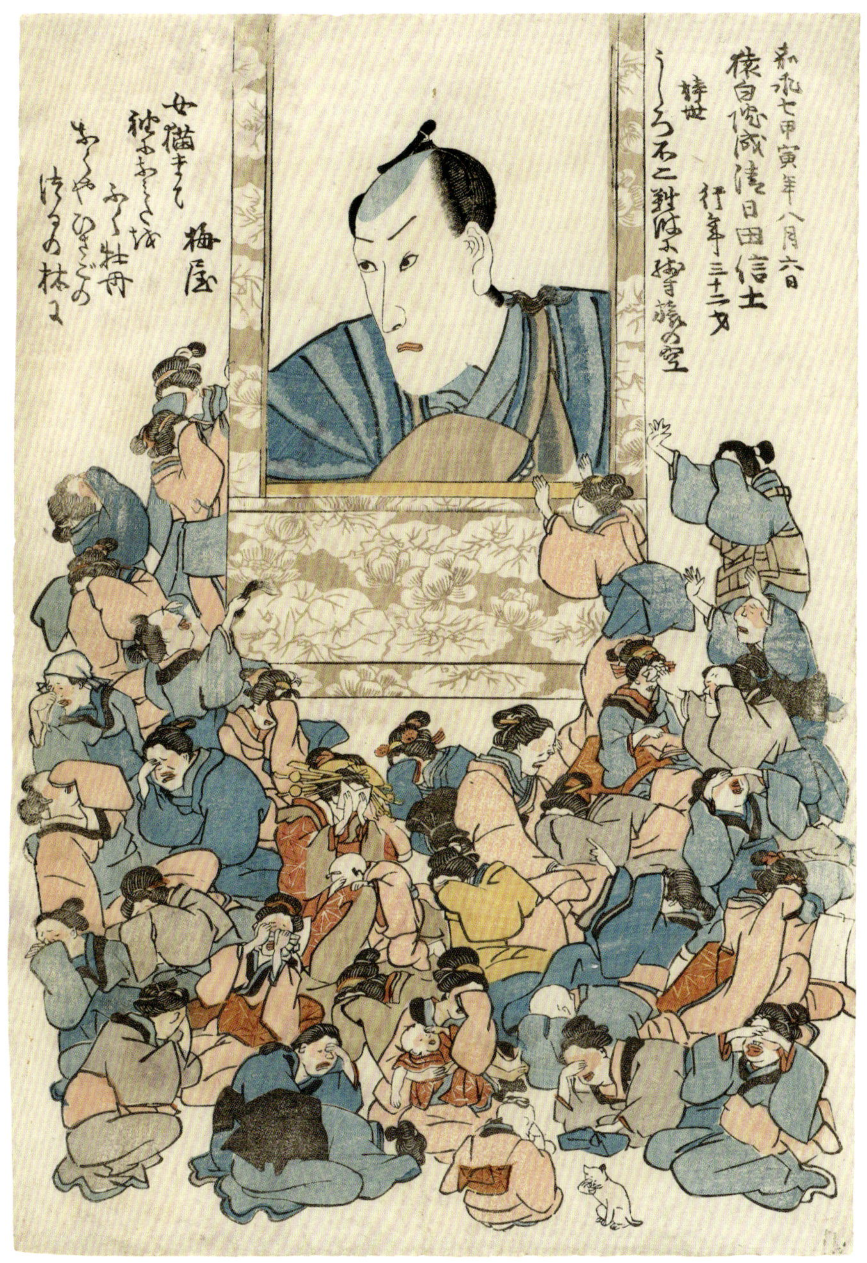

6

Unidentified Edo artist
(active mid-19th century)

Female Admirers Weeping before a Large
Memorial Portrait of the Actor Ichikawa
Danjūrō VIII, 1856

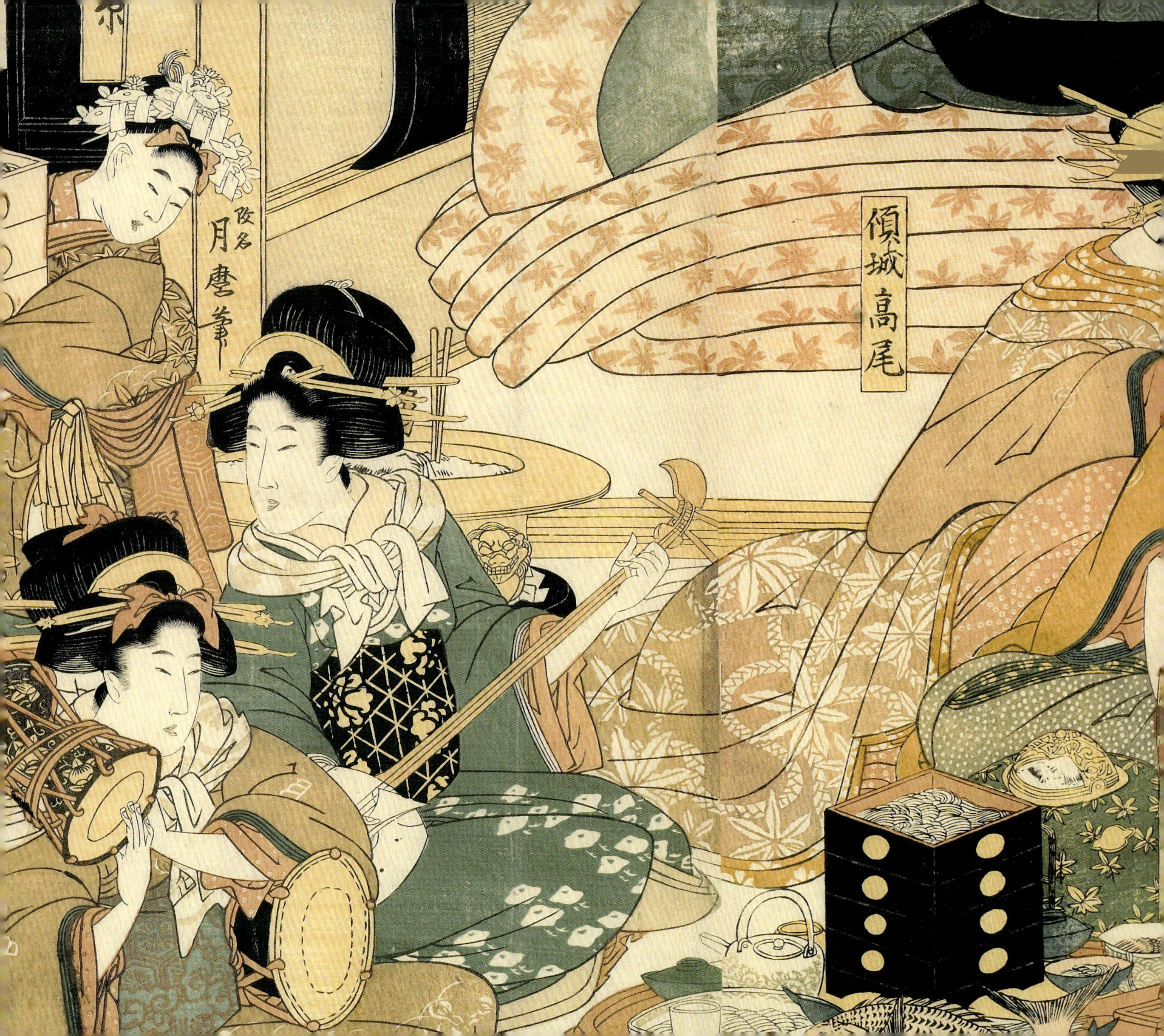
傾城高尾
改名 月麿筆

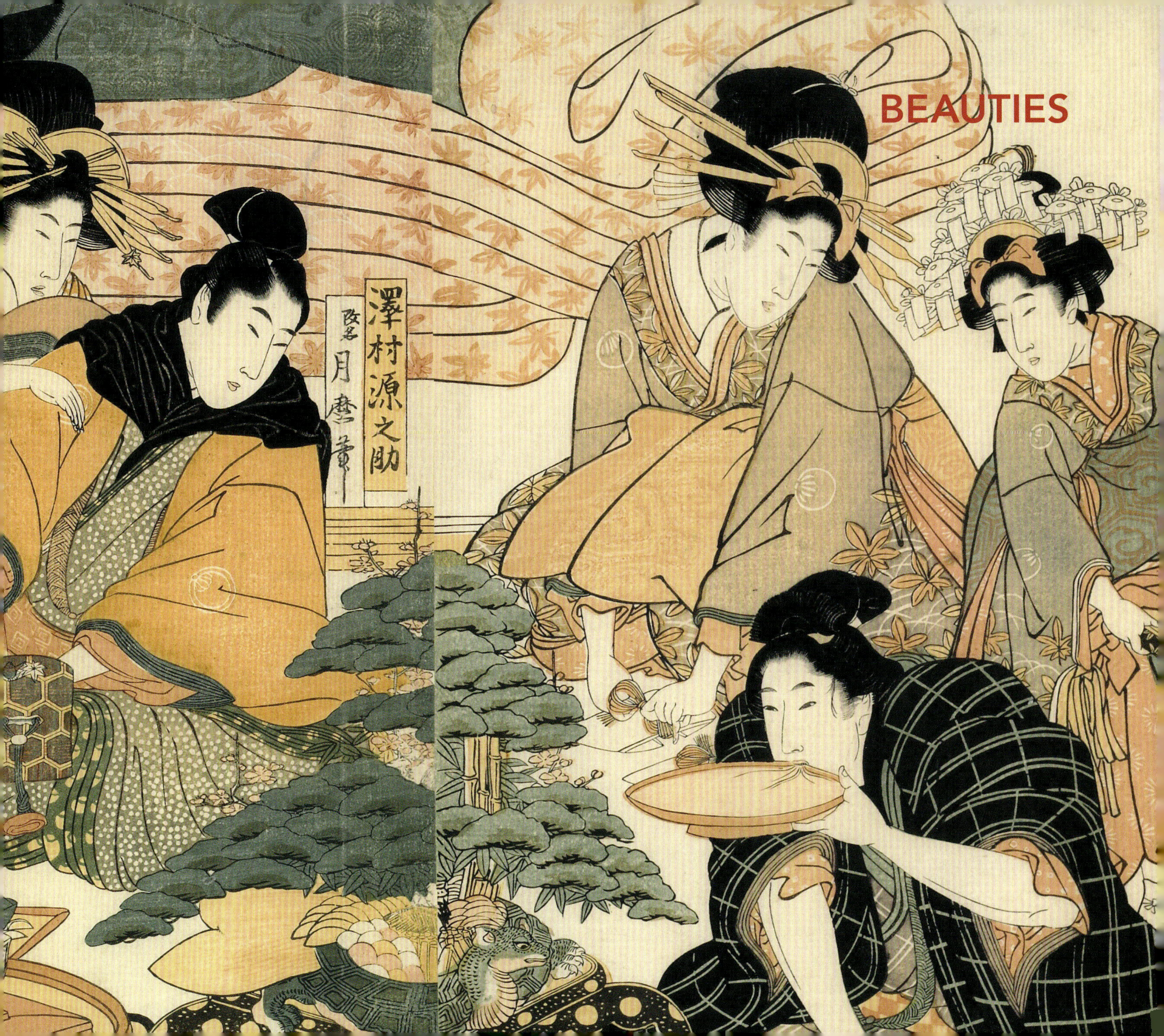
BEAUTIES
澤村源之助
磐月麿畫

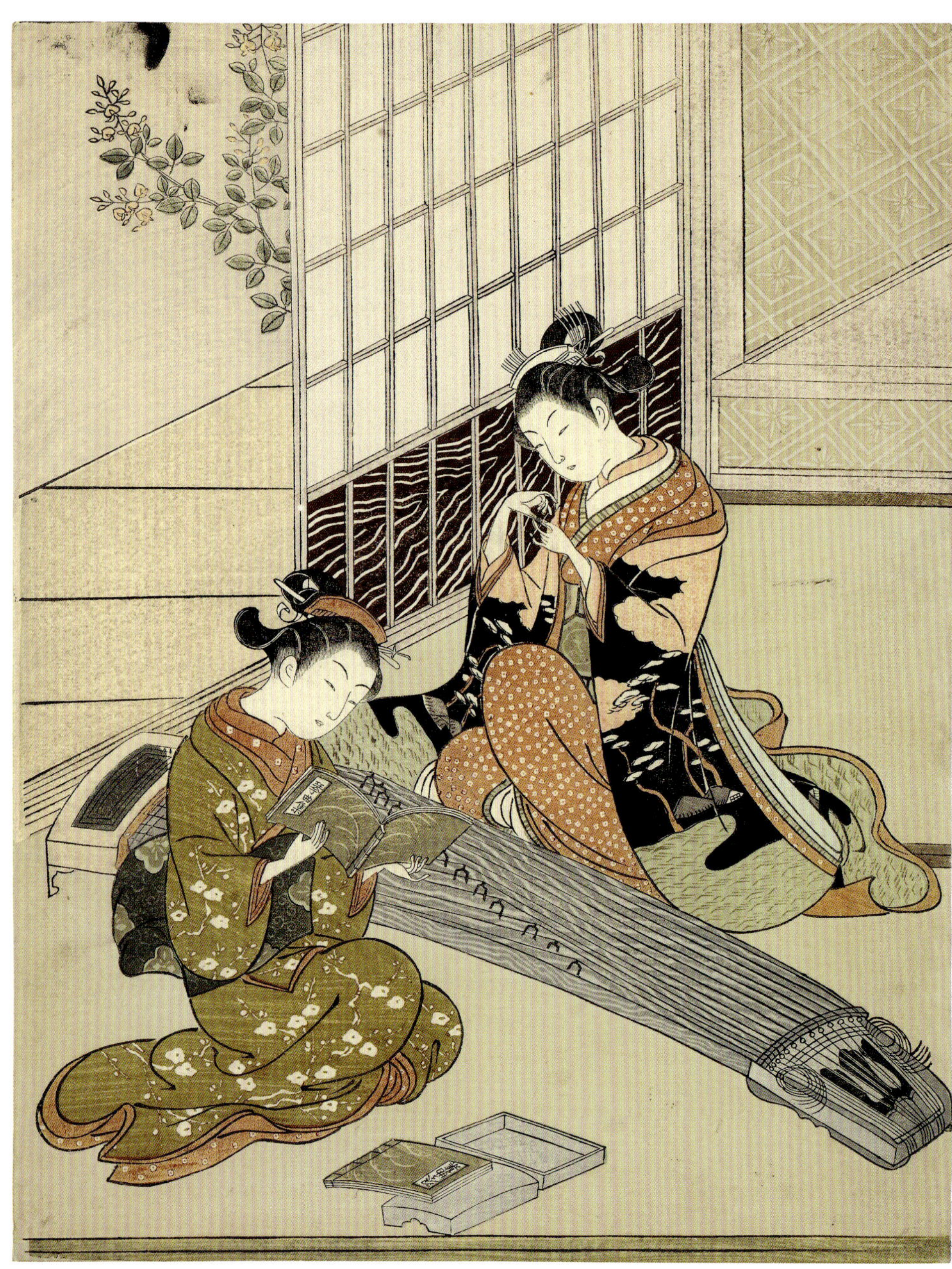

7
Suzuki Harunobu (1725–1770)
The Descending Geese of the Koto Bridge,
from the series *Eight Parlor Views*, 1766

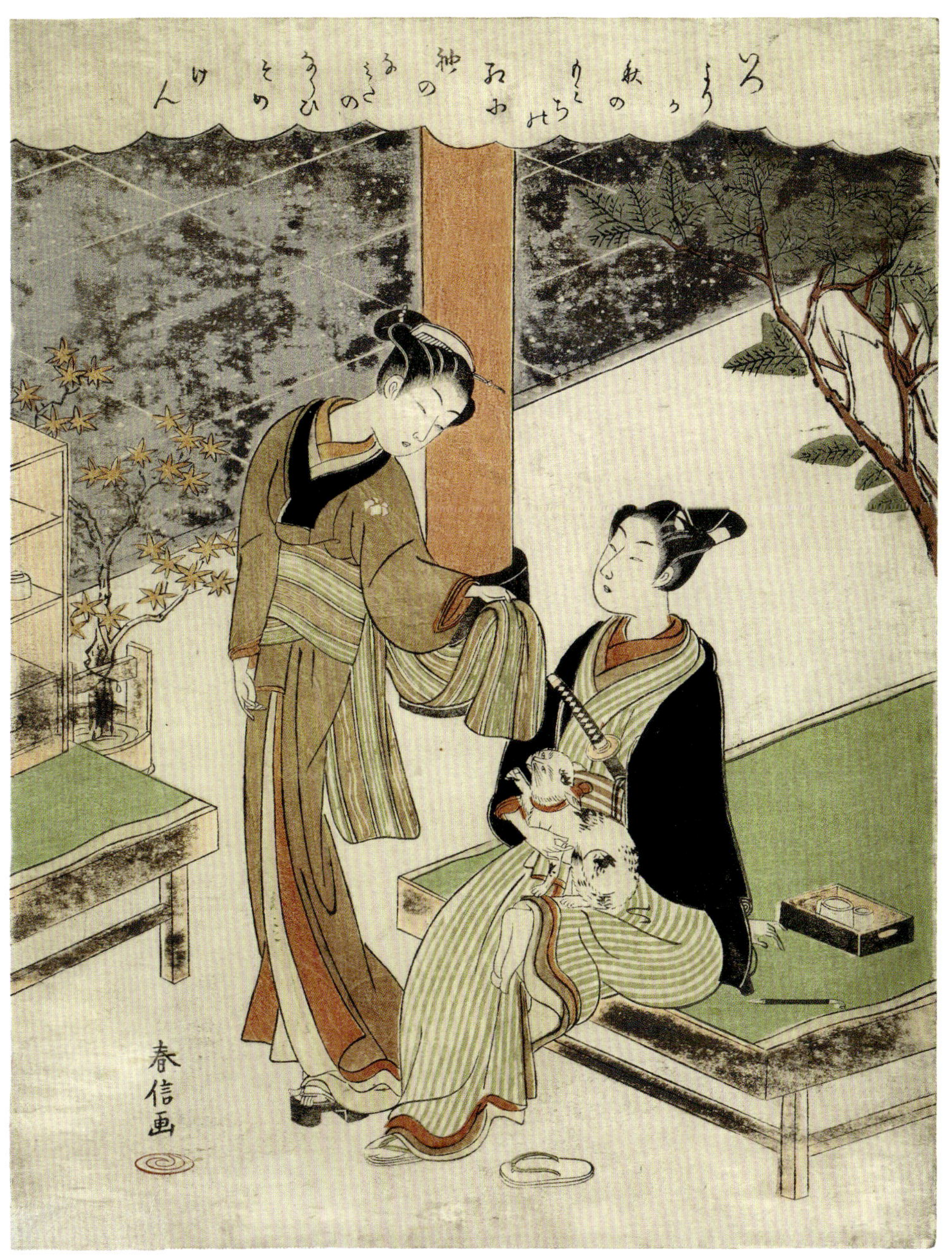

8

Suzuki Harunobu (1725–1770)

Osen Playing with a Cat Held by a Visitor
to Her Tea Shop, ca. 1768–1770

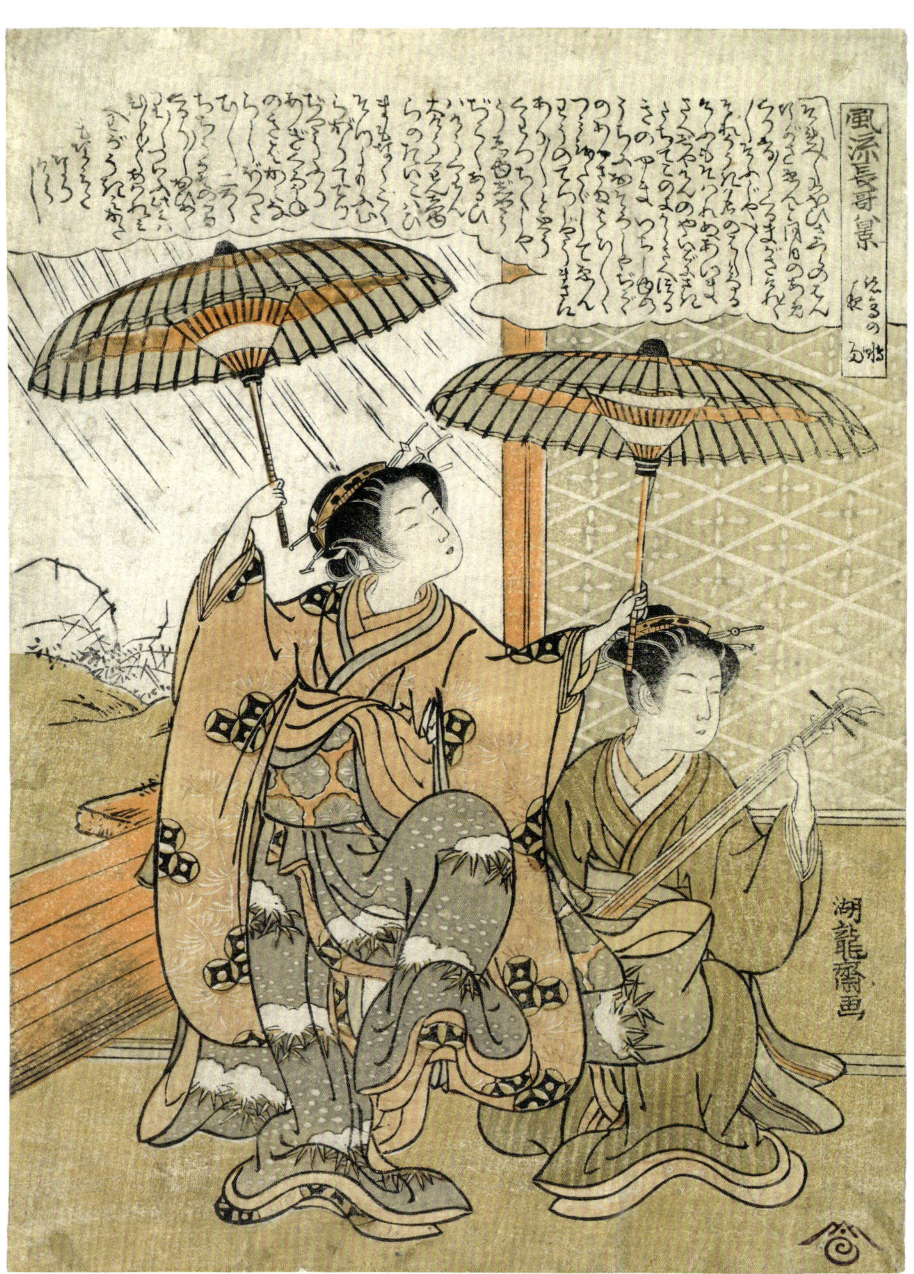

9

Isoda Koryūsai (active 1764–1788)

Night Rain, from the series *Eight Elegant Views of Nagauta Performances*, ca. 1772–1776

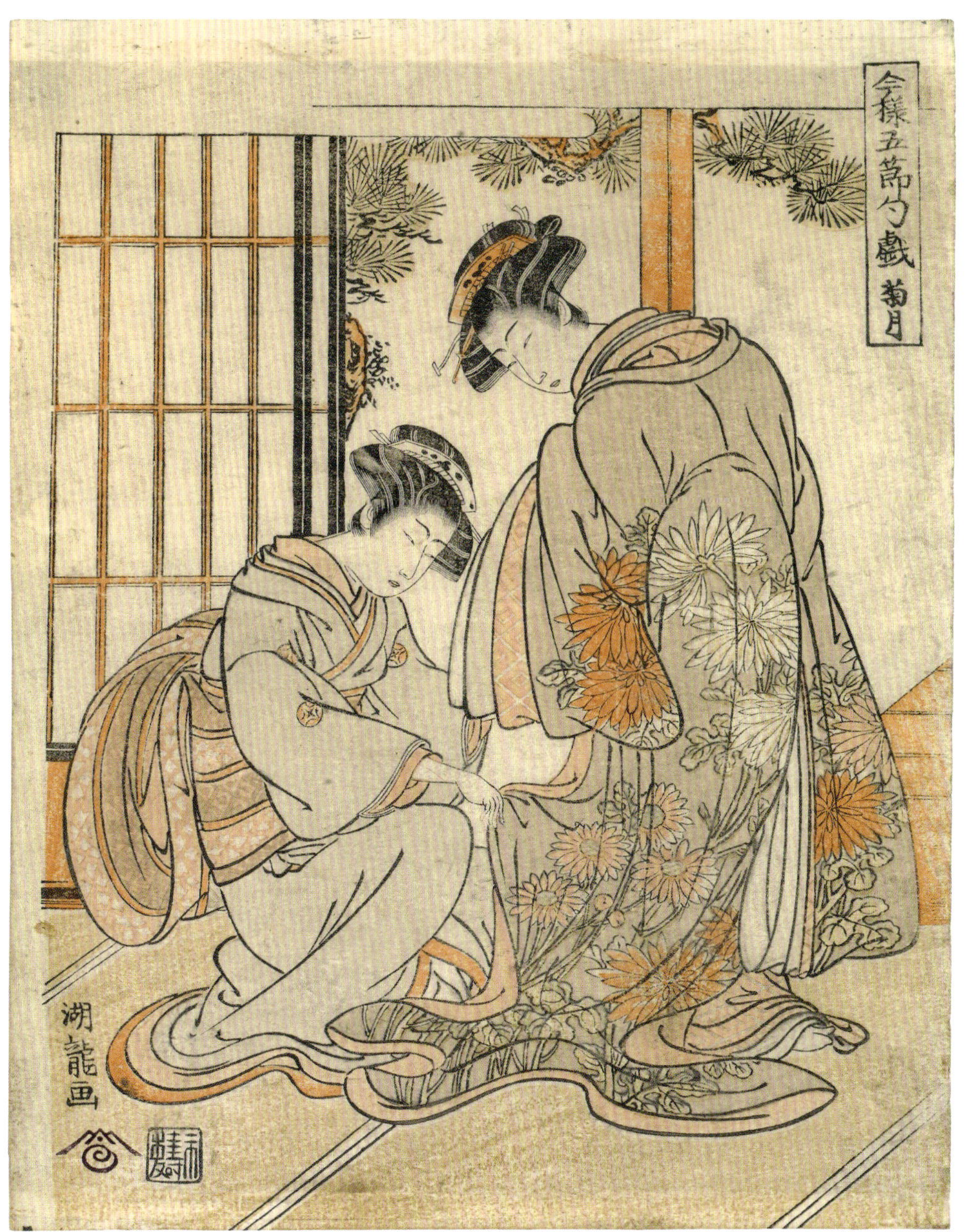

10

Isoda Koryūsai (active 1764–1788)

The Chrysanthemum Festival (Ninth Month),
from the series *Modern Amusements for the
Five Seasonal Festivals*, ca. 1775–1780

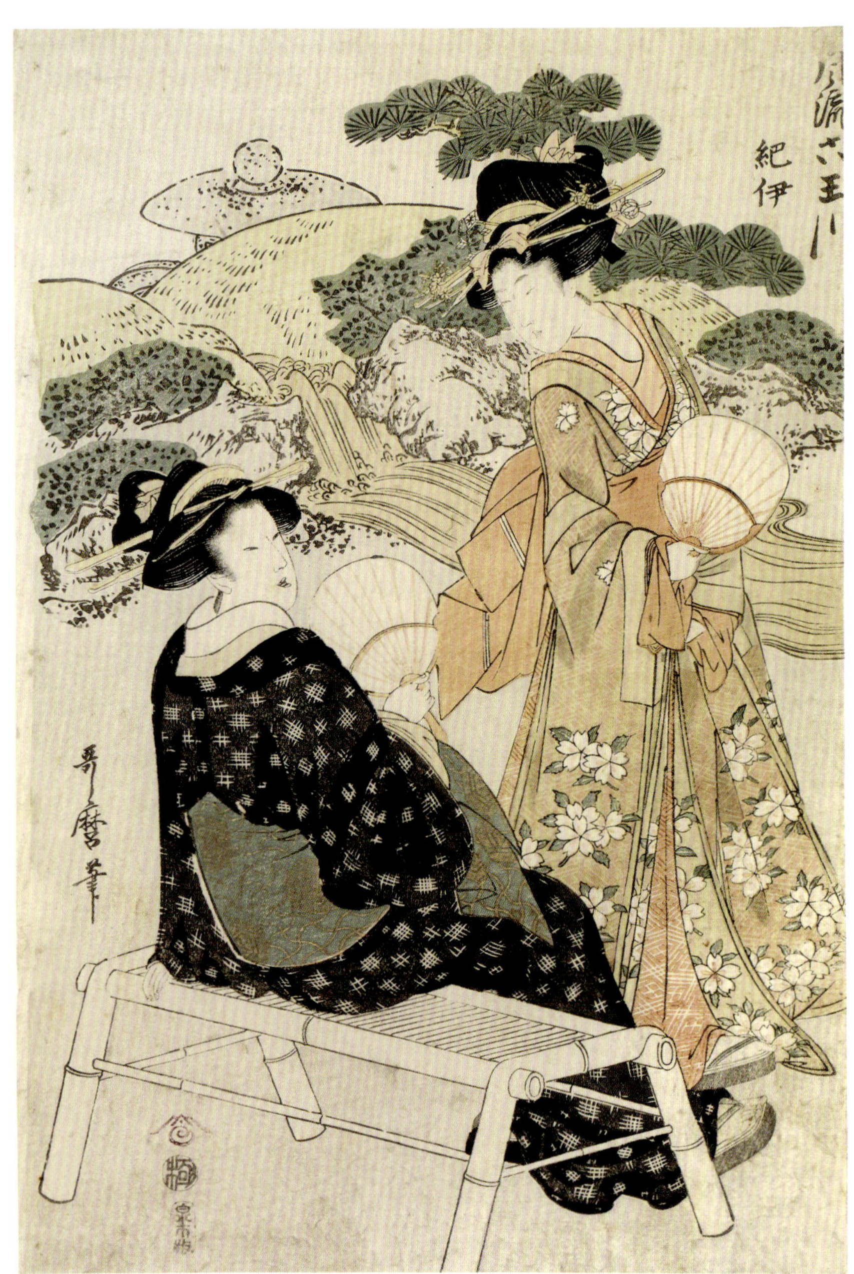

11

Kitagawa Utamaro (ca. 1754–1806)
Two Women with Fans beside a Stream, from
the series *The Six Elegant Tama Rivers*,
ca. 1802–1805

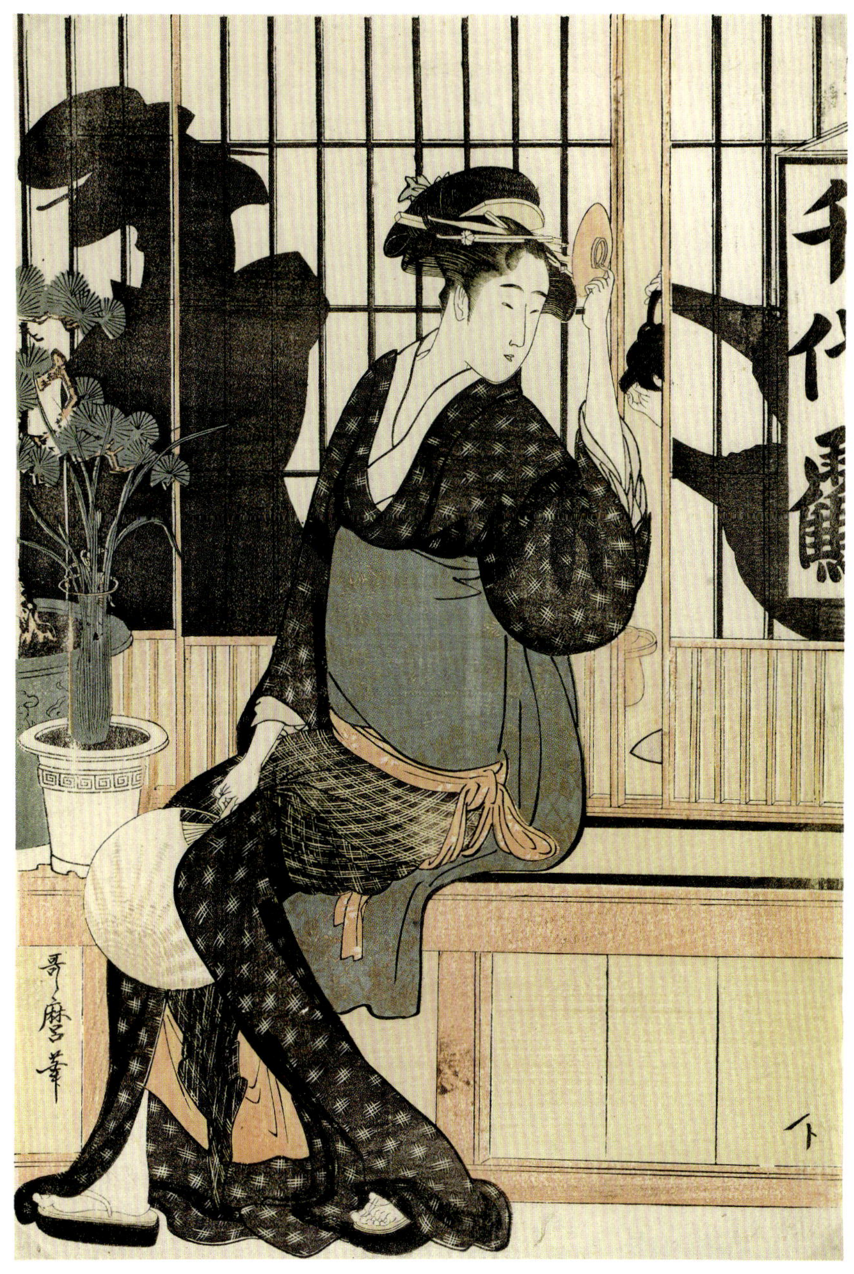

12

Kitagawa Utamaro (ca. 1754–1806)

The Chiyozuru Teahouse–Orise, from an untitled
series of teahouses and waitresses, ca. 1794–1795

13

Kitagawa Tsukimaro (active ca. 1800–1818, d. 1830)

The Courtesan Takao Entertaining the Actors Sawamura Gennosuke and Iwai Kiyotarō at the Miuraya, ca. 1805

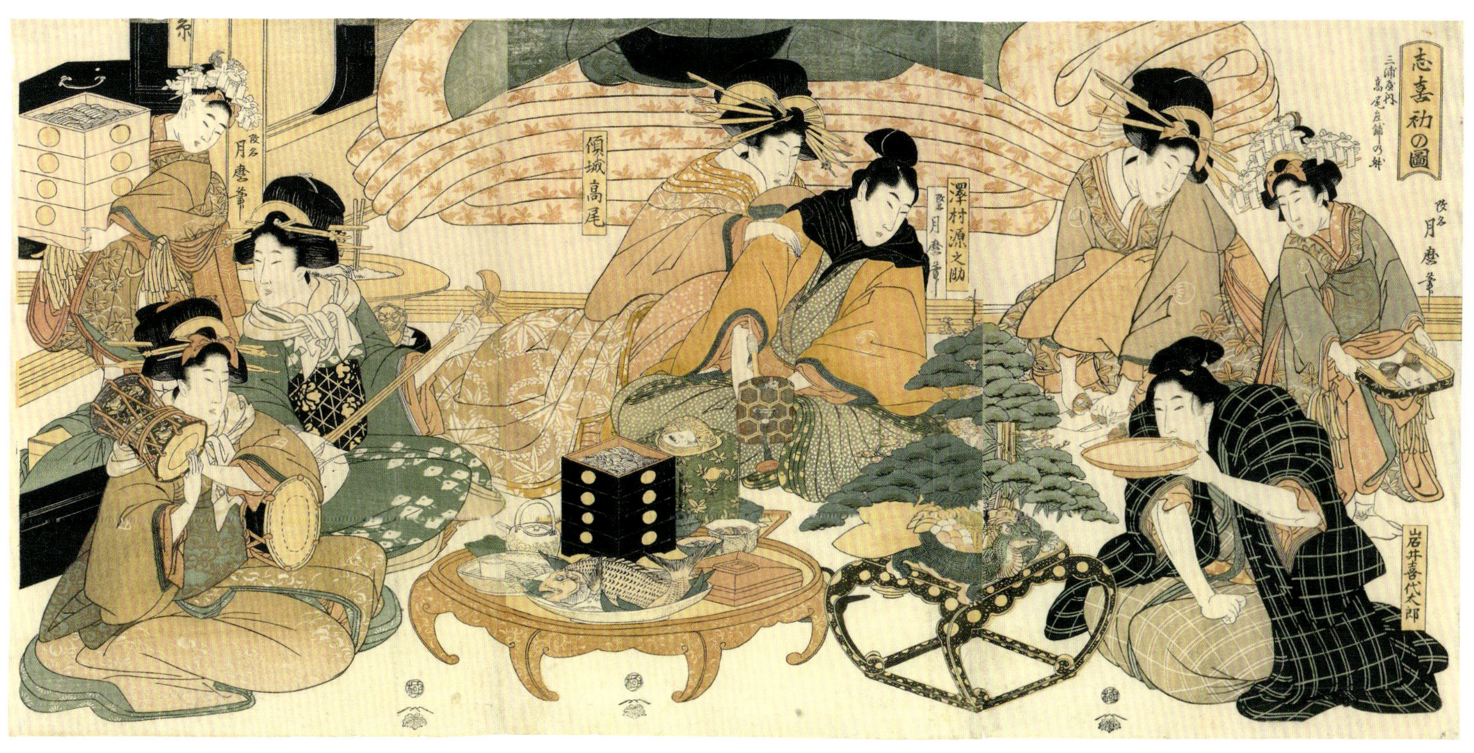
志喜初の圖
三浦屋内
高尾左籠半の丞
傾城高尾
澤村源之助
改名 月麿筆
改名 月麿筆
岩井喜代太郎

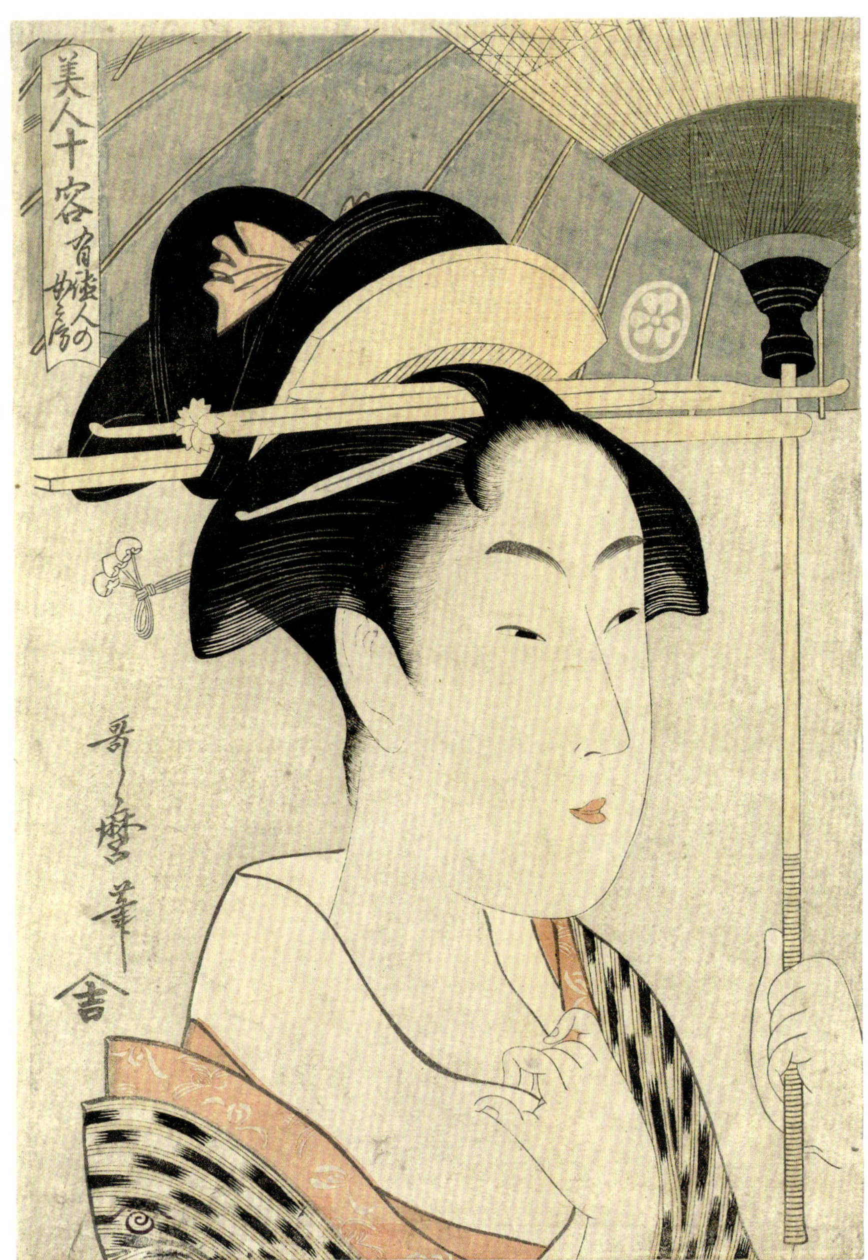

14
Kitagawa Utamaro (ca. 1754–1806)
Wife of a Virtuous Man, from the series
Ten Beautiful Faces, ca. 1797–1800

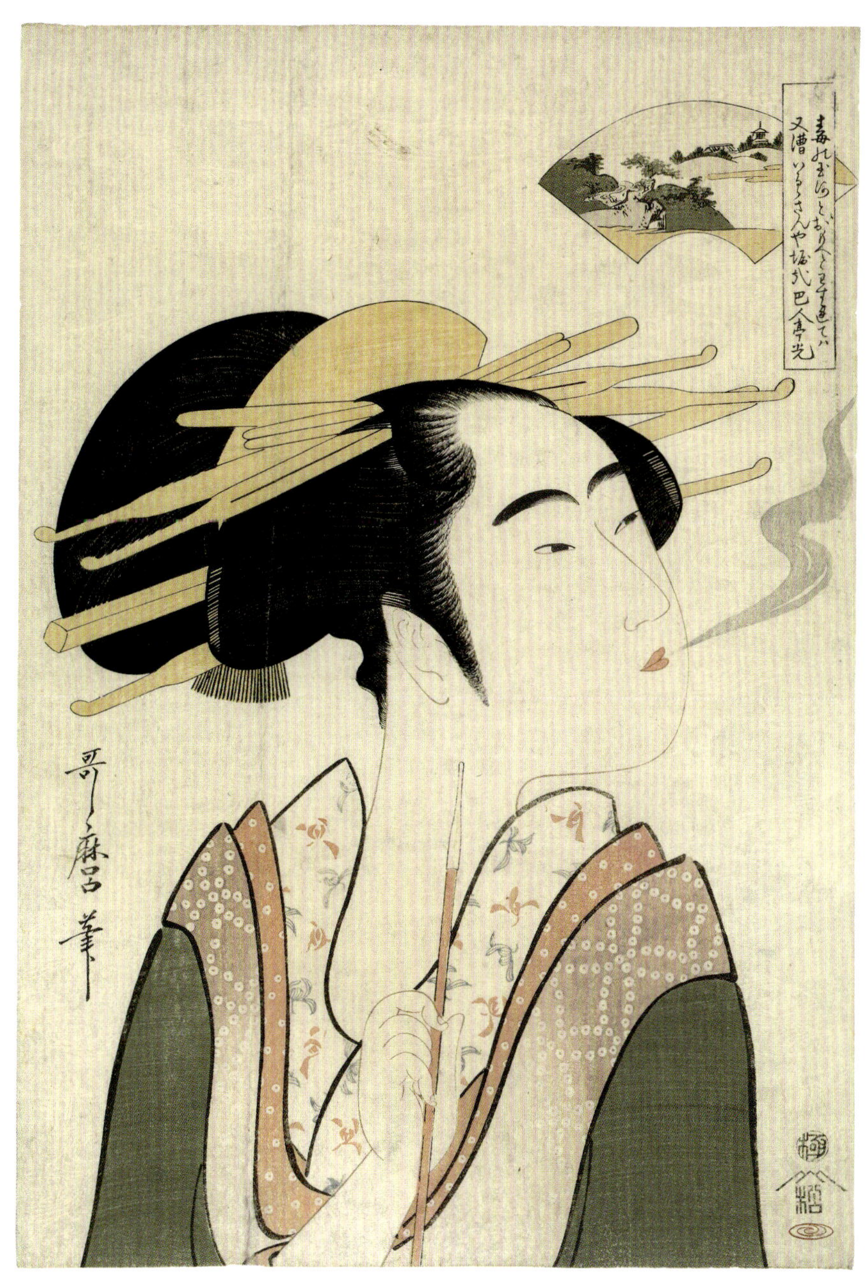

15

Kitagawa Utamaro (ca. 1754–1806)

*Tama River at Mount Kōya (Courtesan
Smoking a Pipe)*, from an untitled series
on the six Tama rivers, ca. 1795–1796

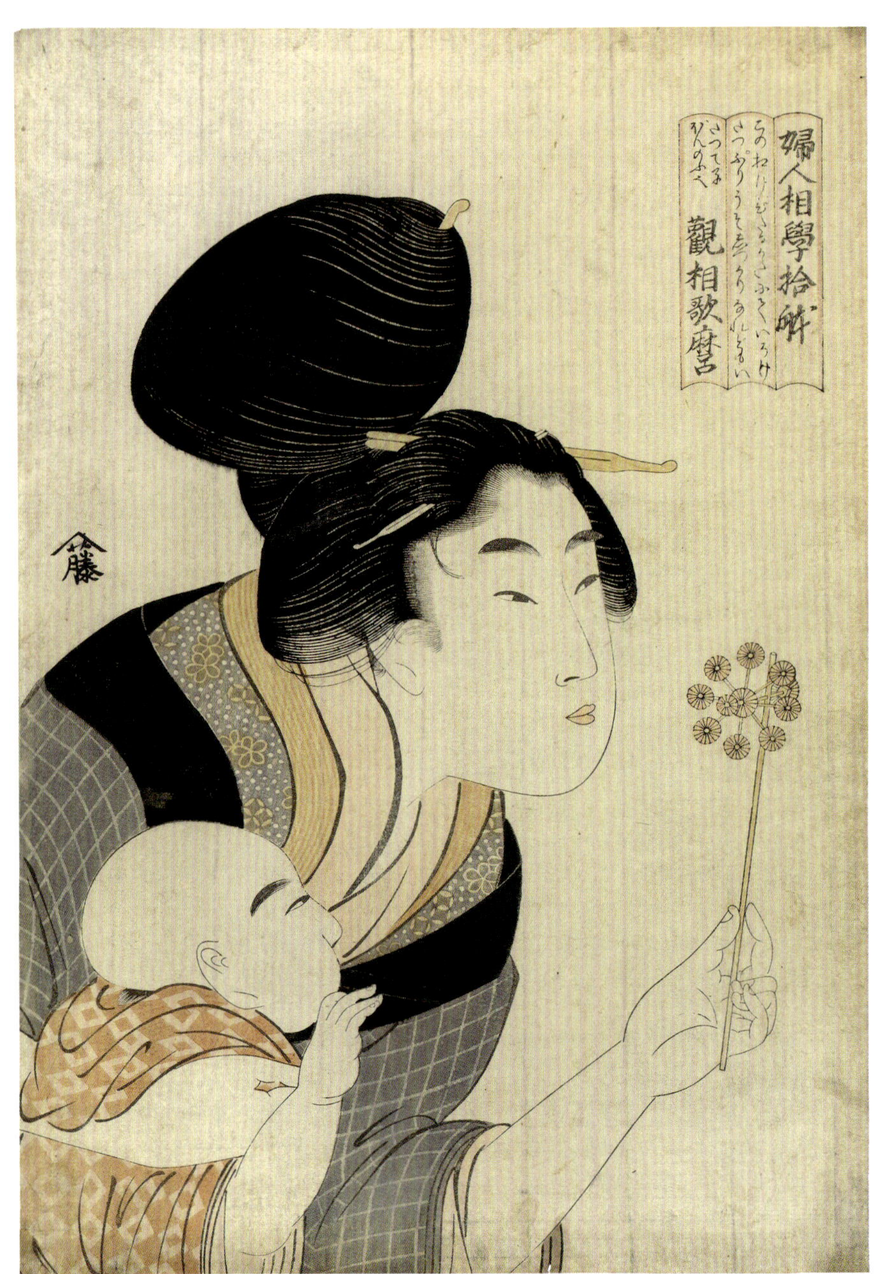

16

Kitagawa Utamaro (ca. 1754–1806)
Woman Blowing a Pinwheel, from the series
Physiognomies of Ten Women, 1792–1793

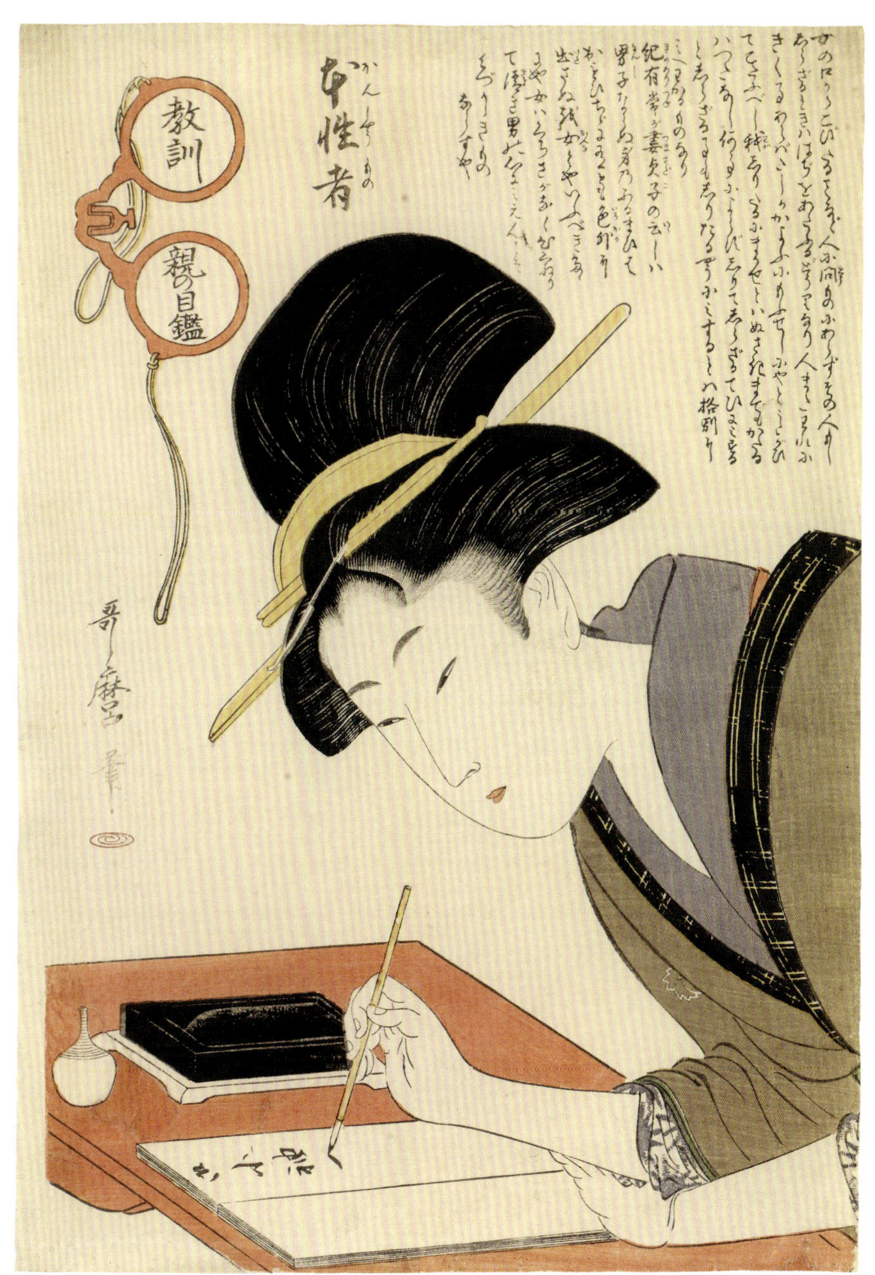

17

Kitagawa Utamaro (ca. 1754–1806)

A Woman of Character, from the series *Moral Instruction Seen through a Parent's Eyes*, ca. 1798–1802

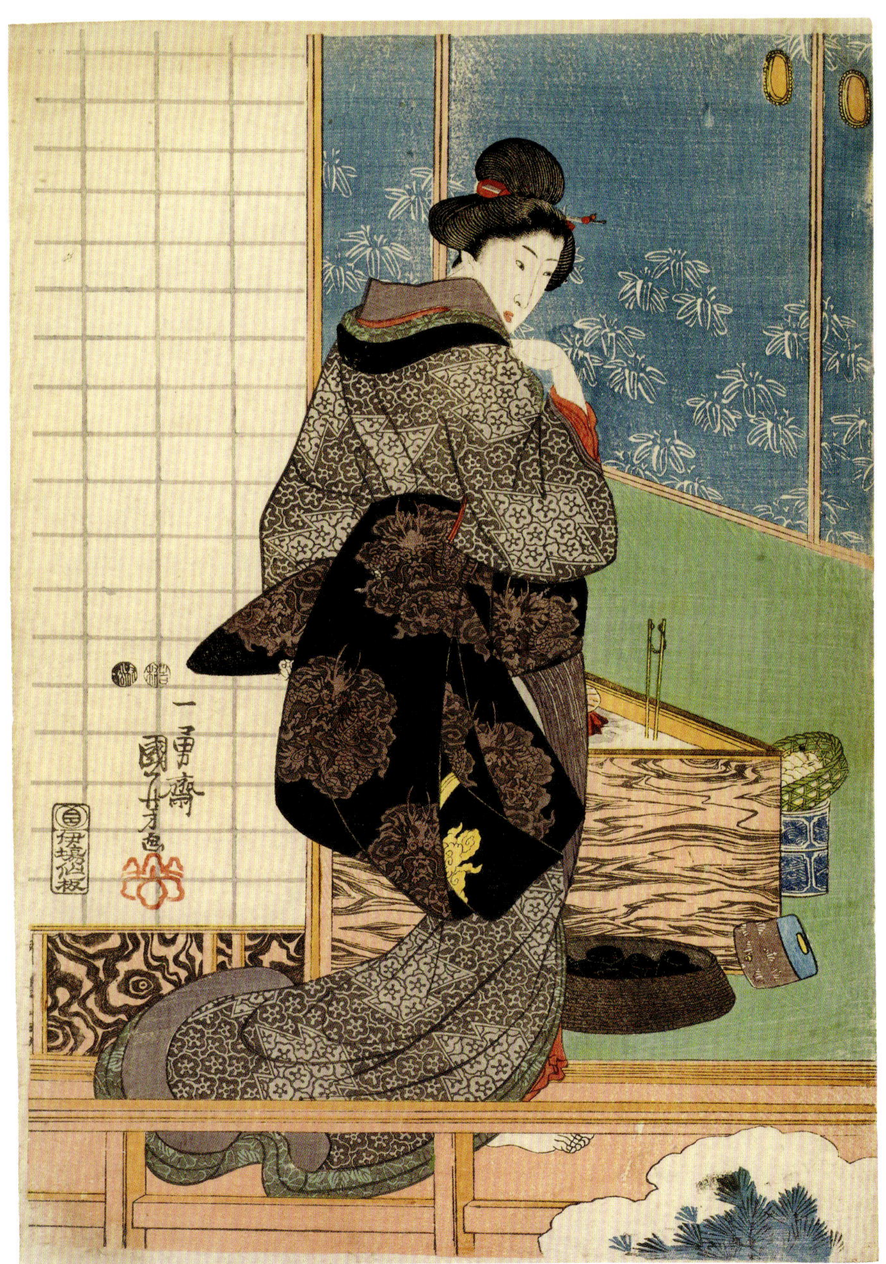

18

Utagawa Kuniyoshi (1798–1861)
Snowy Morning, from the series *Among Snow, Moon, and Flowers*, one sheet from a triptych, ca. 1847–1848

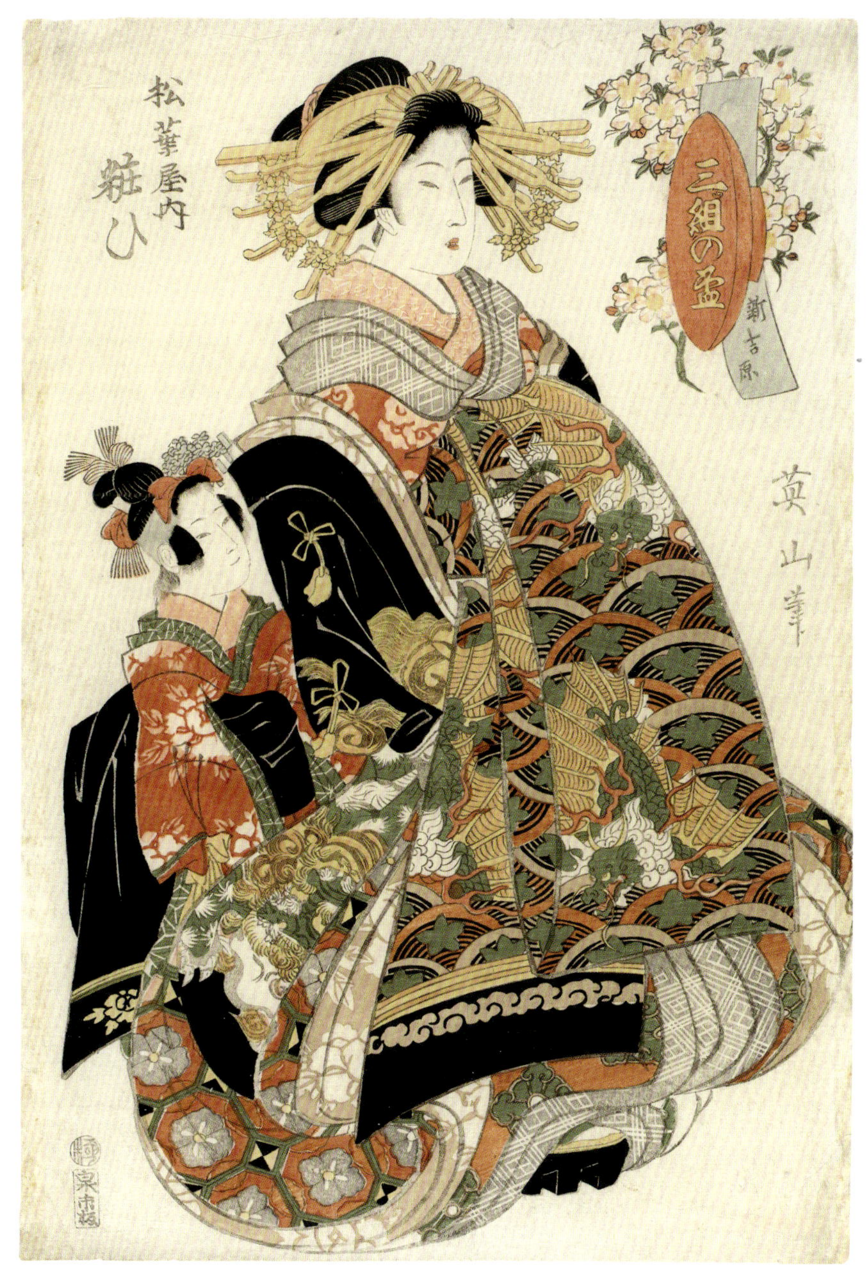

19

Kikukawa Eizan (1787–1867)

Yosooi of the Matsubaya, from the series *Three Wine Cups in the New Yoshiwara*, ca. 1815–1825

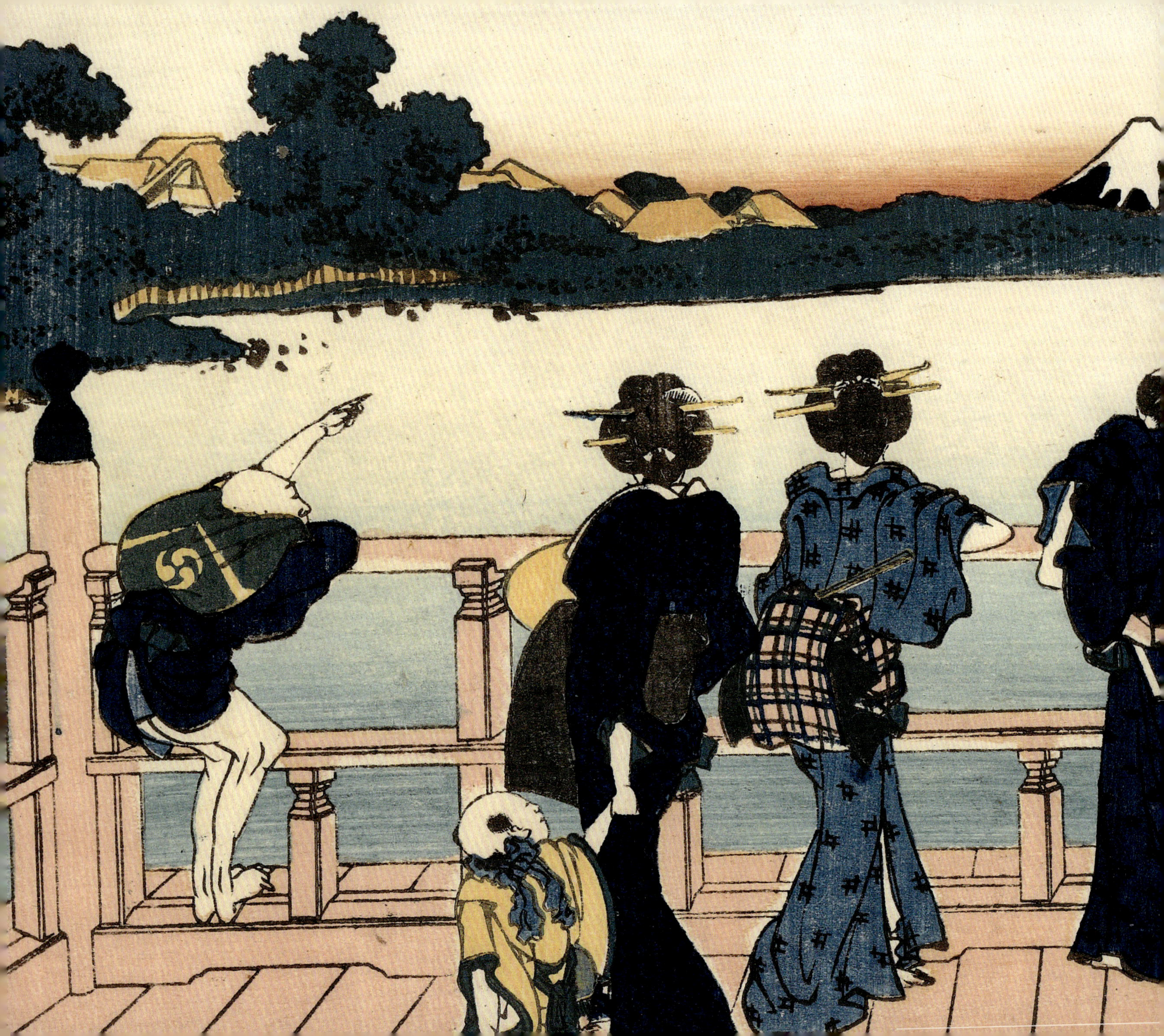

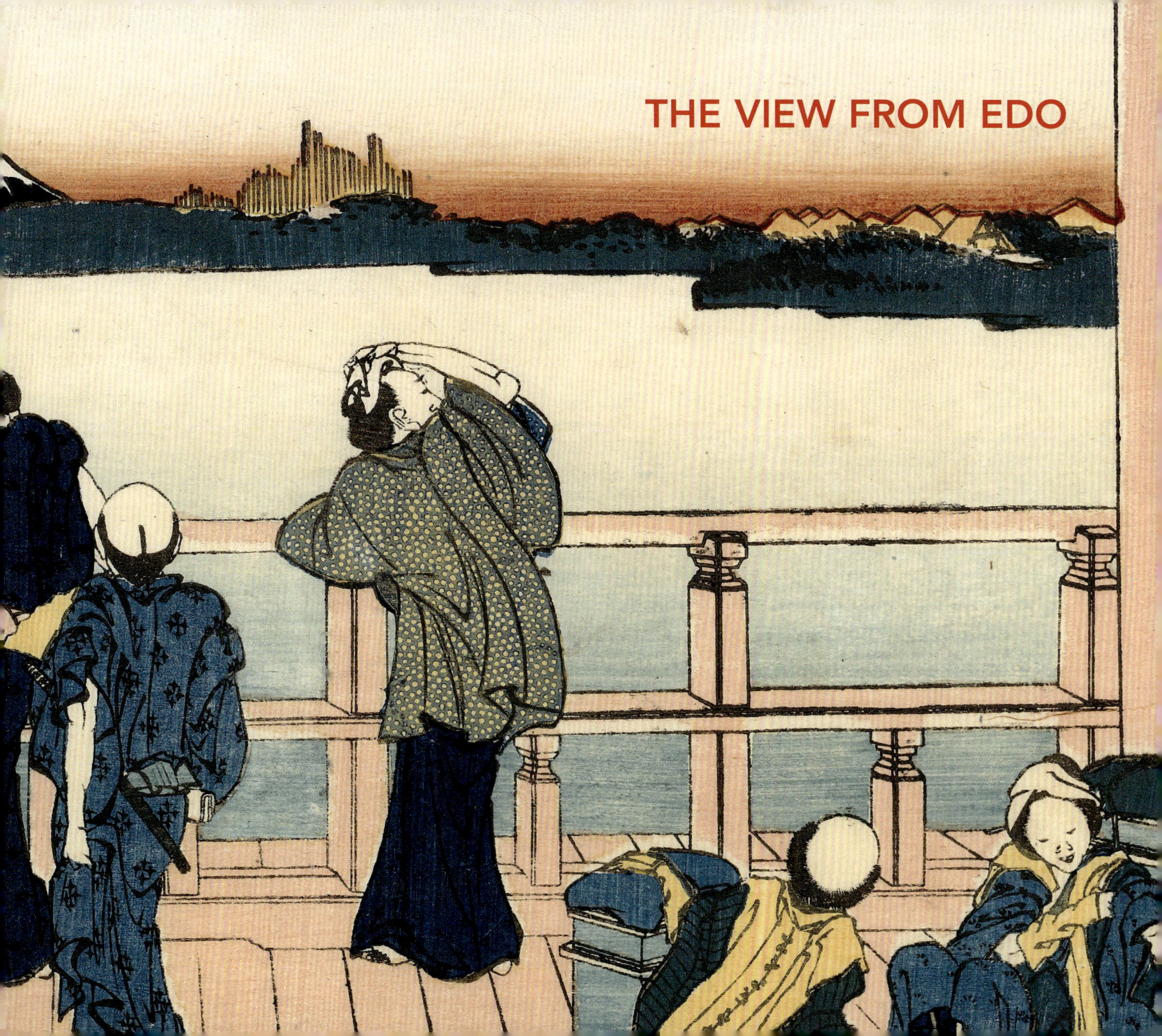
THE VIEW FROM EDO

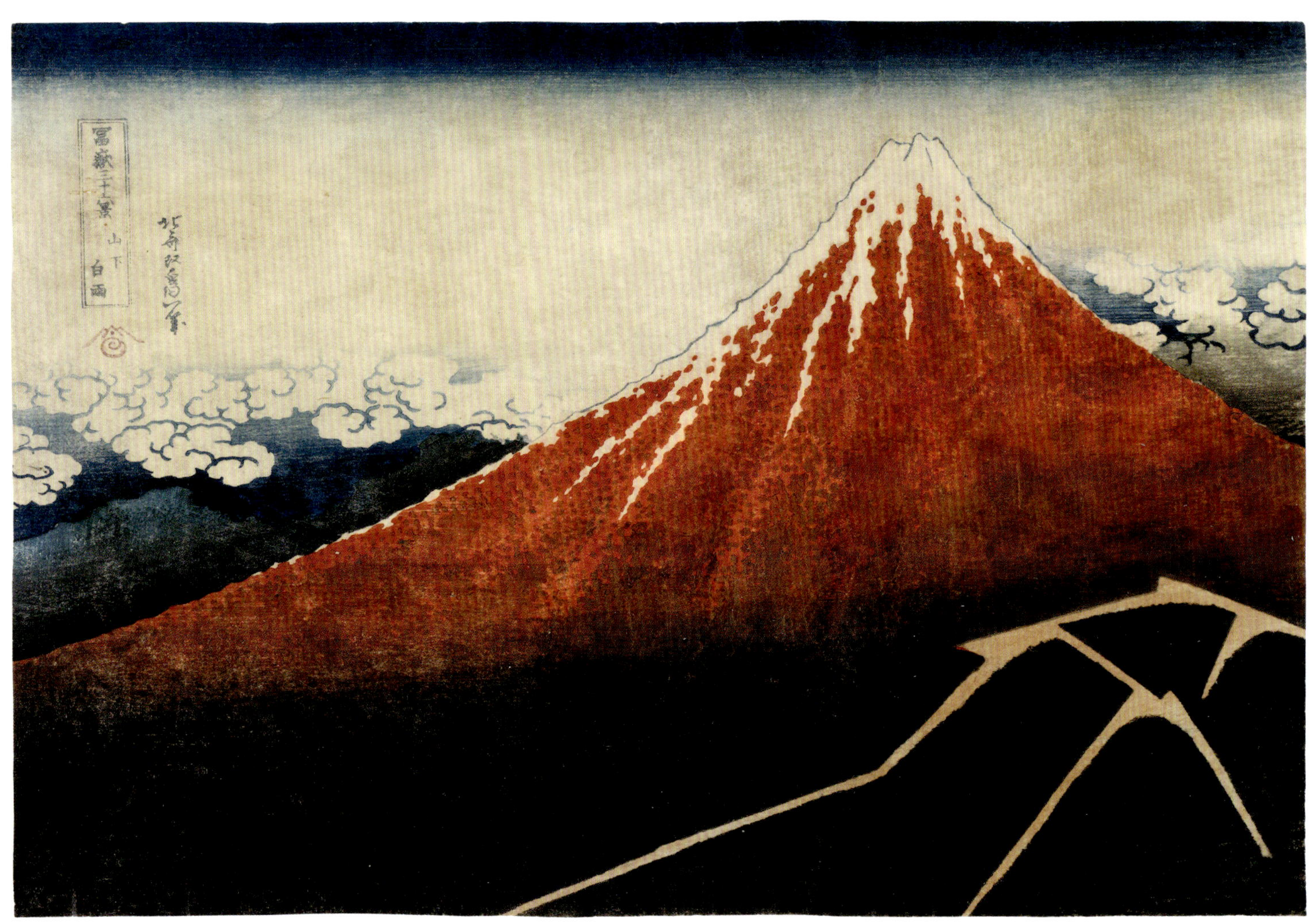

20

Katsushika Hokusai (1760–1849)

Storm below the Mountain, from the series
Thirty-Six Views of Mount Fuji, ca. 1830–1832

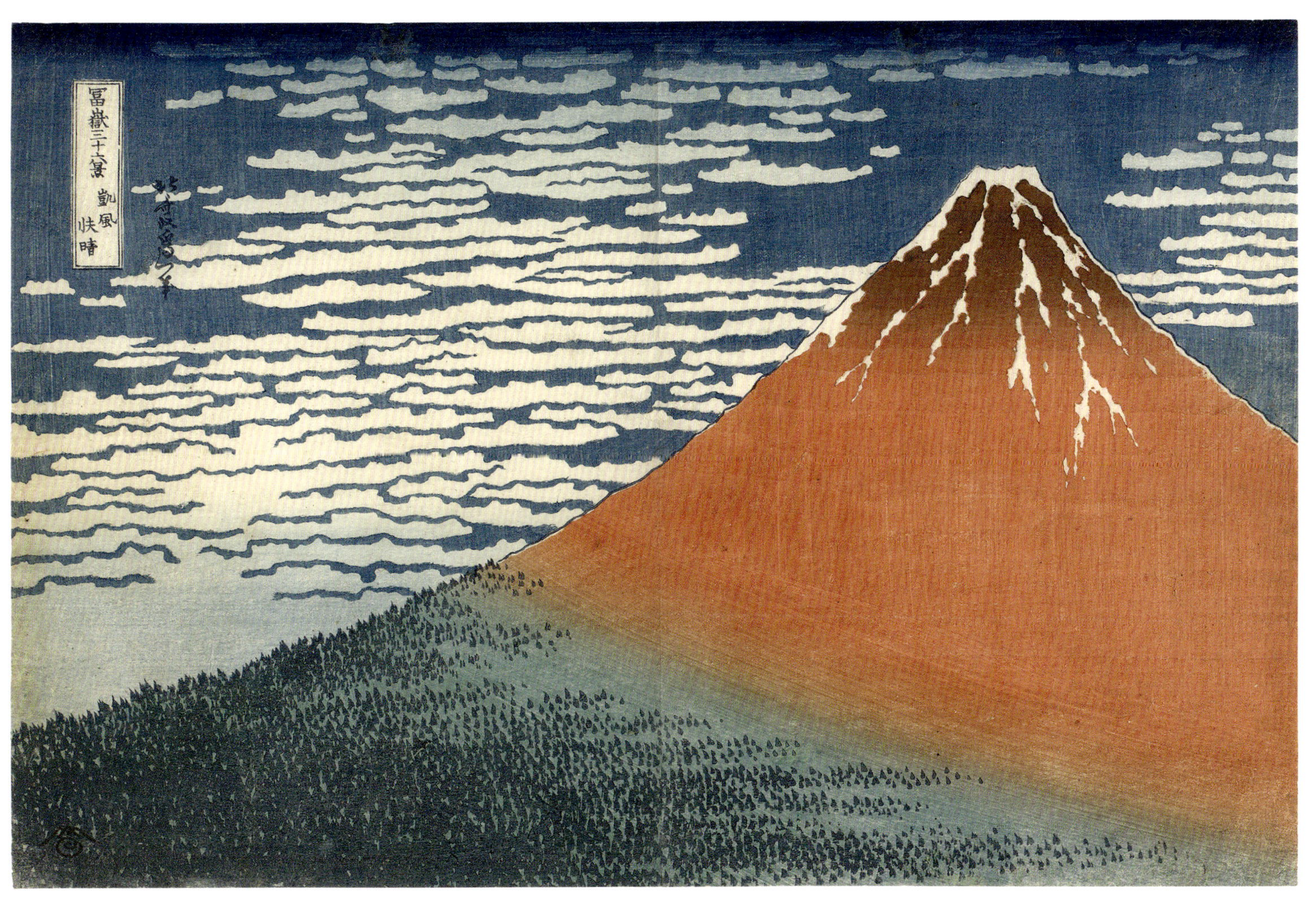

21

Katsushika Hokusai (1760–1849)

Fuji in Clear Weather, from the series
Thirty-Six Views of Mount Fuji, ca. 1830–1832

22

Utagawa Toyoharu (1735–1814)
The Cool of the Evening near Ryōgoku Bridge in Edo,
from the series *Perspective Pictures*, ca. 1770–1780

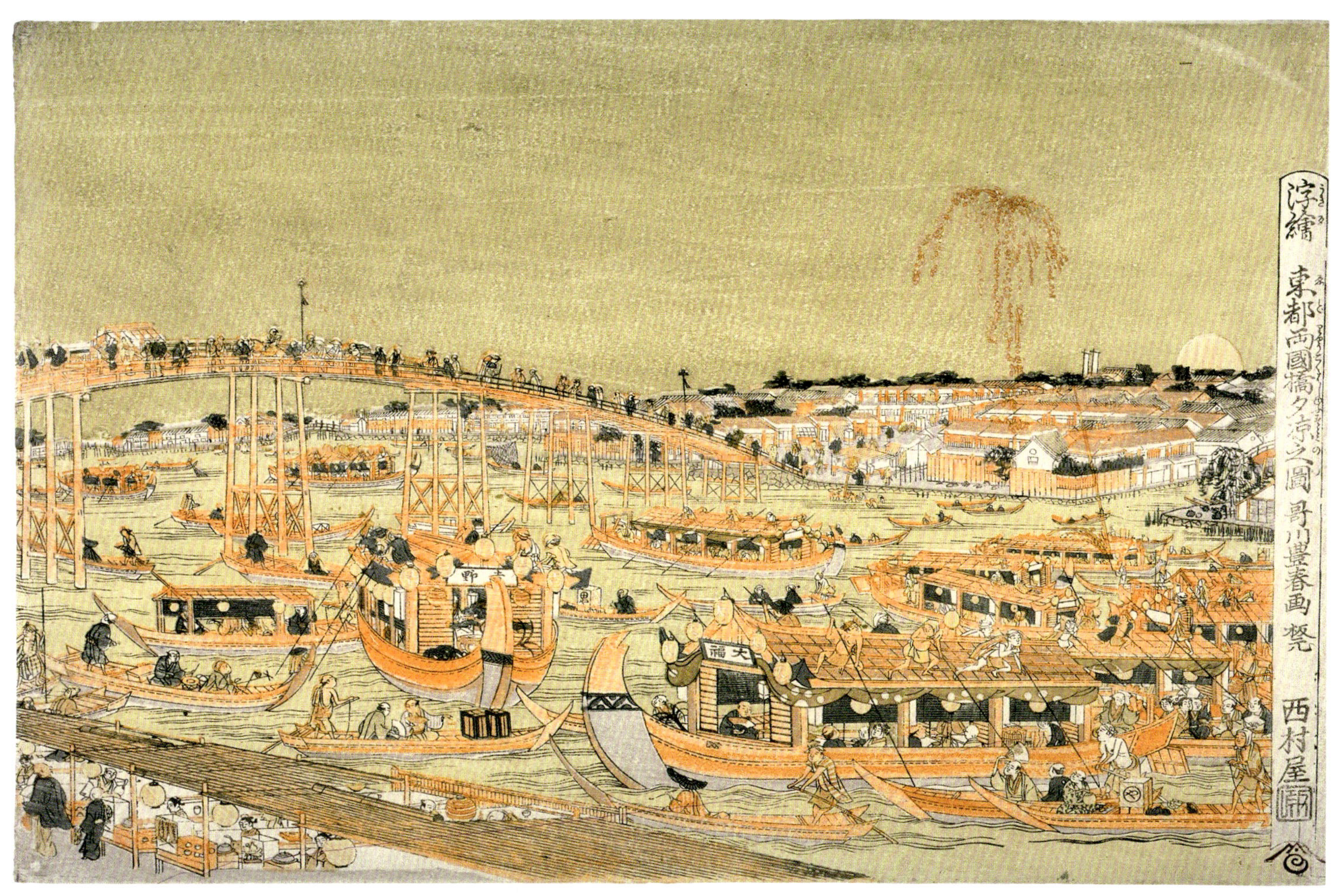

浮繪 東都両國橋夕涼之圖 哥川豊春画
西村屋

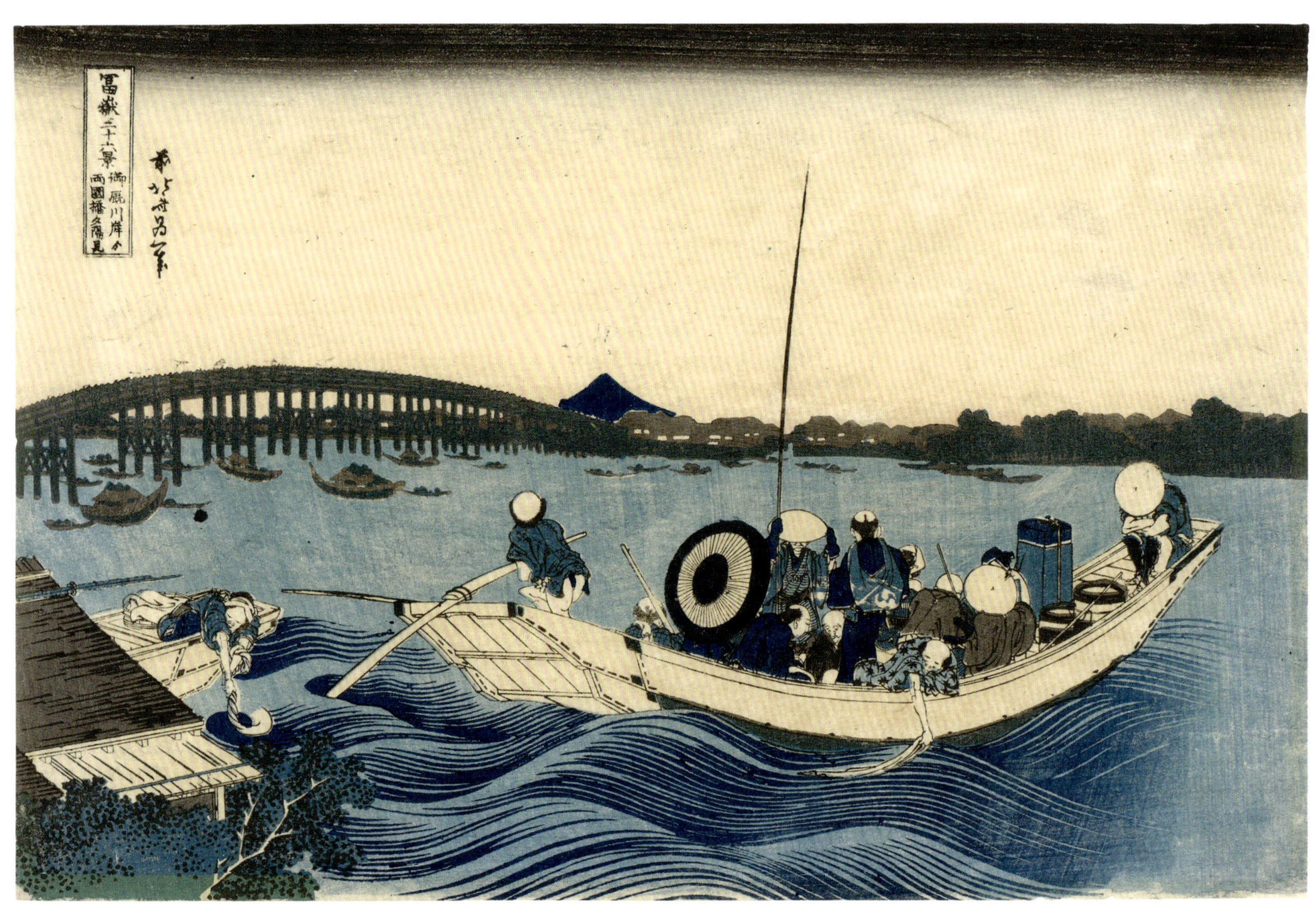

23

Katsushika Hokusai (1760–1849)

Fuji from Onmaya Embankment with Sunset over Ryōgoku Bridge,
from the series *Thirty-Six Views of Mount Fuji*, ca. 1830–1832

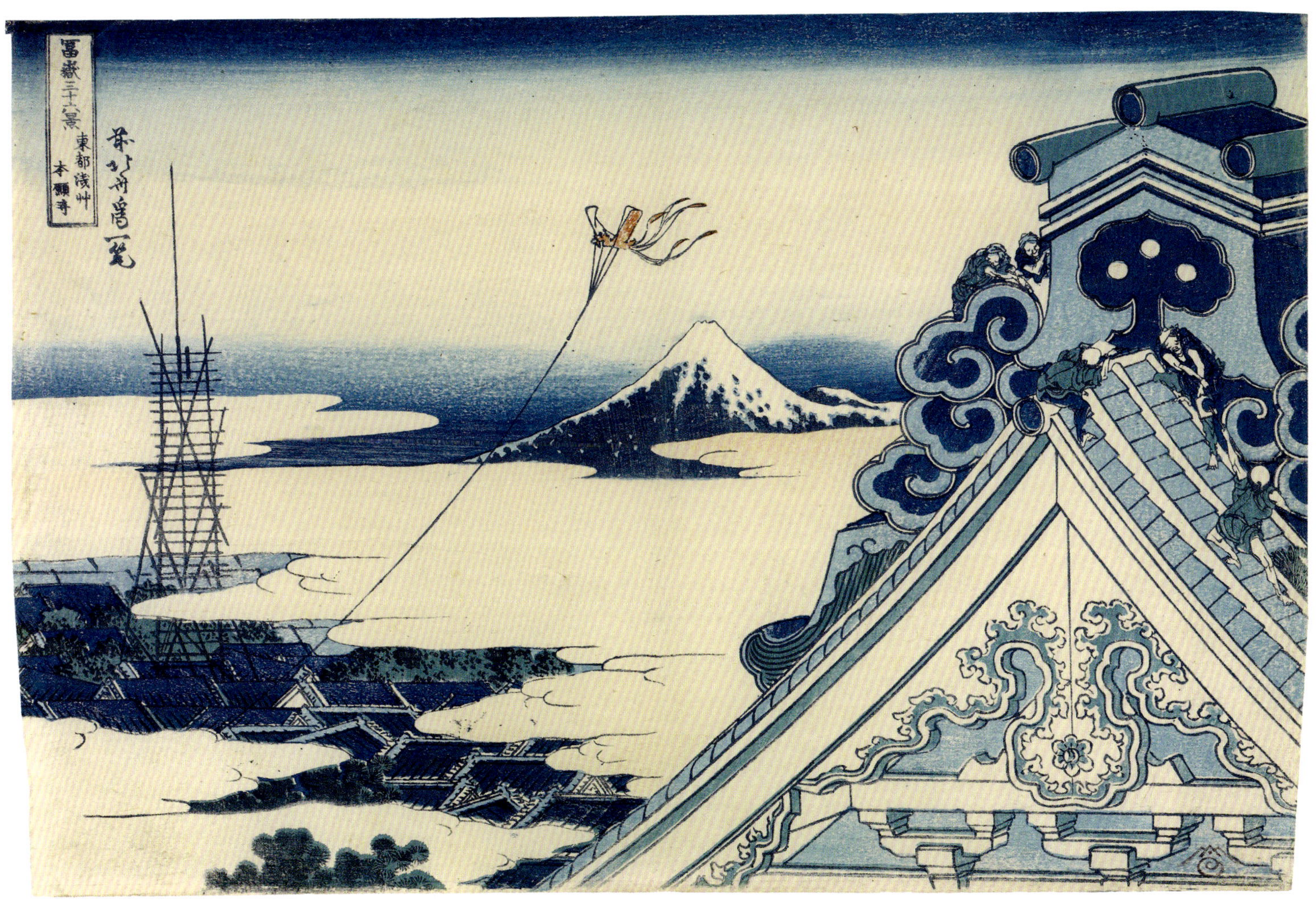

24

Katsushika Hokusai (1760–1849)

Fuji from the Hongan Temple at Asakusa in Edo, from the series
Thirty-Six Views of Mount Fuji, ca. 1830–1832

Katsushika Hokusai (1760–1849)

Under the Wave off Kanagawa (The Great Wave), from the series
Thirty-Six Views of Mount Fuji, ca. 1830–1832

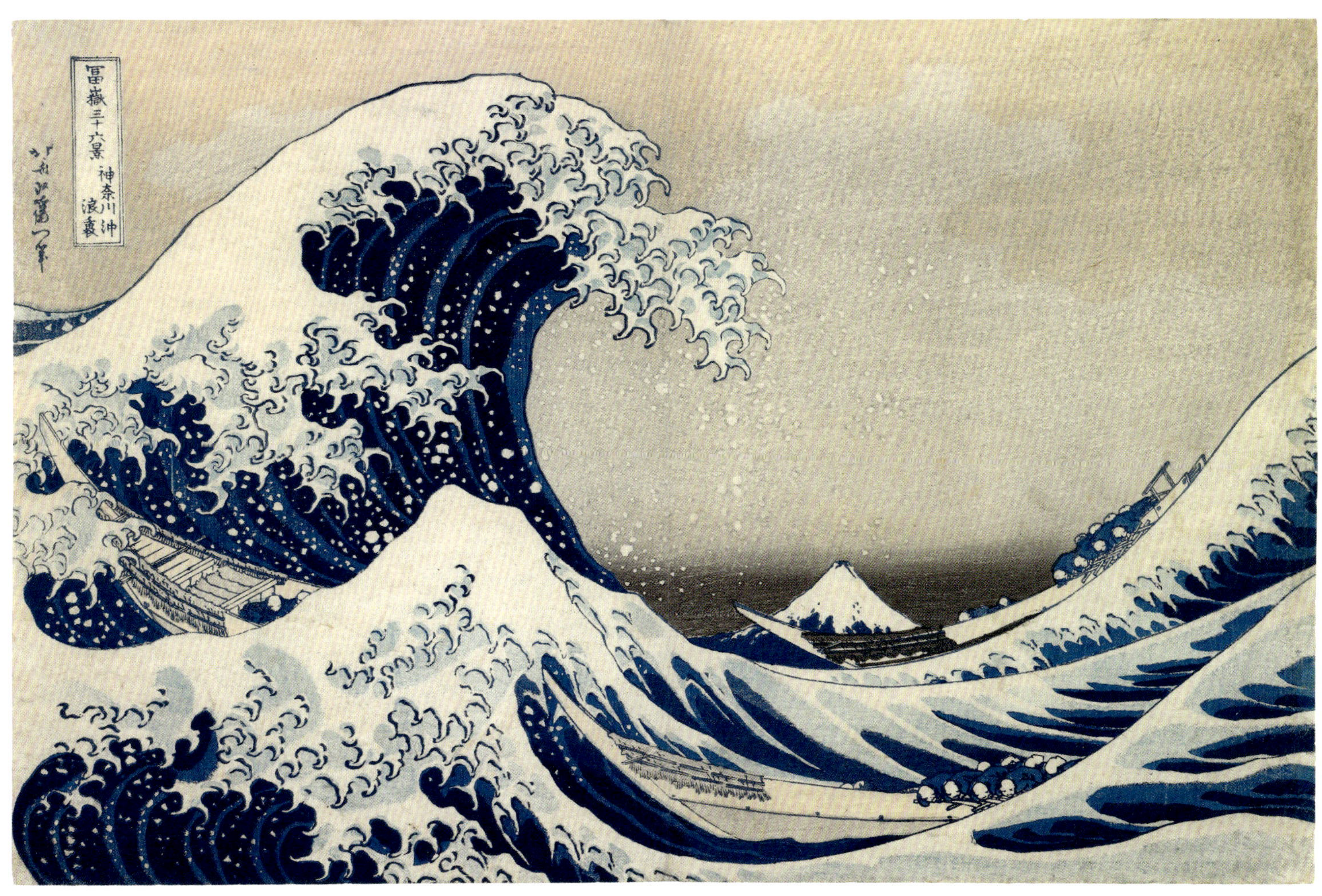冨嶽三十六景 神奈川沖浪裏
北斎改爲一筆

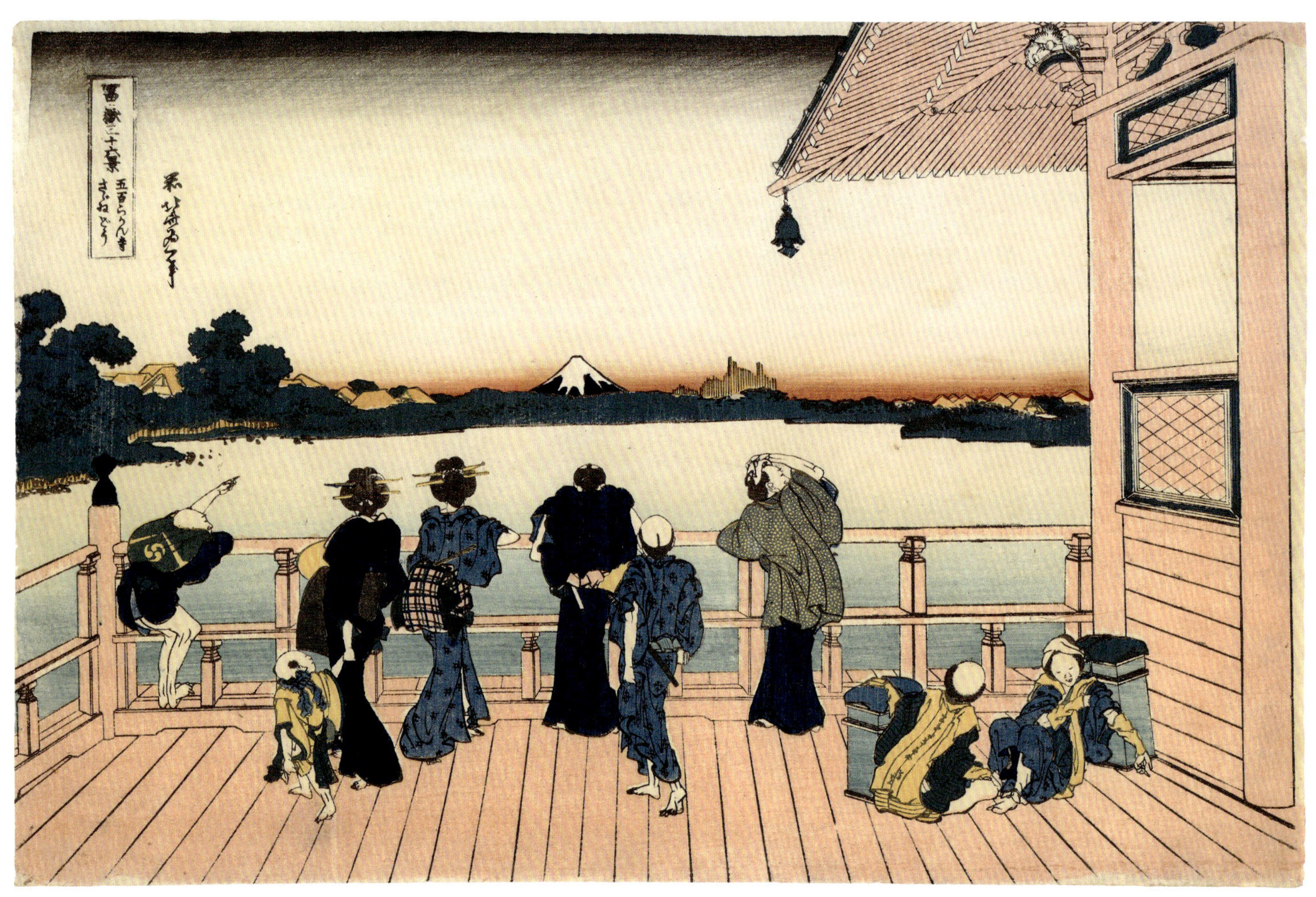

26

Katsushika Hokusai (1760–1849)

Fuji from the Sazai Hall at the Temple of the Five Hundred Rakan, from the series *Thirty-Six Views of Mount Fuji*, ca. 1830–1832

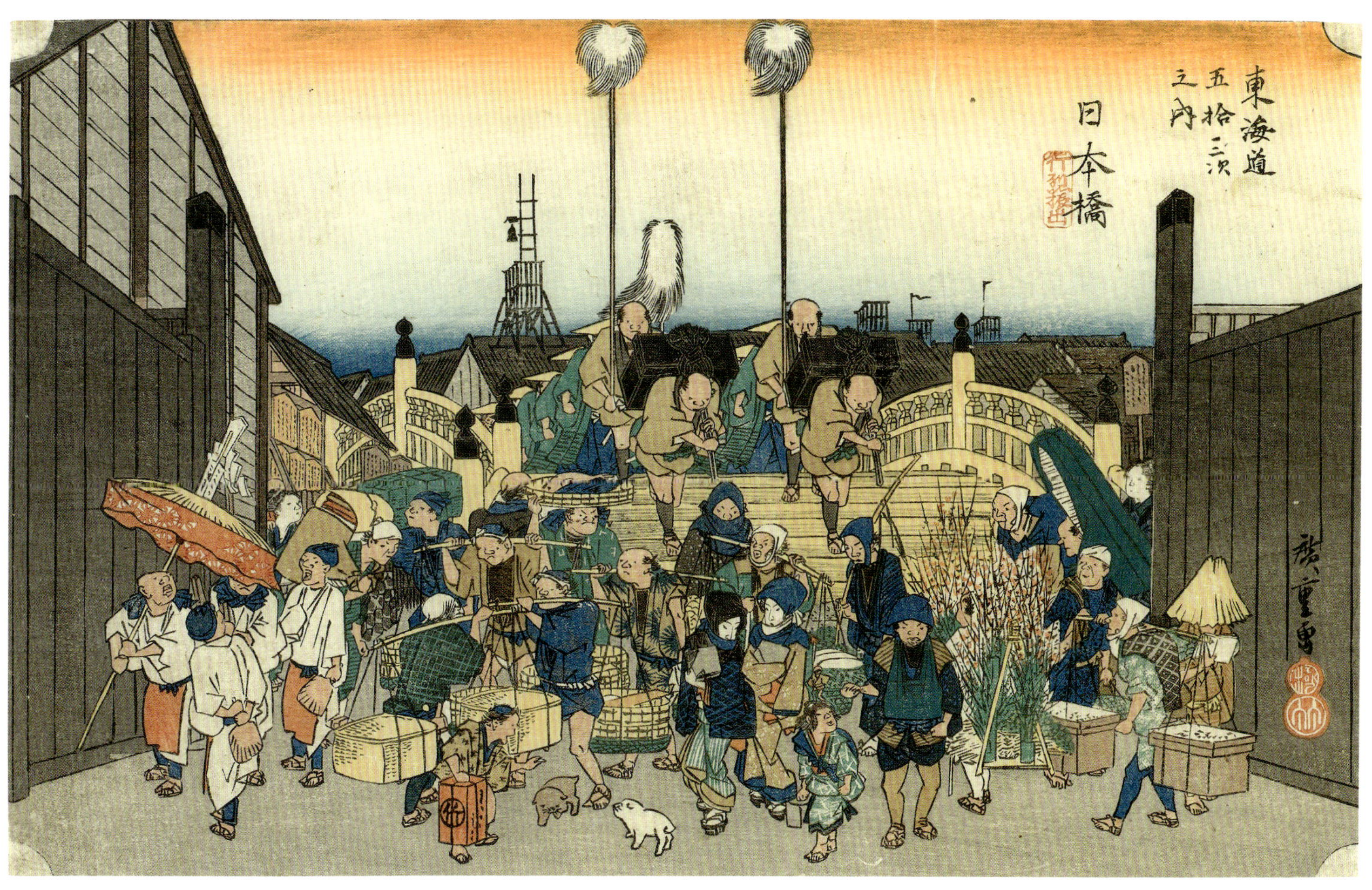

27

Utagawa Hiroshige (1797–1858)

A Daimyō Procession Setting Forth from Nihonbashi, from the
series *Fifty-Three Stations of the Tōkaidō*, ca. 1831–1834

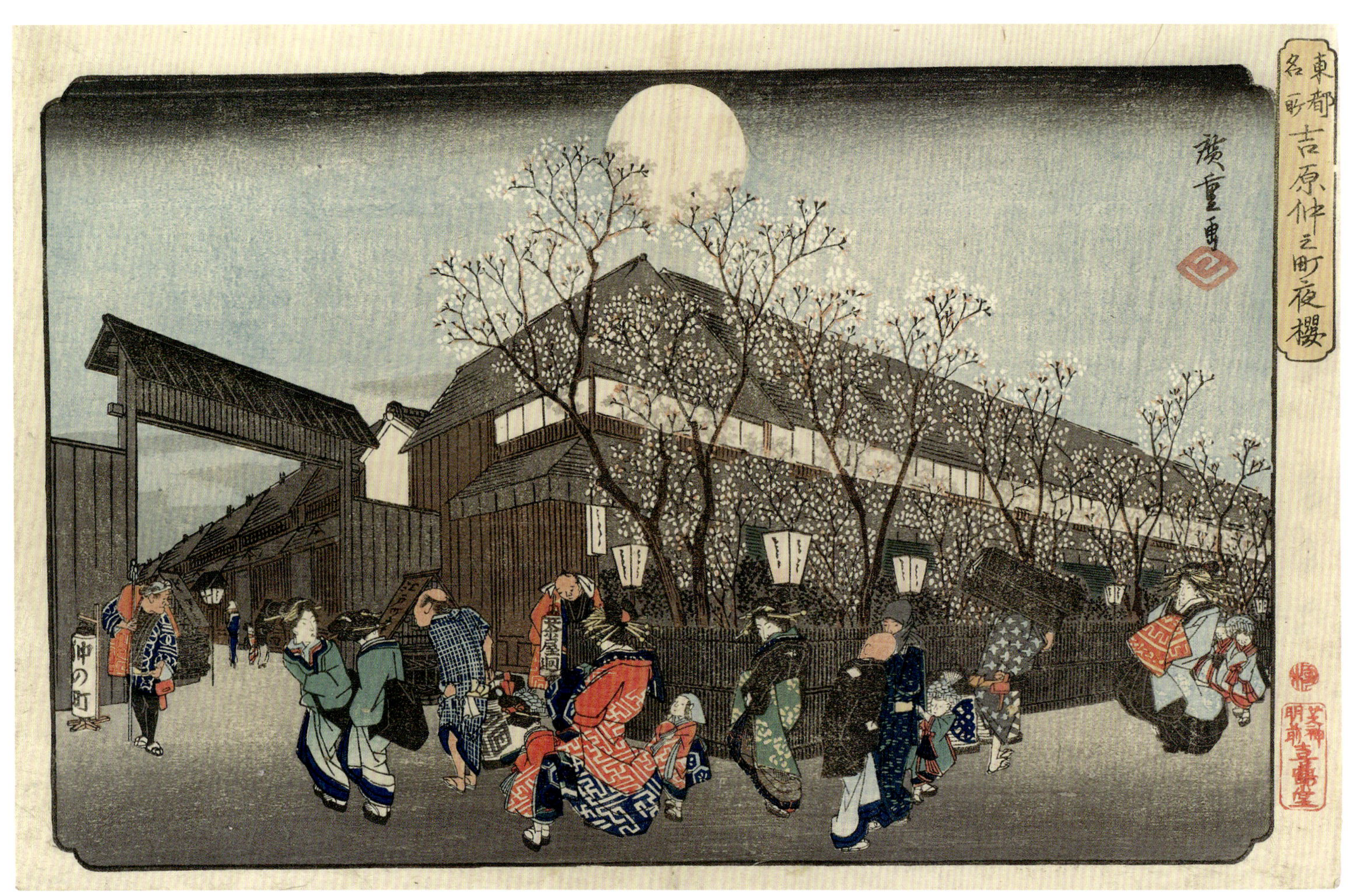

28

Utagawa Hiroshige (1797–1858)

Cherry Blossoms at Night at Nakanochō in the Yoshiwara, from the series
Famous Places in the Eastern Capital, ca. 1834–1835

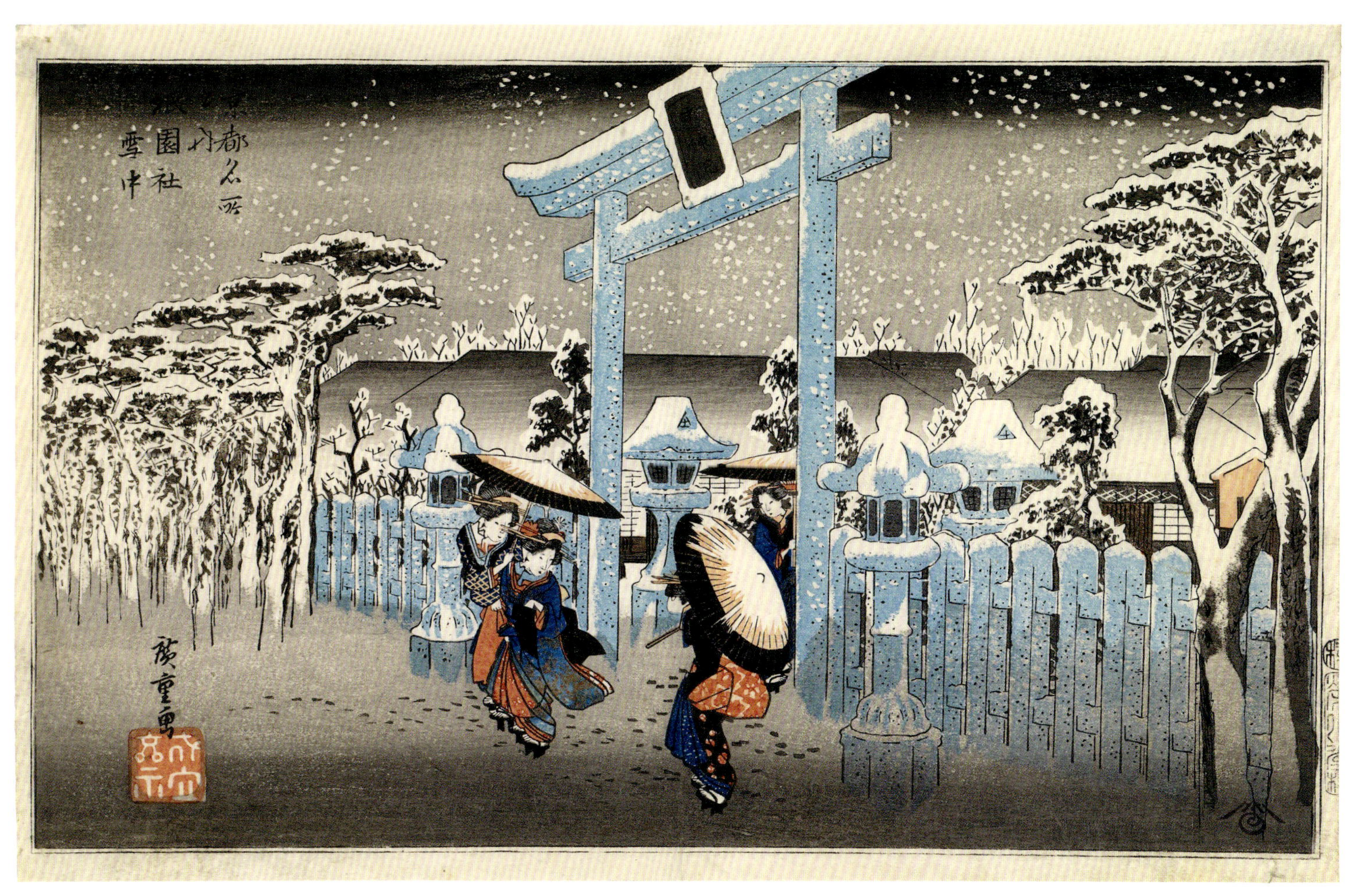

29

Utagawa Hiroshige (1797–1858)

Gion Shrine in the Snow, from the series
Famous Places in Kyoto, ca. 1834

Utagawa Kuniyoshi (1798–1861)

Pleasure Boat and Fireworks on the Sumida River, from the book
The Pillowed Boudoir, 1839

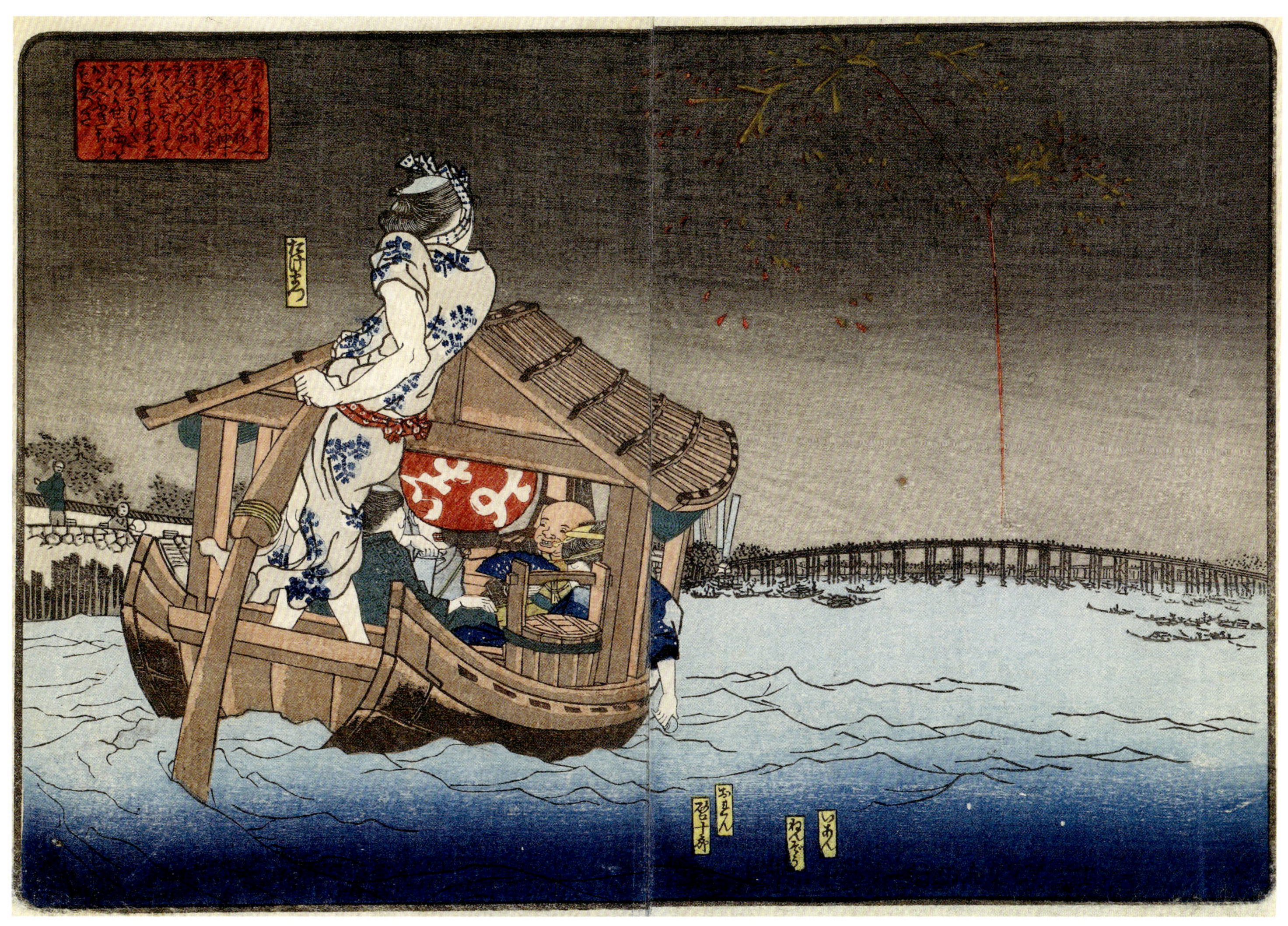

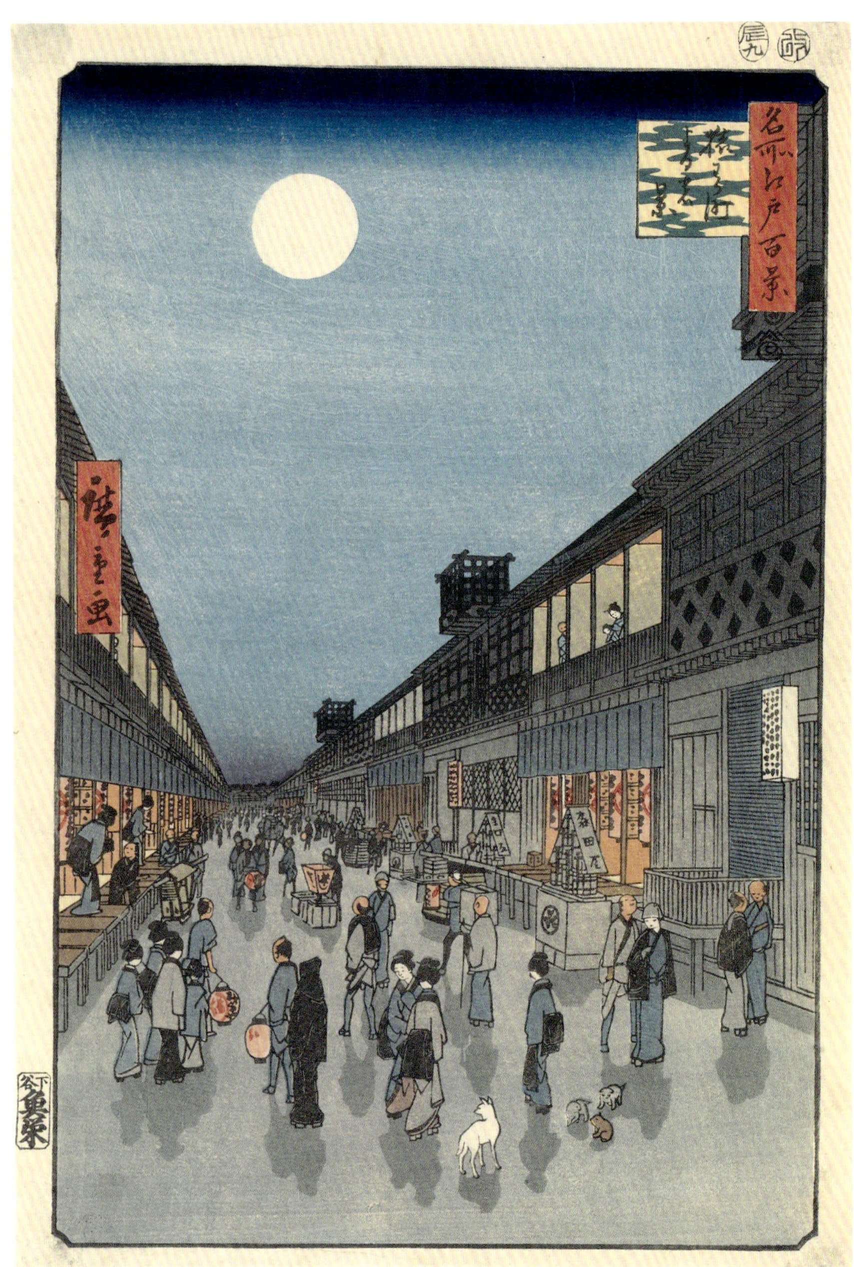

31

Utagawa Hiroshige (1797–1858)
Night View of Saruwaka Street, from the series
One Hundred Views of Famous Places in Edo,
1856

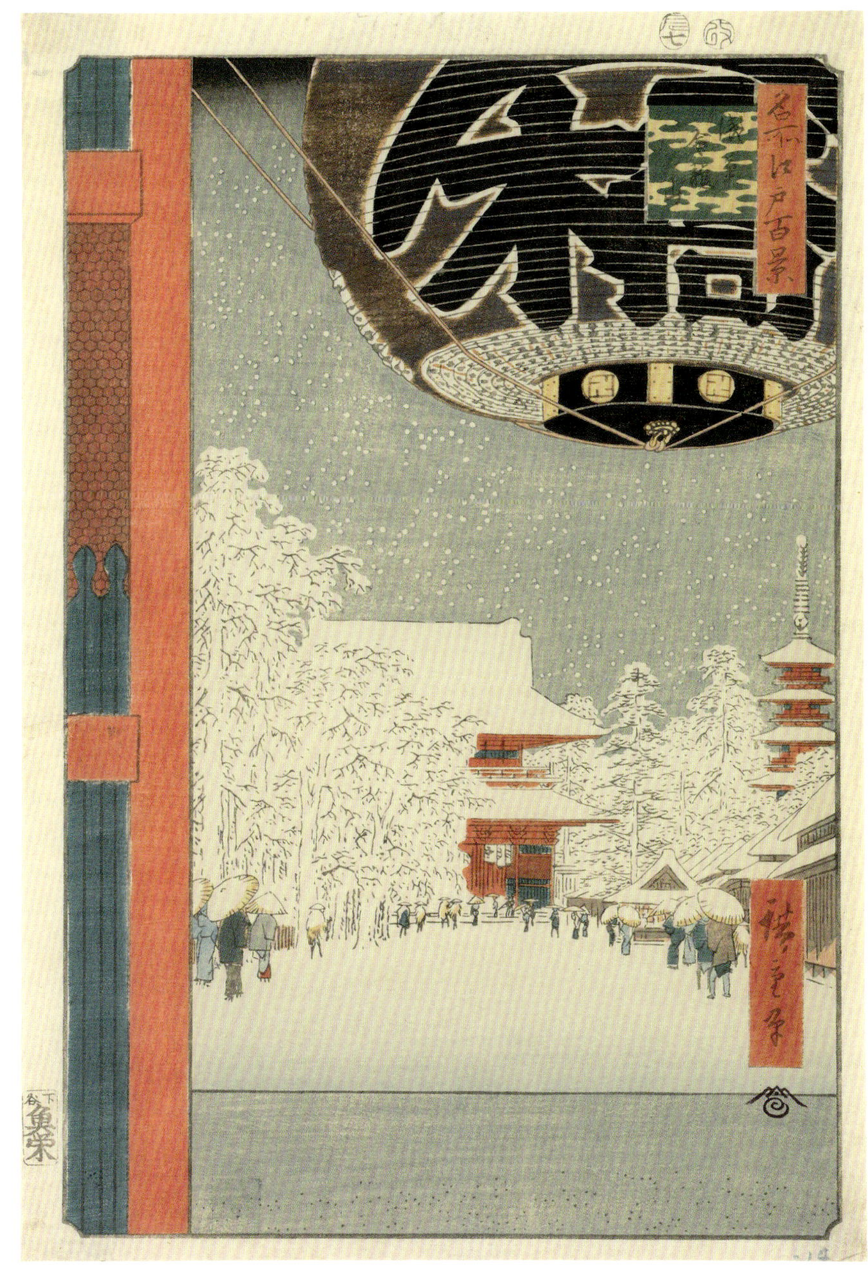

32
Utagawa Hiroshige (1797–1858)
Kinryūzan Temple in Asakusa, from the series
One Hundred Views of Famous Places in Edo,
1856

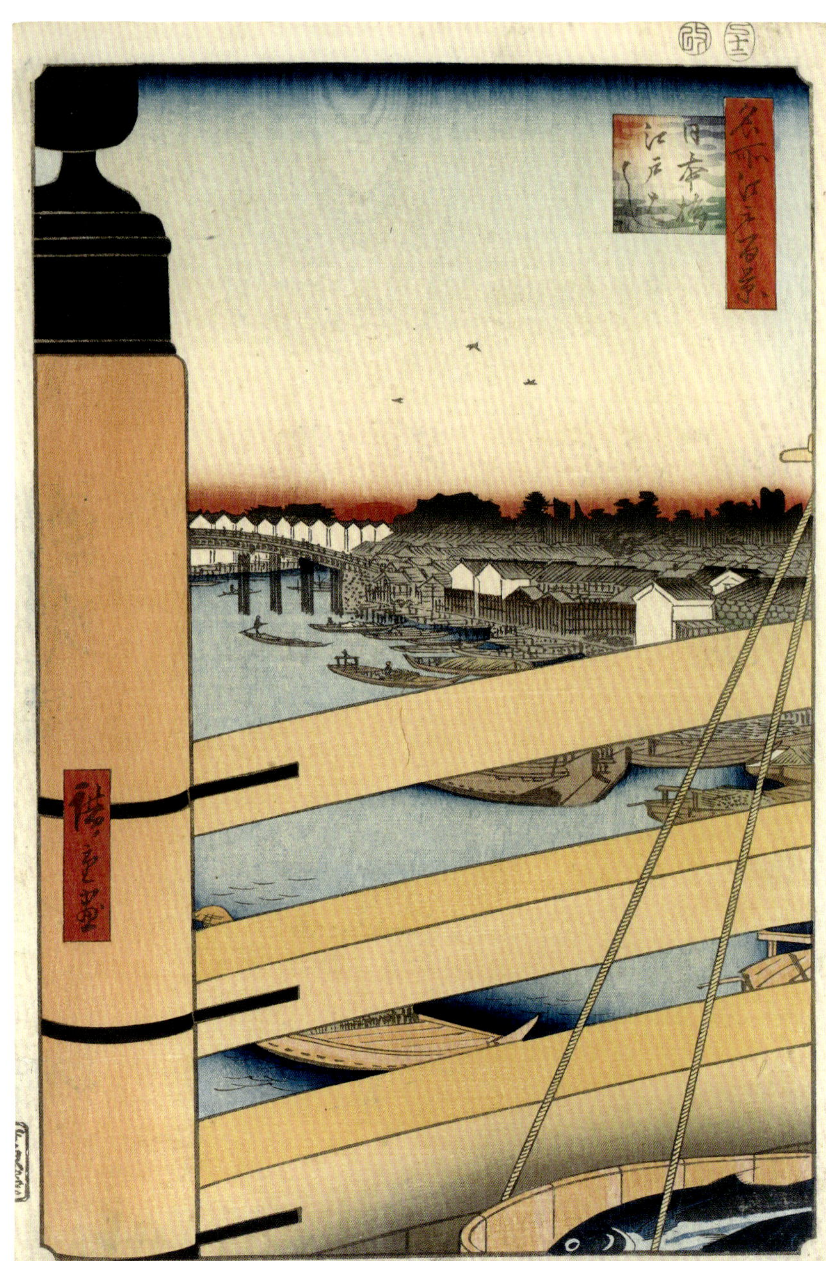

33
Utagawa Hiroshige (1797–1858)
Edo Bridge from Nihon Bridge, from the series
One Hundred Views of Famous Places in Edo,
1857

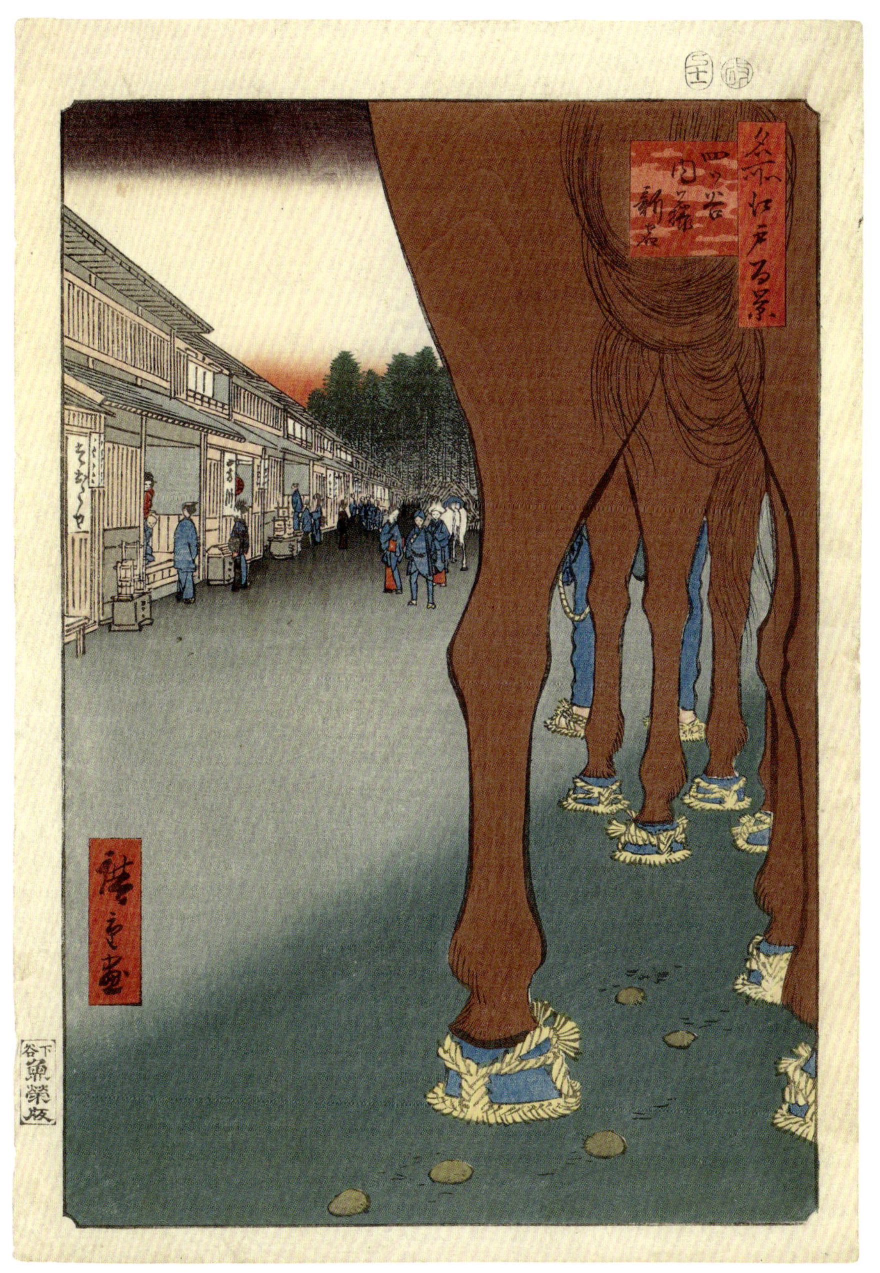

34
Utagawa Hiroshige (1797–1858)
Naitō, New Station at Yotsuya, from the series
One Hundred Views of Famous Places in Edo,
1857

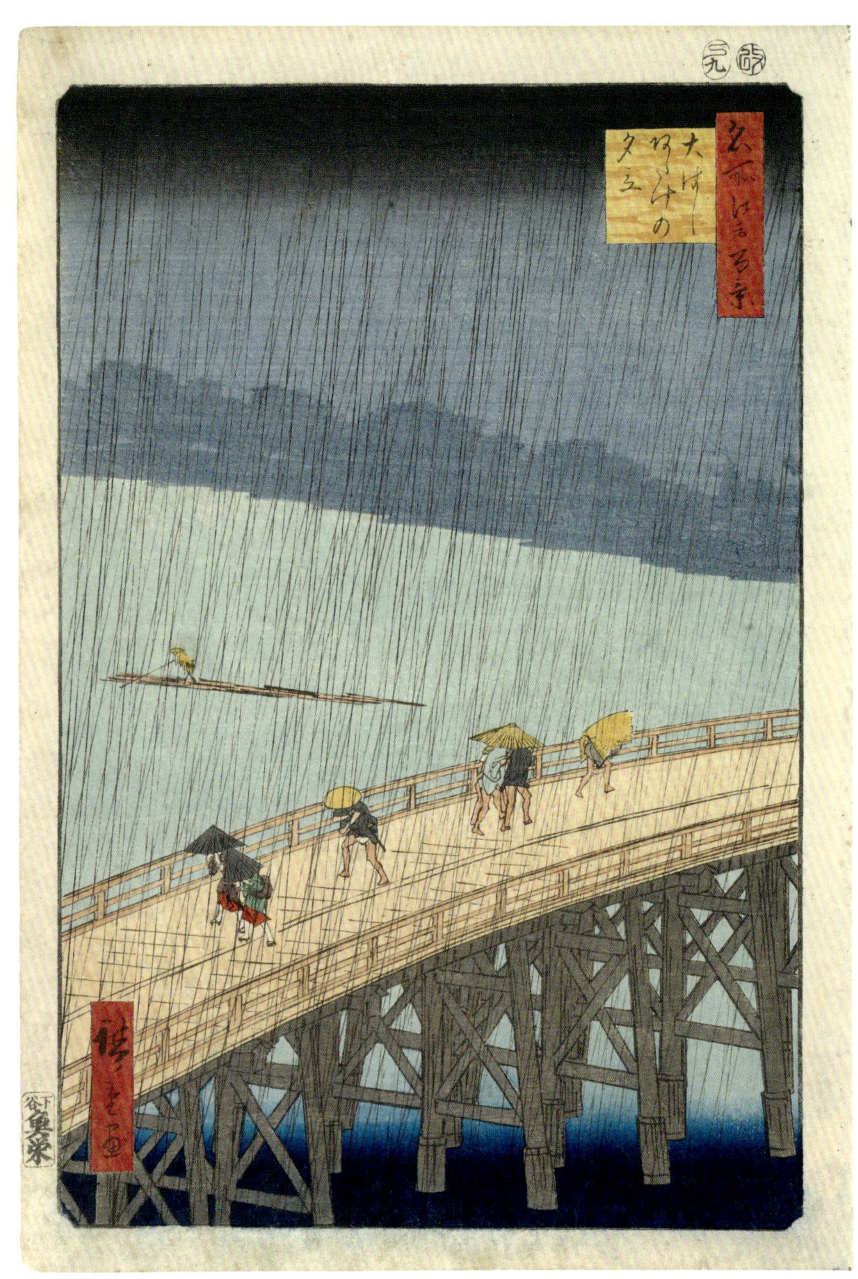

35

Utagawa Hiroshige (1797–1858)

Evening Rain at Atake on the Great Bridge, from the series *One Hundred Views of Famous Places in Edo*, 1857

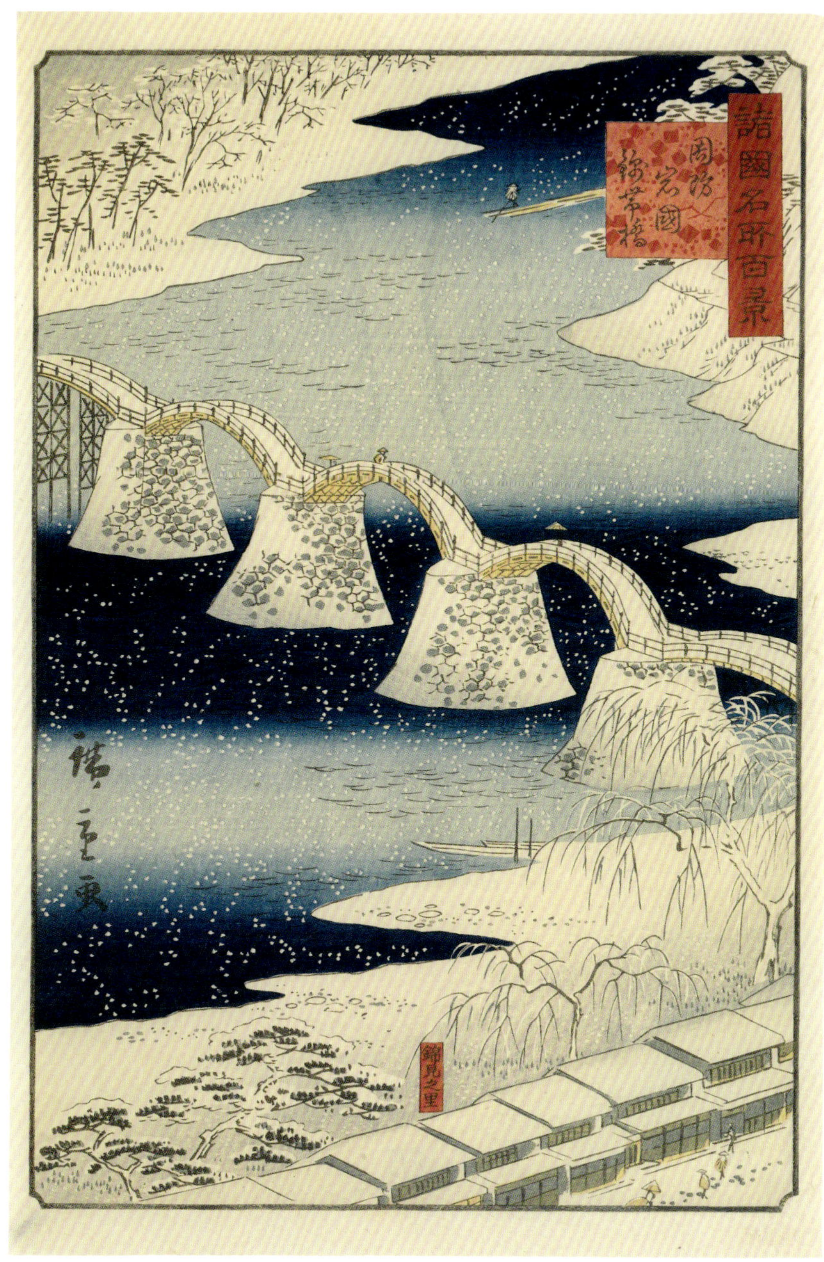

36

Utagawa Hiroshige II (1826–1869)

Kintai Bridge at Iwakuni in Suō Province,
from the series *One Hundred Famous Places
in the Provinces*, 1859

37

Utagawa Hiroshige (1797–1858)

No. 11 Hakone: Holding Pine Torches at Night, from the series *Fifty-Three Stations of the Tōkaidō*, ca. 1851–1852

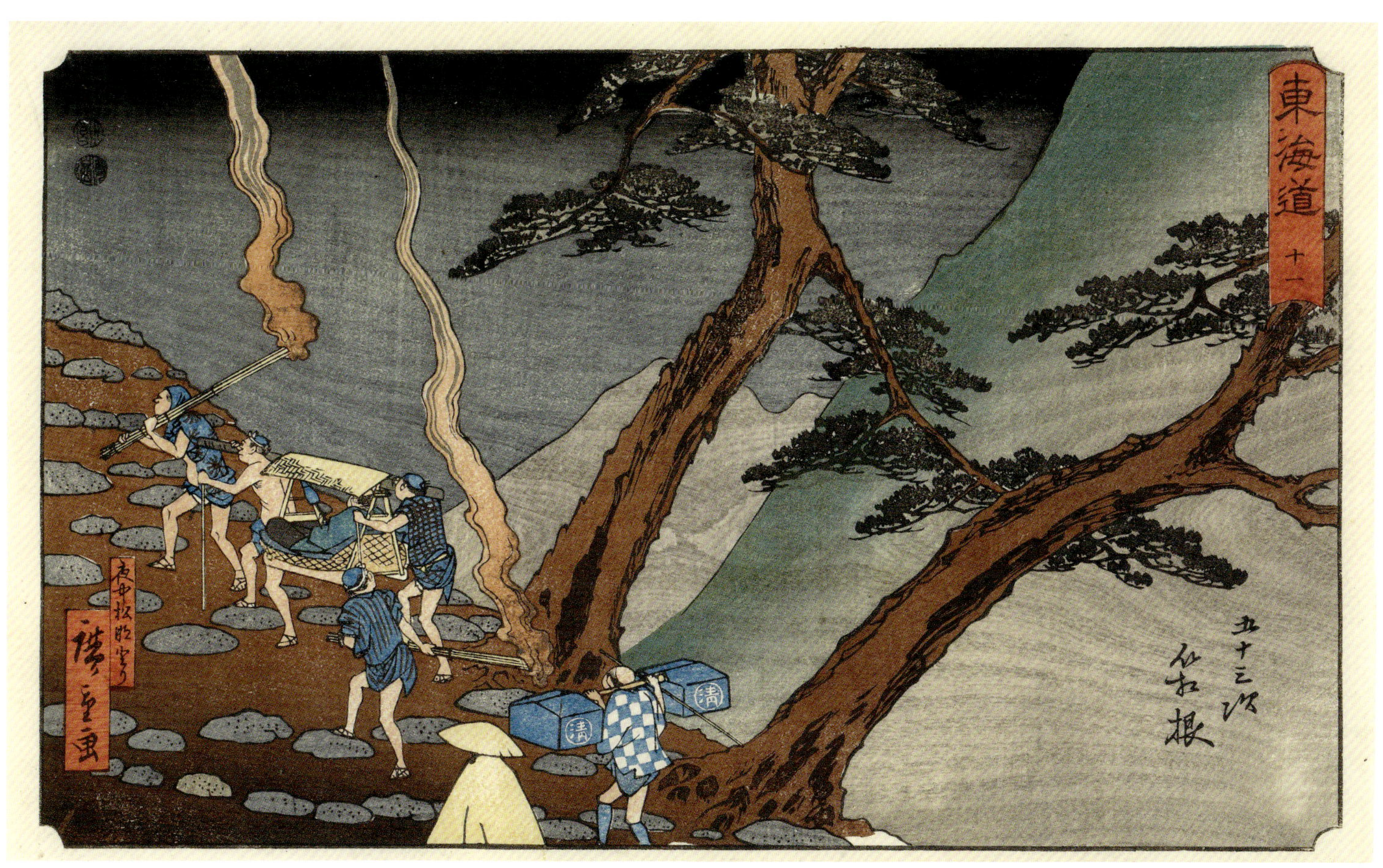

東海道
十一
五十三次
箱根
夜中松明之図
廣重画

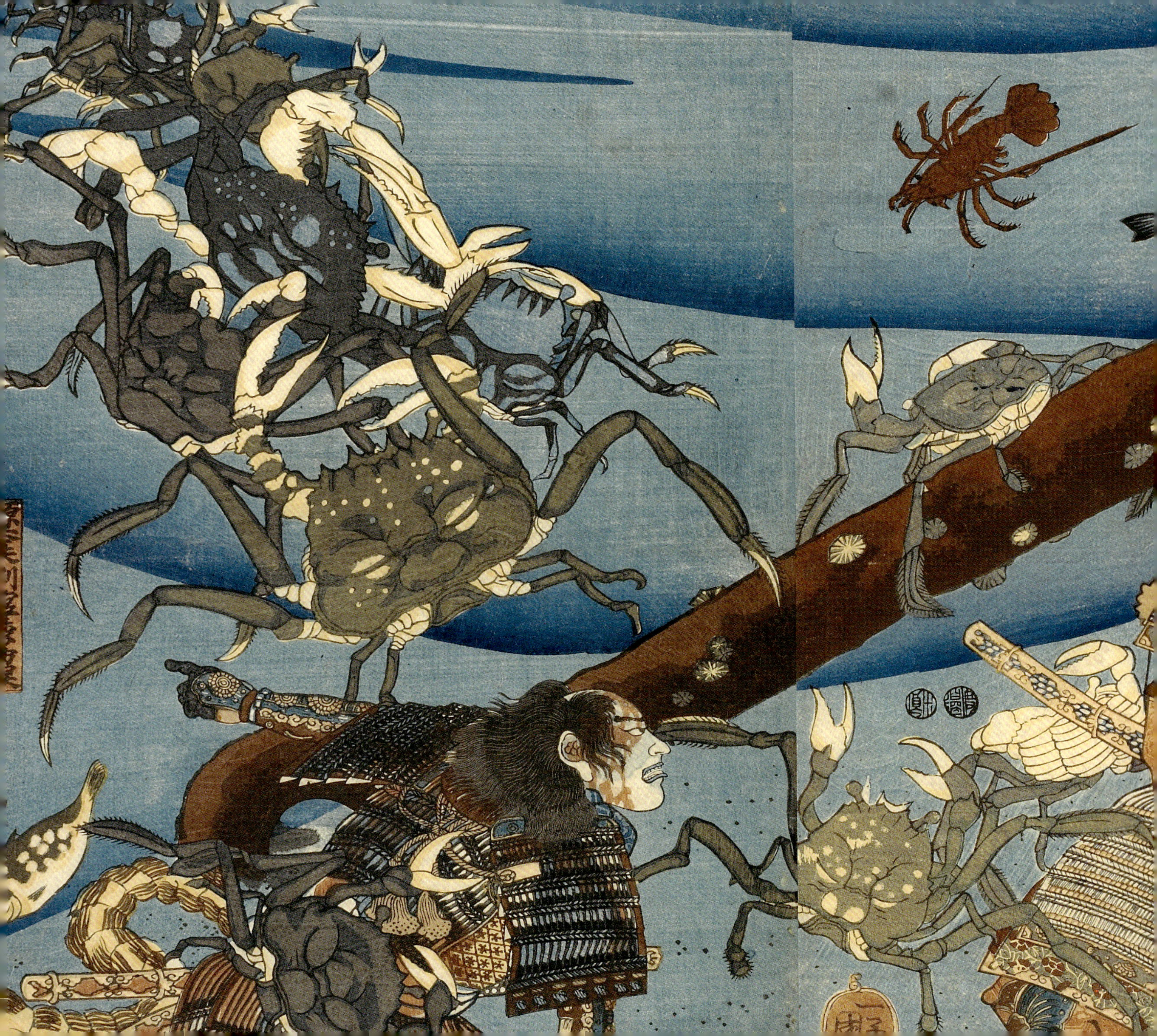

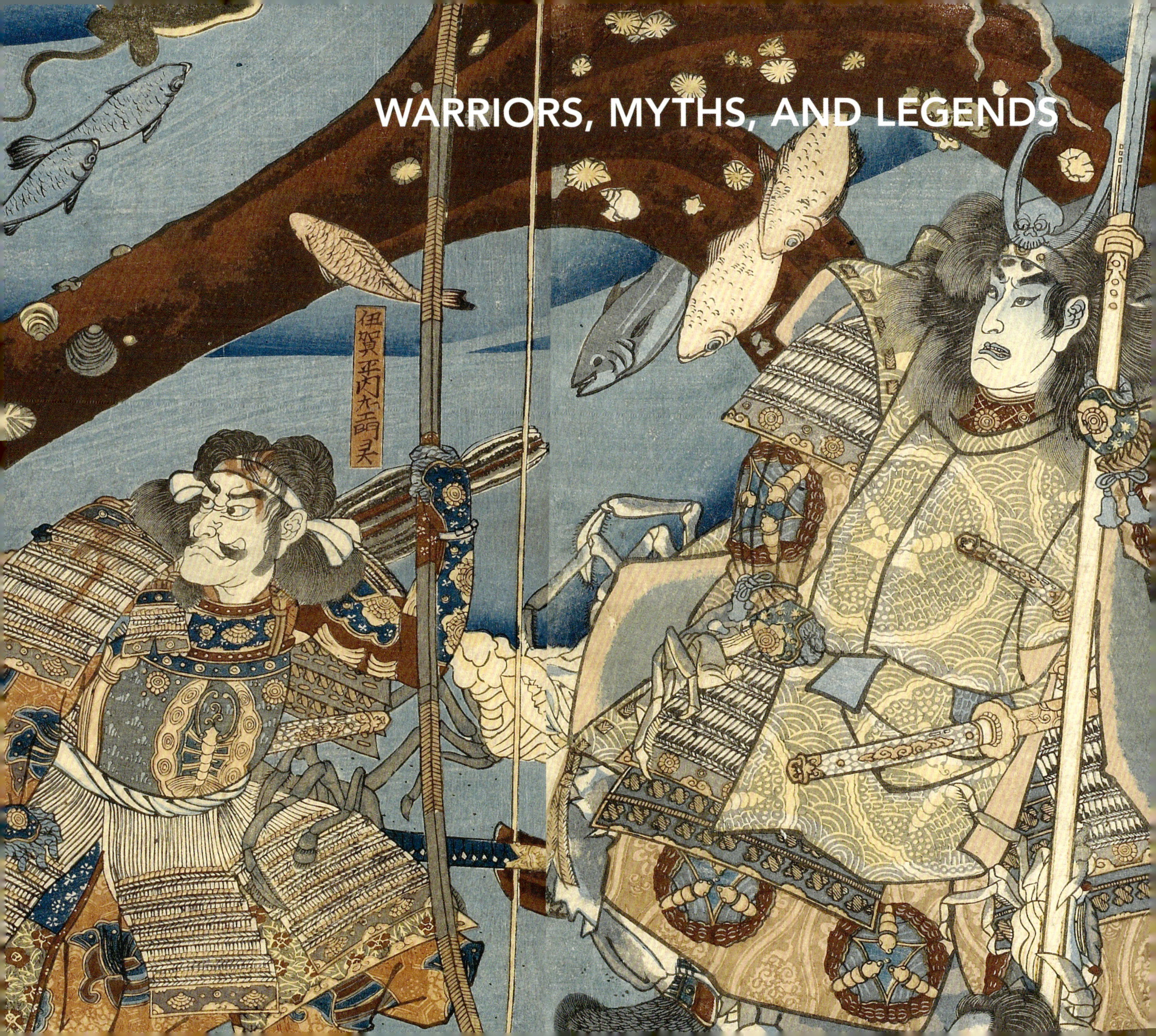

WARRIORS, MYTHS, AND LEGENDS

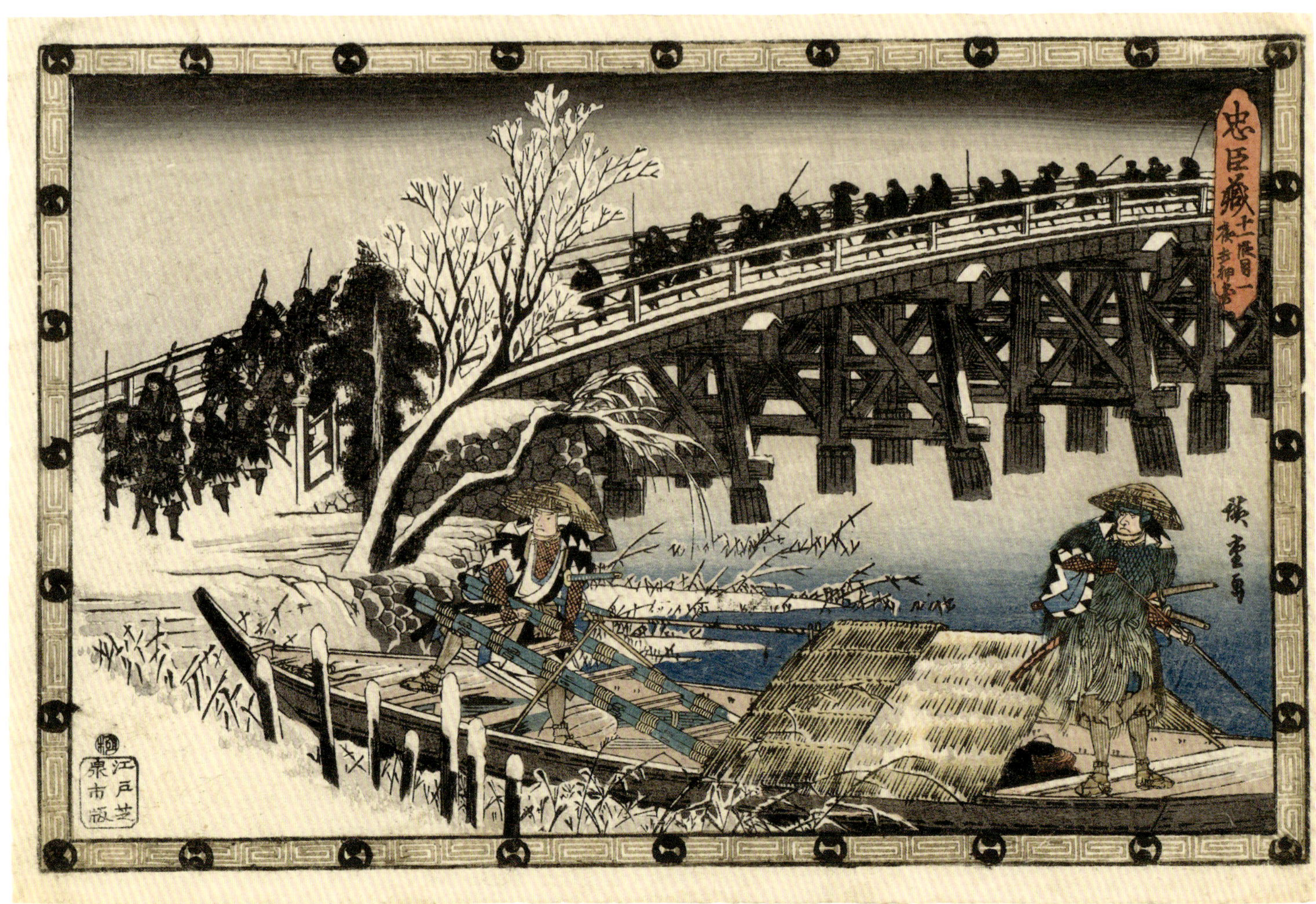

38

Utagawa Hiroshige (1797–1858)

Act 11, Gathering before the Night Attack, from the series *The Treasury of Loyal Retainers (Chūshingura)*, ca. 1835–1836

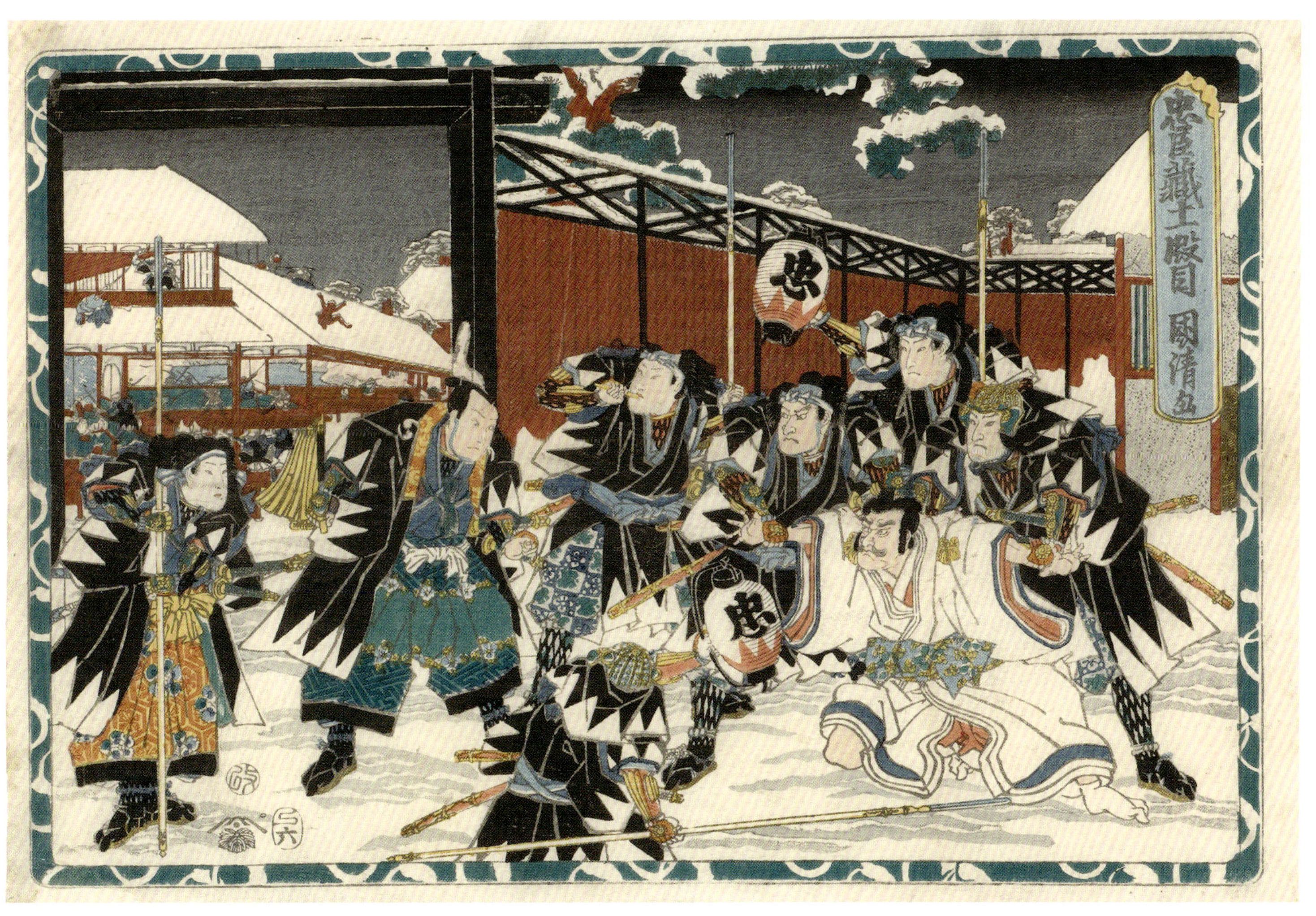

39

Utagawa Kunikiyo II (1850–1887)

Act 11, from the series *The Treasury of Loyal Retainers (Chūshingura)*, 1857

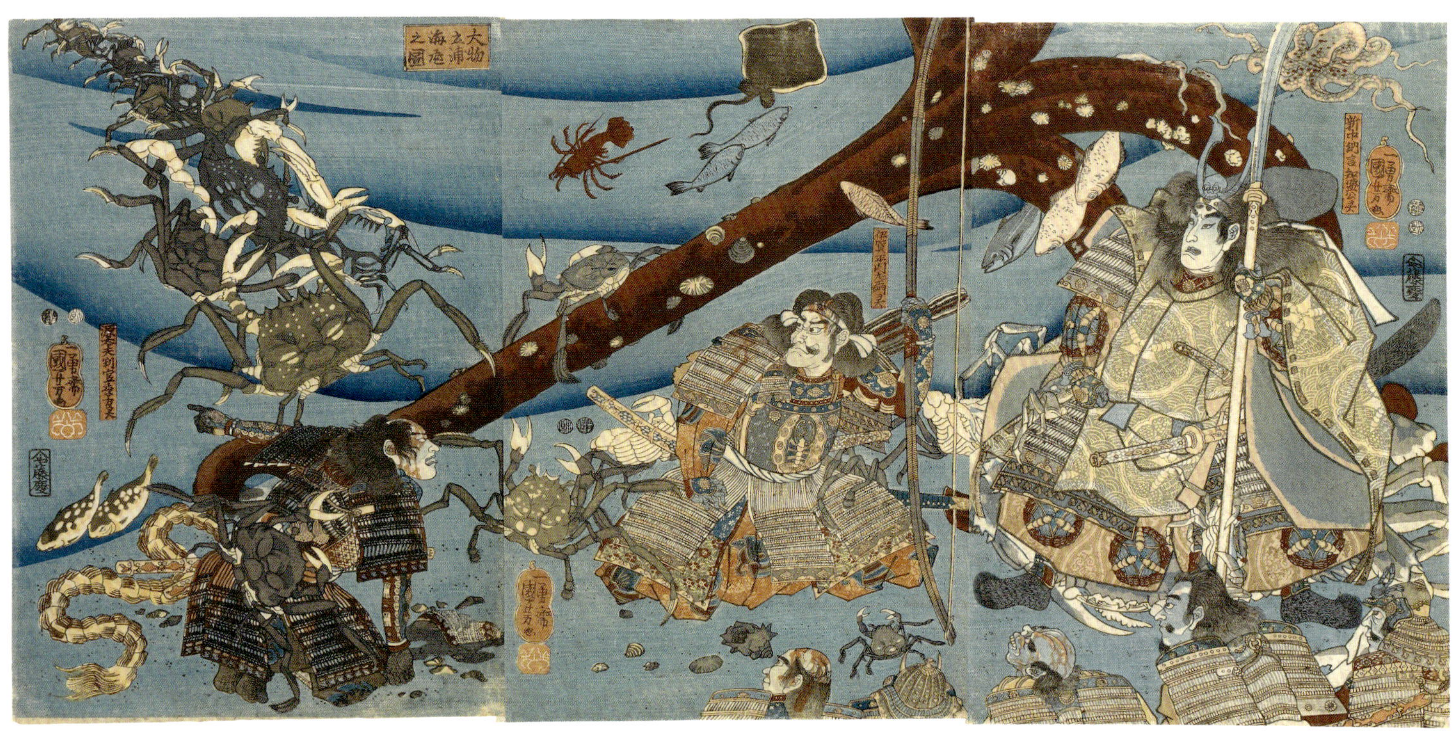

40

Utagawa Kuniyoshi (1798–1861)

At the Bottom of the Sea in Daimotsu Bay, ca. 1851–1852

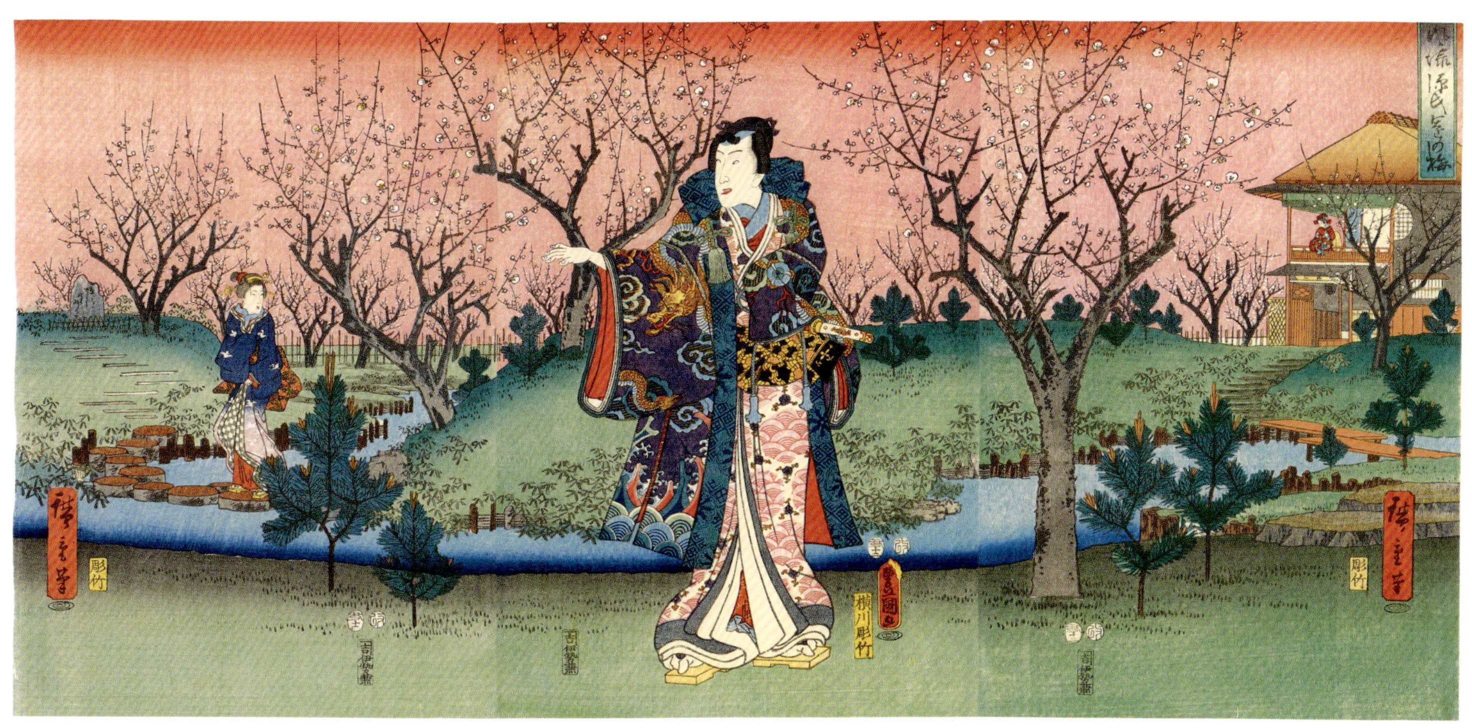

41
Utagawa Hiroshige (1797–1858) and Utagawa Kunisada (1786–1864)
The Plum Orchard, from the series *Elegant Prince Genji*, 1853

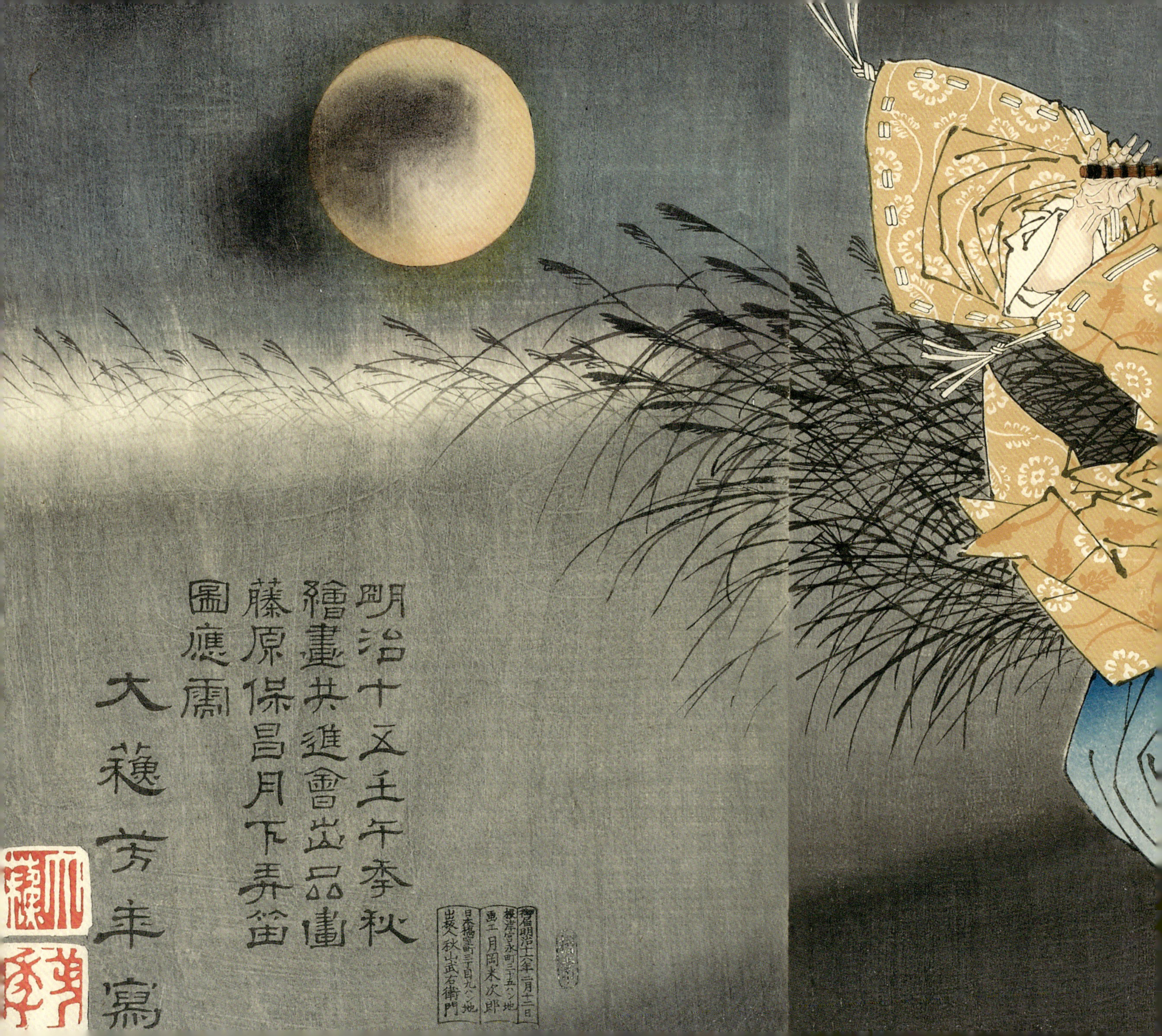

明治十五壬午季秋
繪畫共進會出品畫
藤原保昌月下弄笛
圖應需
大蘇芳年寫

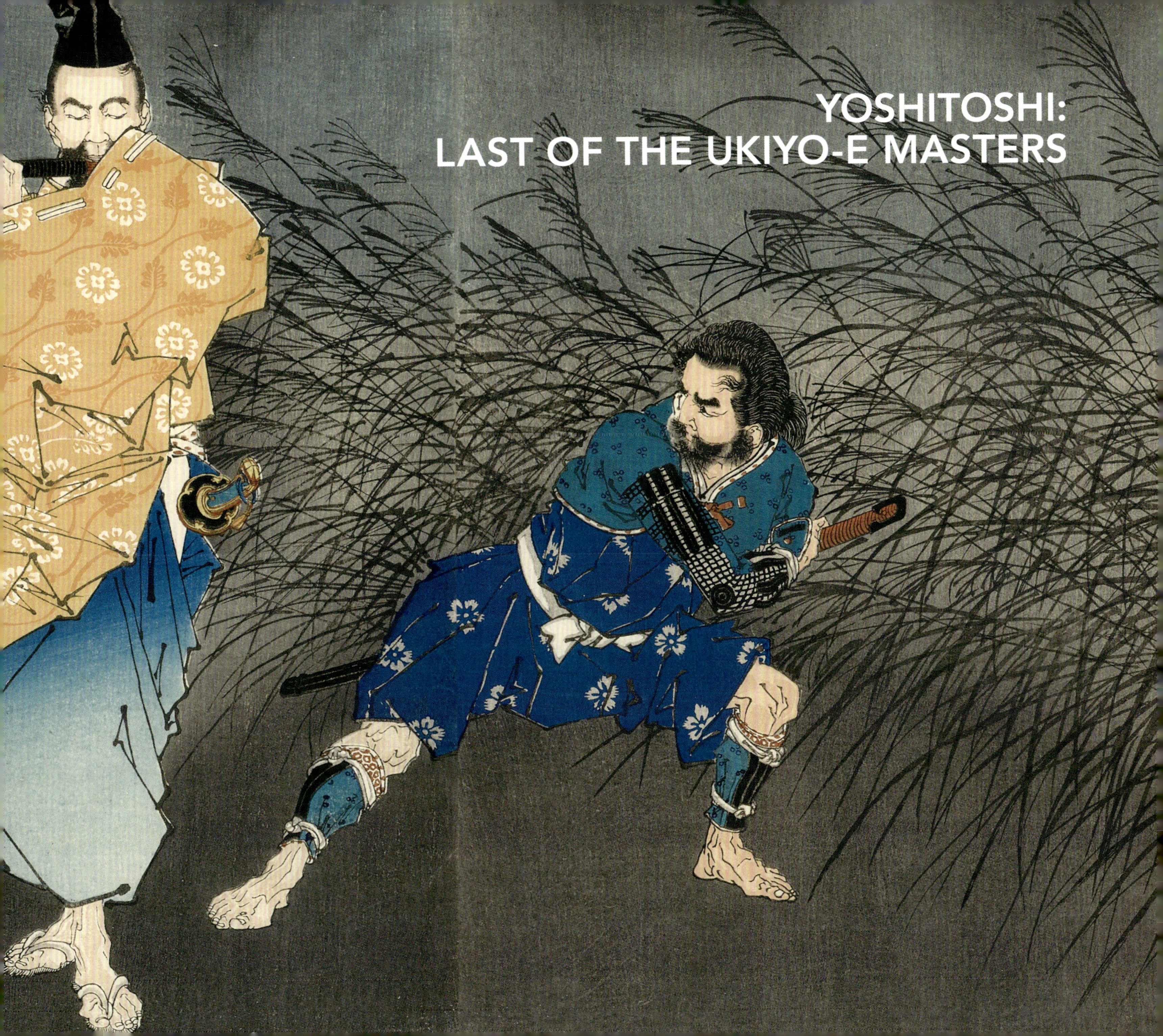

YOSHITOSHI:
LAST OF THE UKIYO-E MASTERS

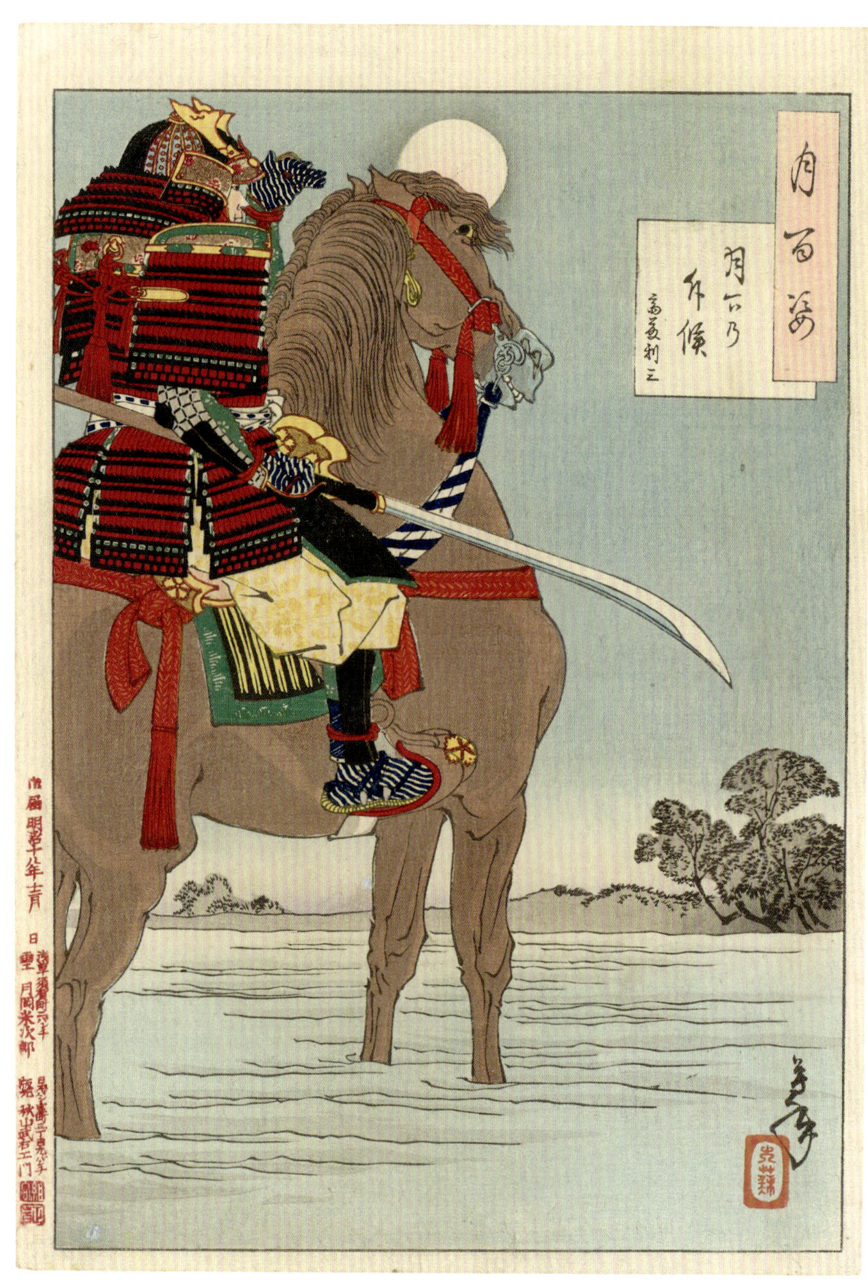

42

Tsukioka Yoshitoshi (1839–1892)

A Moonlight Scouting Patrol, from the series
One Hundred Aspects of the Moon, 1885

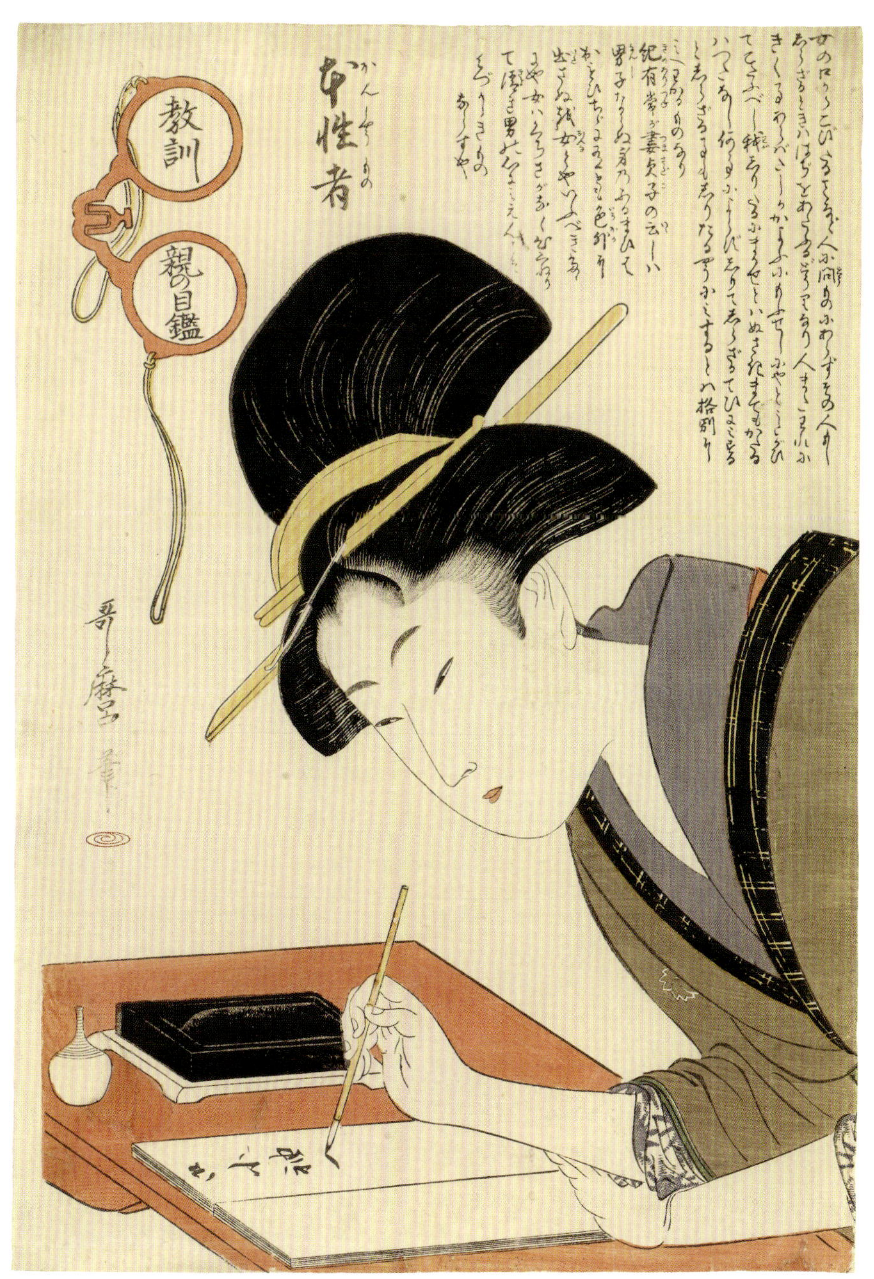

17

Kitagawa Utamaro (ca. 1754–1806)

A Woman of Character, from the series *Moral Instruction Seen through a Parent's Eyes*, ca. 1798–1802

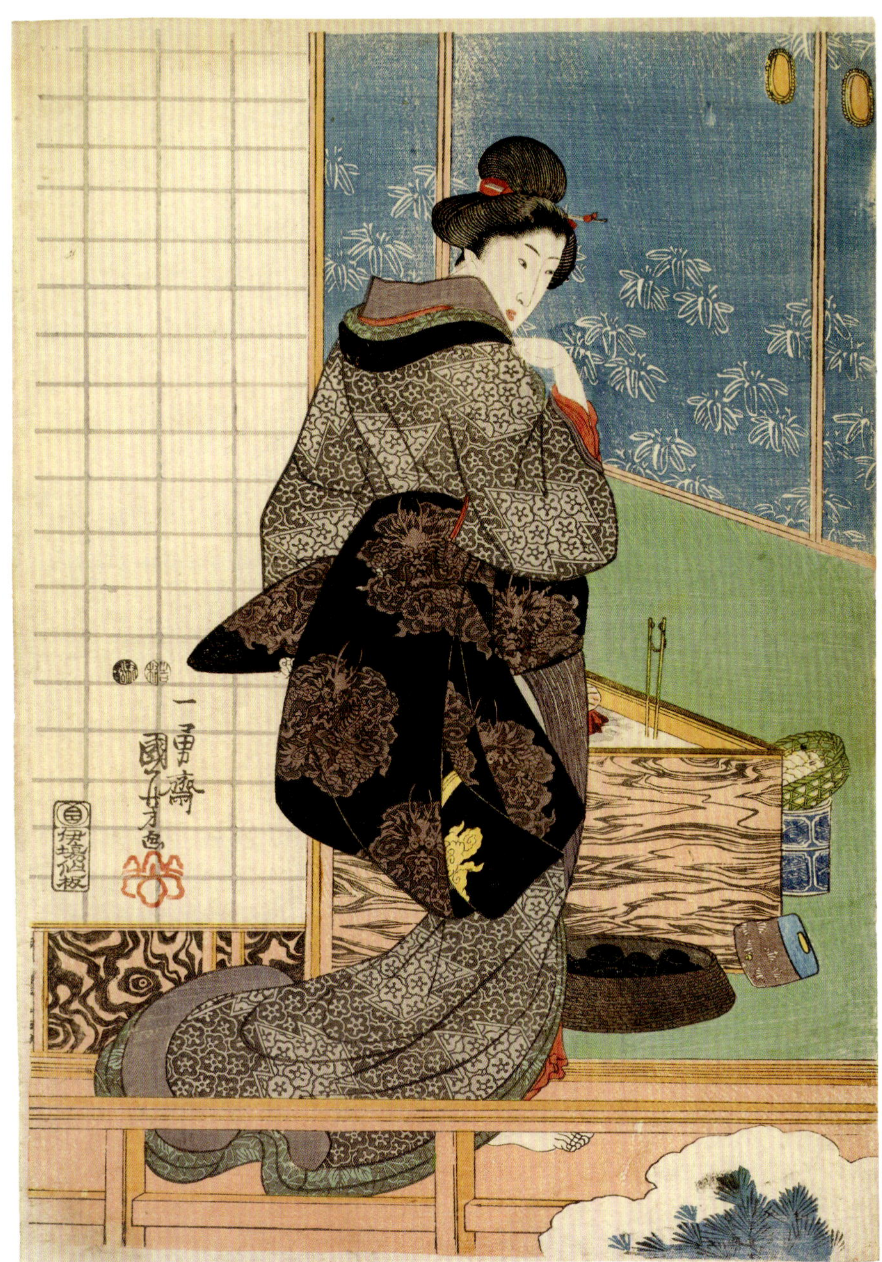

18

Utagawa Kuniyoshi (1798–1861)
Snowy Morning, from the series *Among Snow, Moon, and Flowers*, one sheet from a triptych, ca. 1847–1848

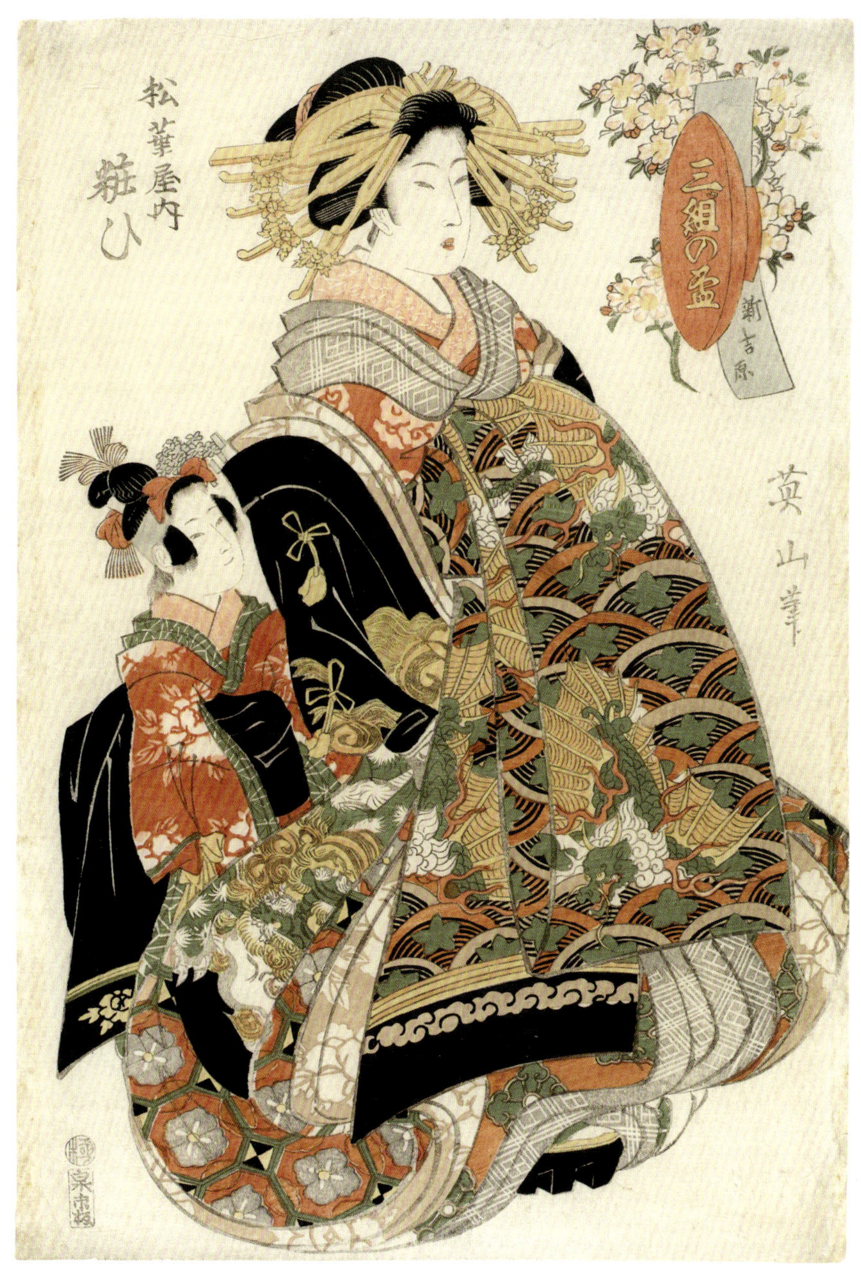

19

Kikukawa Eizan (1787–1867)

Yosooi of the Matsubaya, from the series *Three Wine Cups in the New Yoshiwara*, ca. 1815–1825

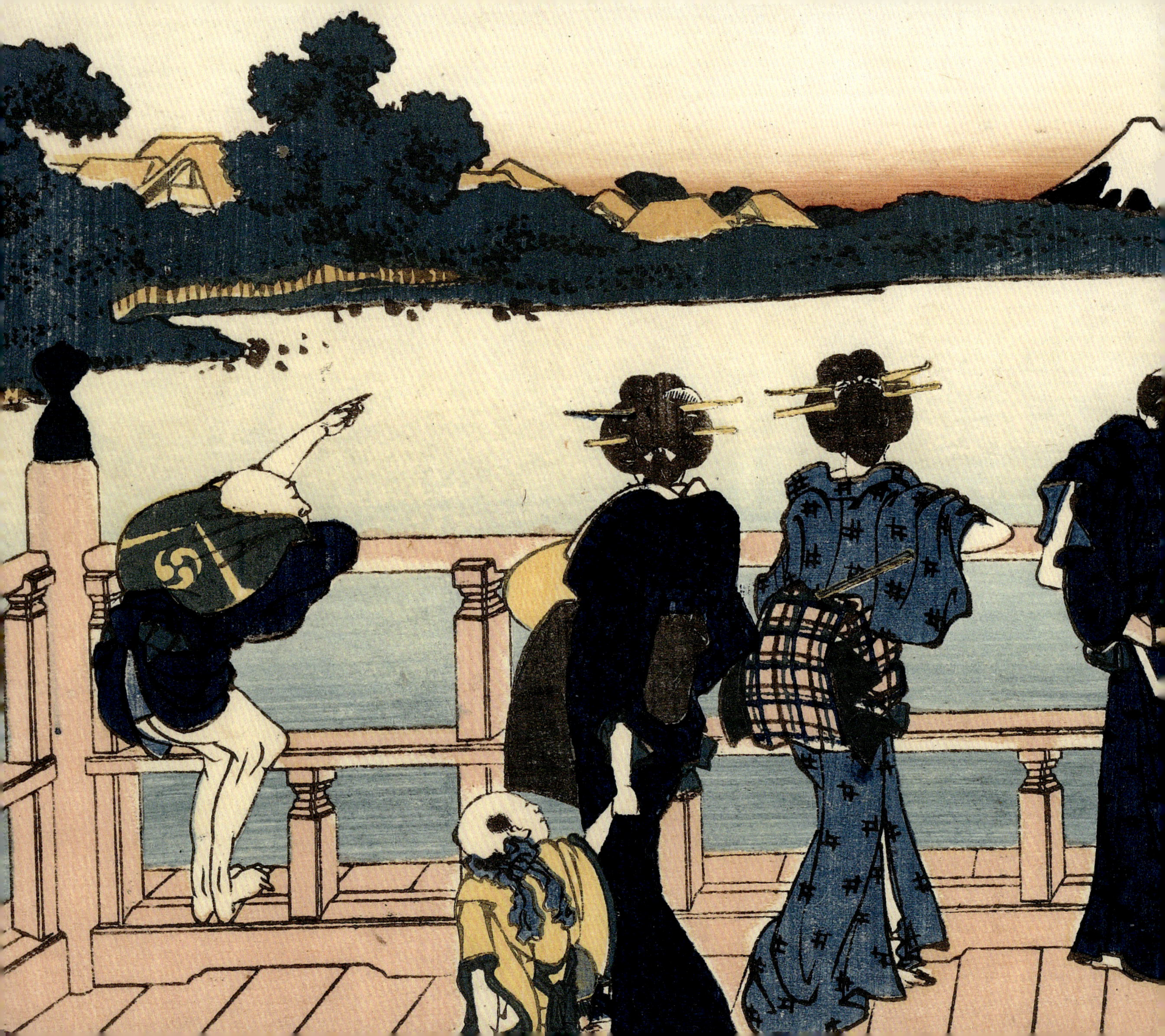

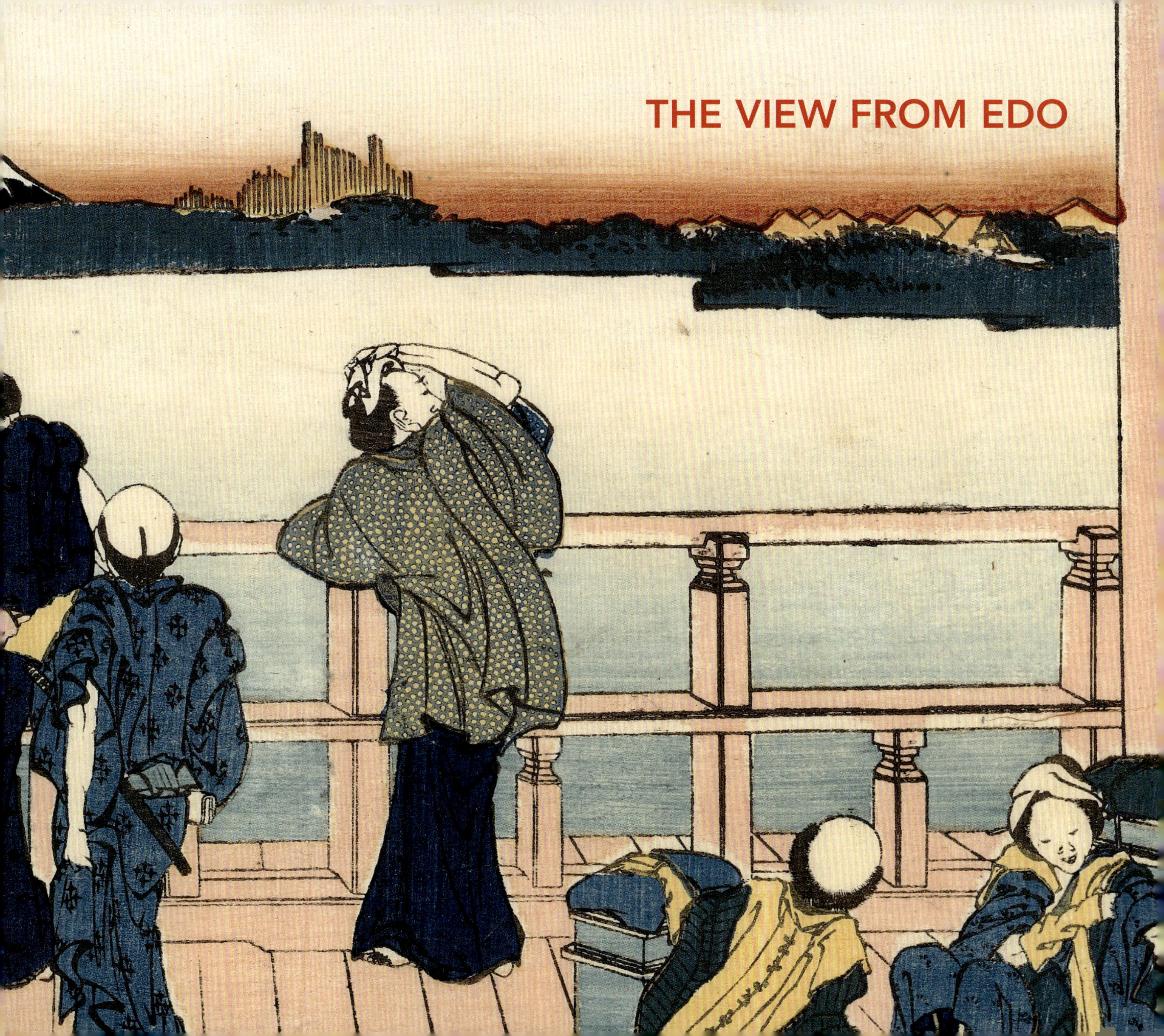
THE VIEW FROM EDO

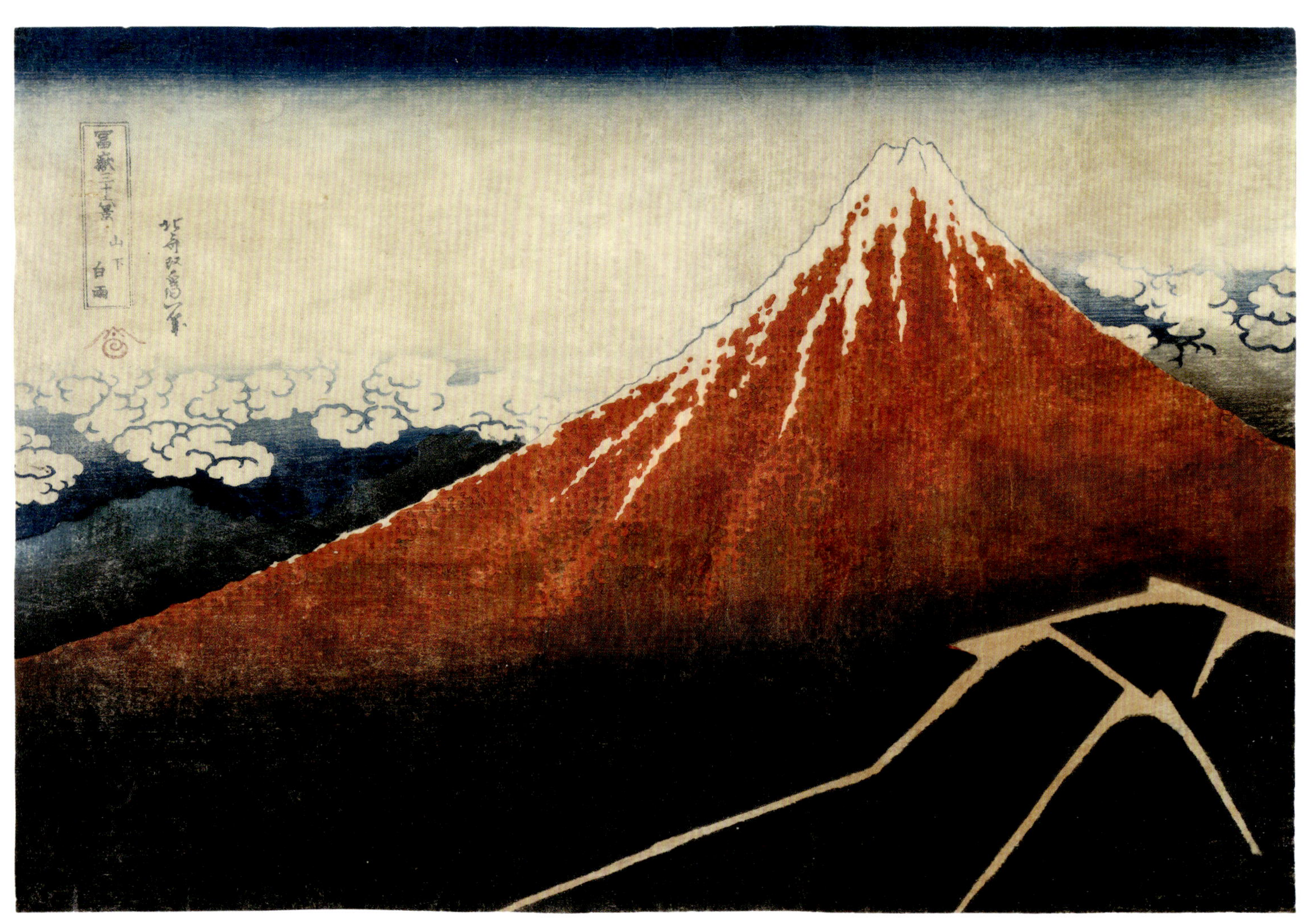

20

Katsushika Hokusai (1760–1849)

Storm below the Mountain, from the series
Thirty-Six Views of Mount Fuji, ca. 1830–1832

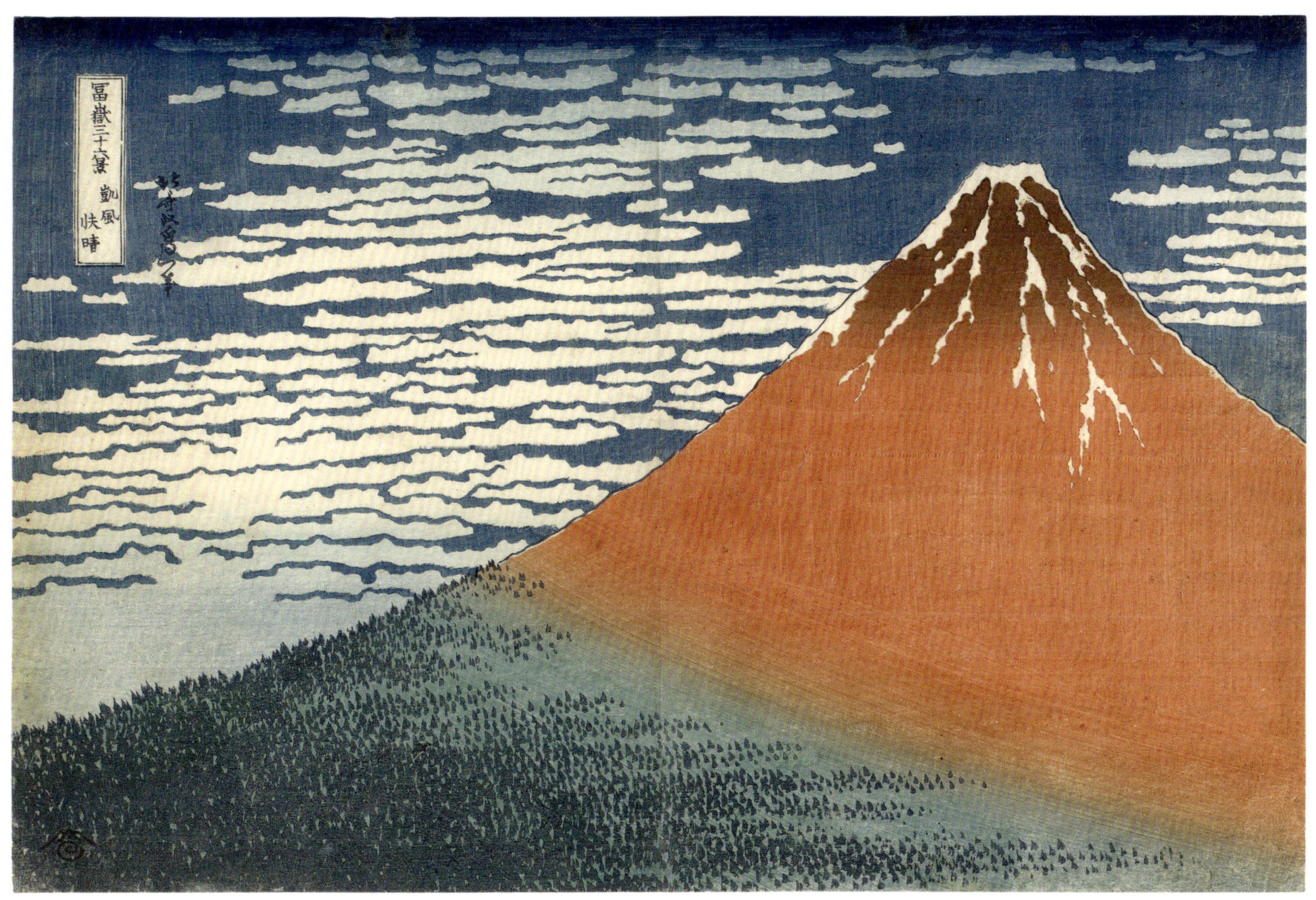

21

Katsushika Hokusai (1760–1849)

Fuji in Clear Weather, from the series
Thirty-Six Views of Mount Fuji, ca. 1830–1832

22

Utagawa Toyoharu (1735–1814)

The Cool of the Evening near Ryōgoku Bridge in Edo,
from the series *Perspective Pictures*, ca. 1770–1780

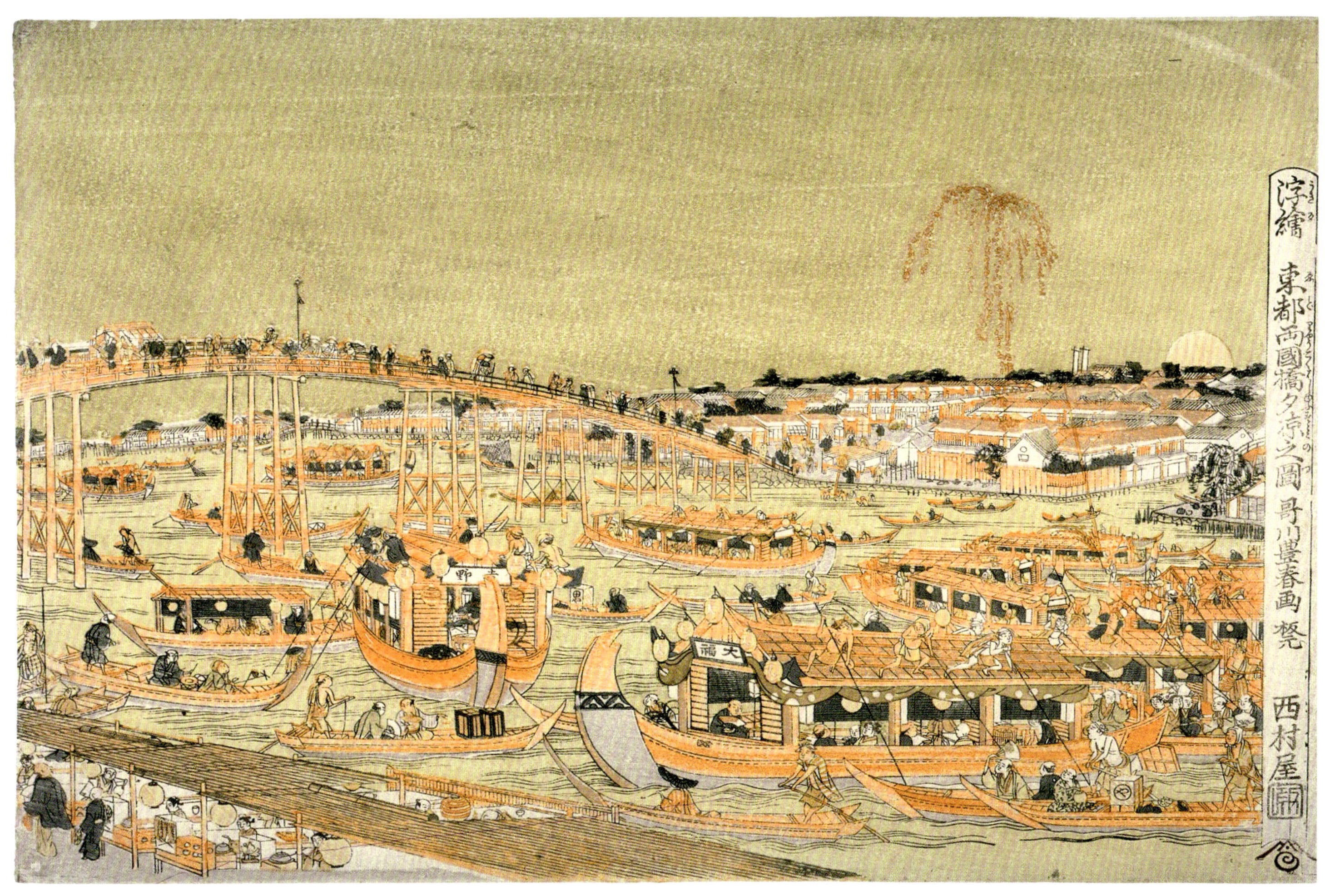

浮繪　東都両國橋夕涼之圖　哥川豊春画
西村屋板

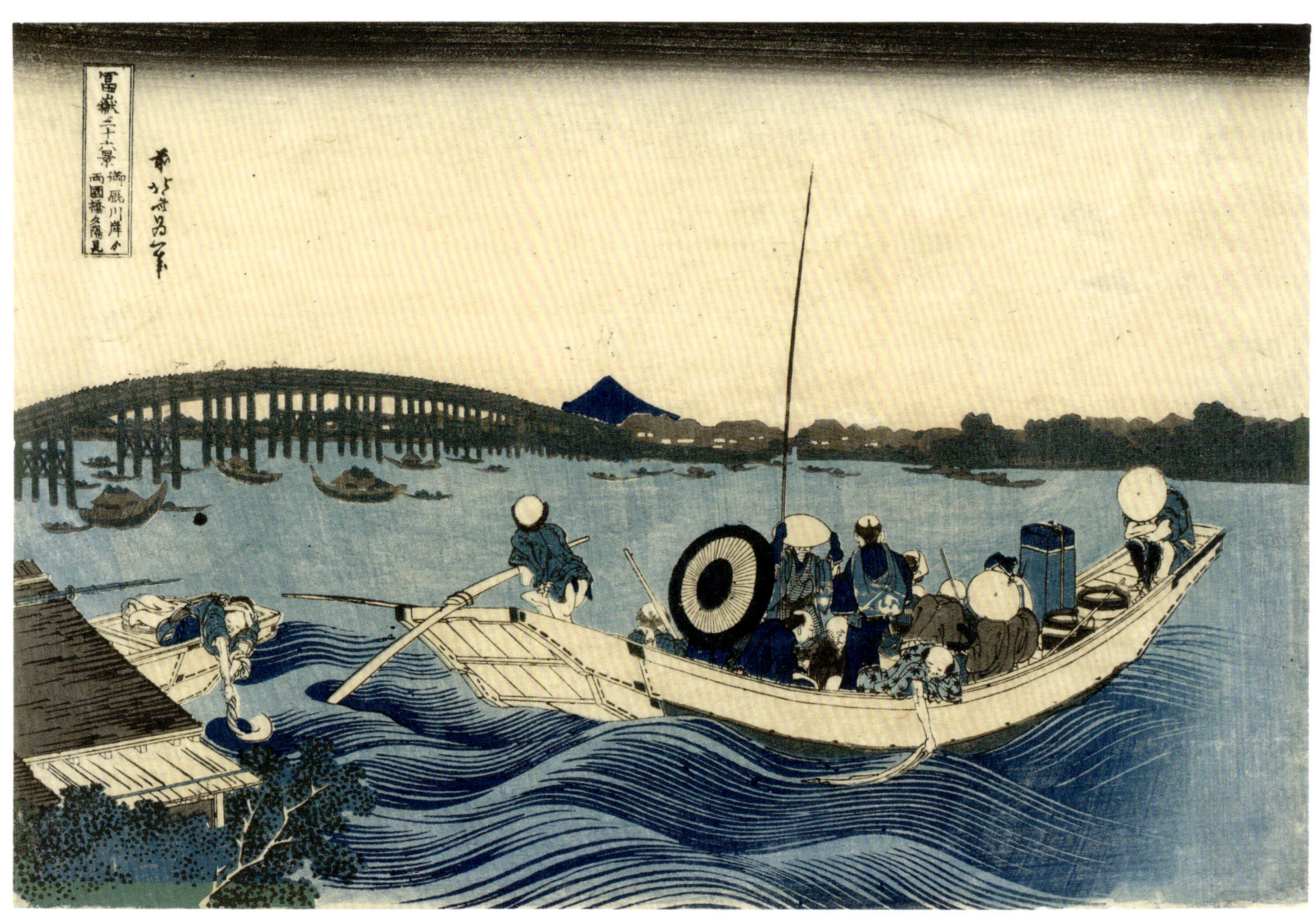

23

Katsushika Hokusai (1760–1849)

Fuji from Onmaya Embankment with Sunset over Ryōgoku Bridge,
from the series *Thirty-Six Views of Mount Fuji,* ca. 1830–1832

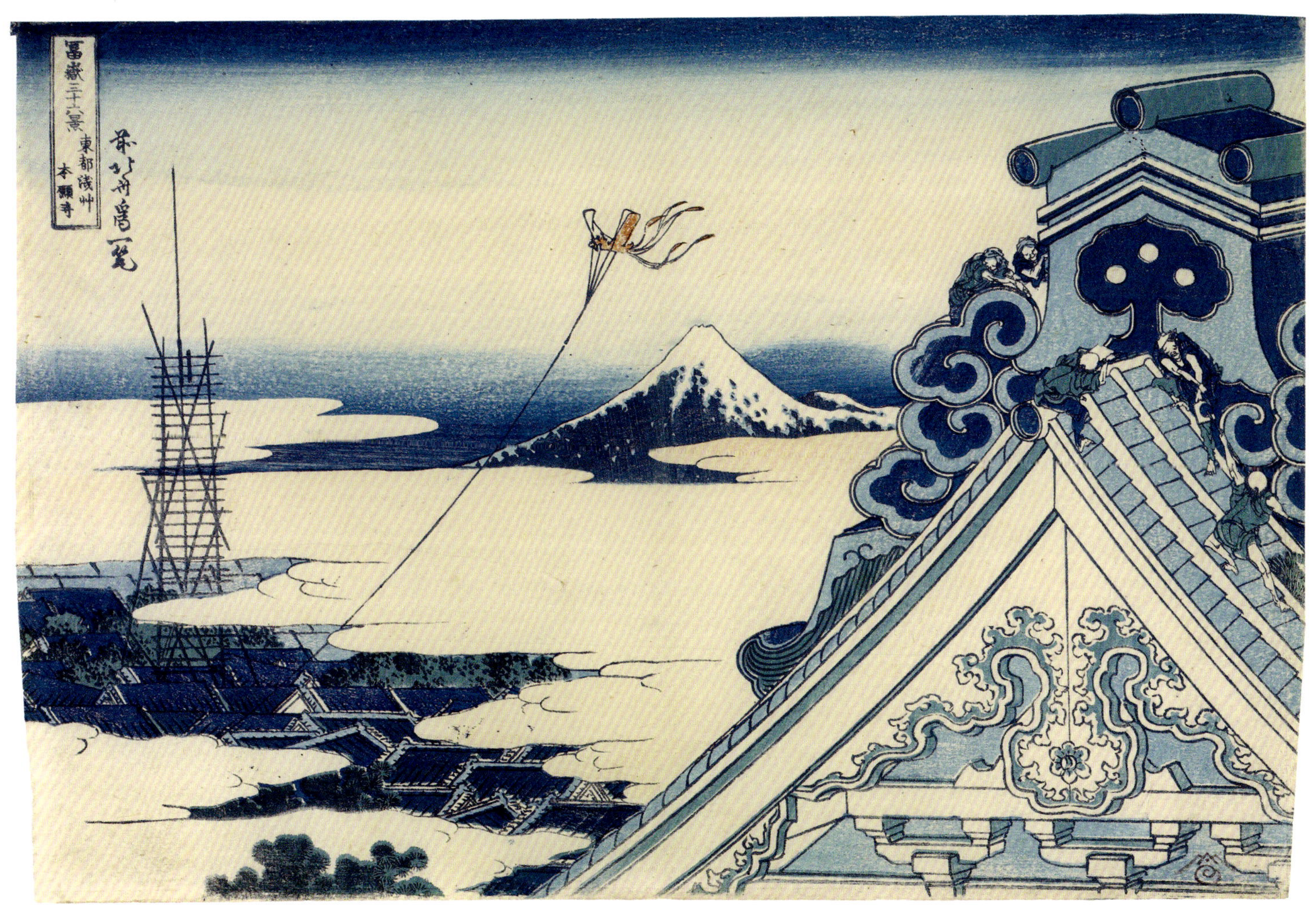

24

Katsushika Hokusai (1760–1849)

Fuji from the Hongan Temple at Asakusa in Edo, from the series
Thirty-Six Views of Mount Fuji, ca. 1830–1832

25

Katsushika Hokusai (1760–1849)

Under the Wave off Kanagawa (The Great Wave), from the series
Thirty-Six Views of Mount Fuji, ca. 1830–1832

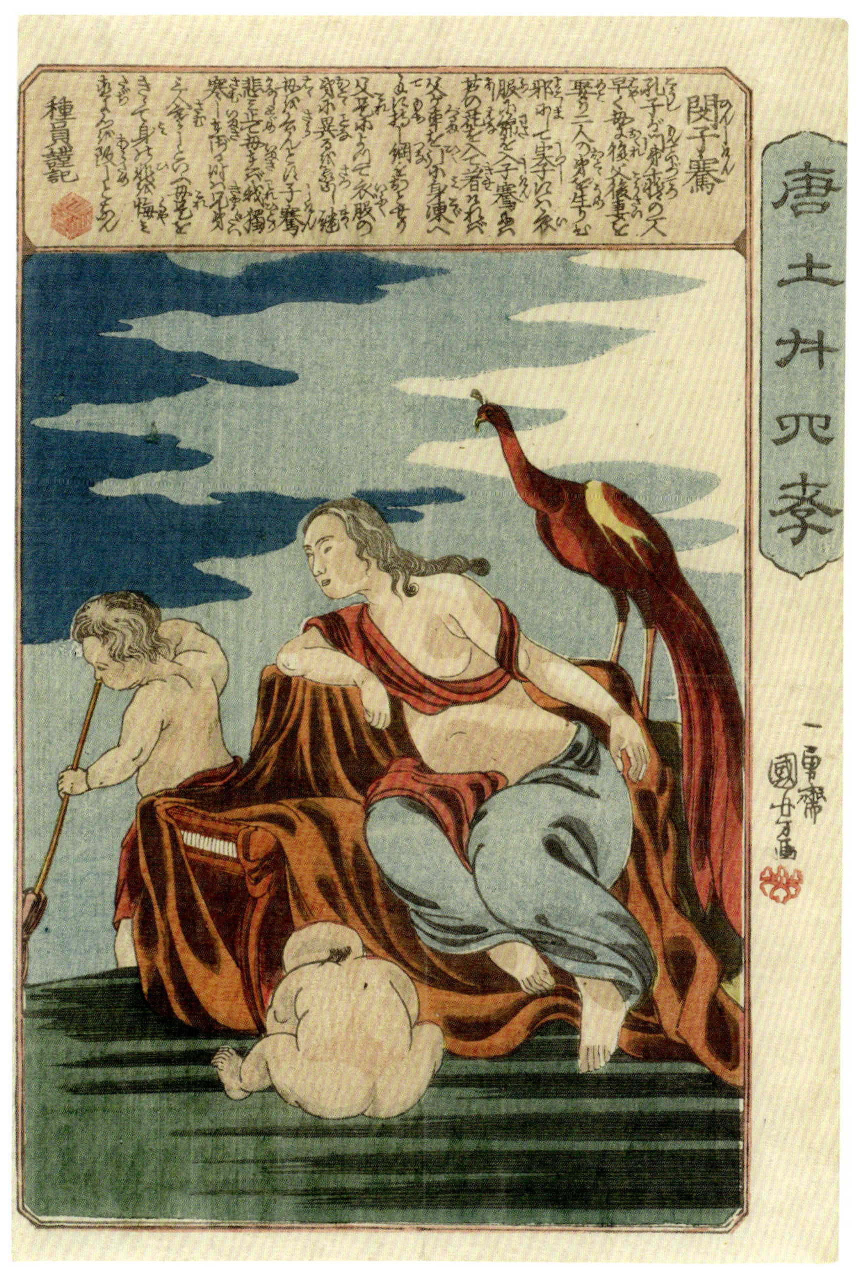

唐土廾四孝
閔子騫
種員謹記
一勇齋
國芳画

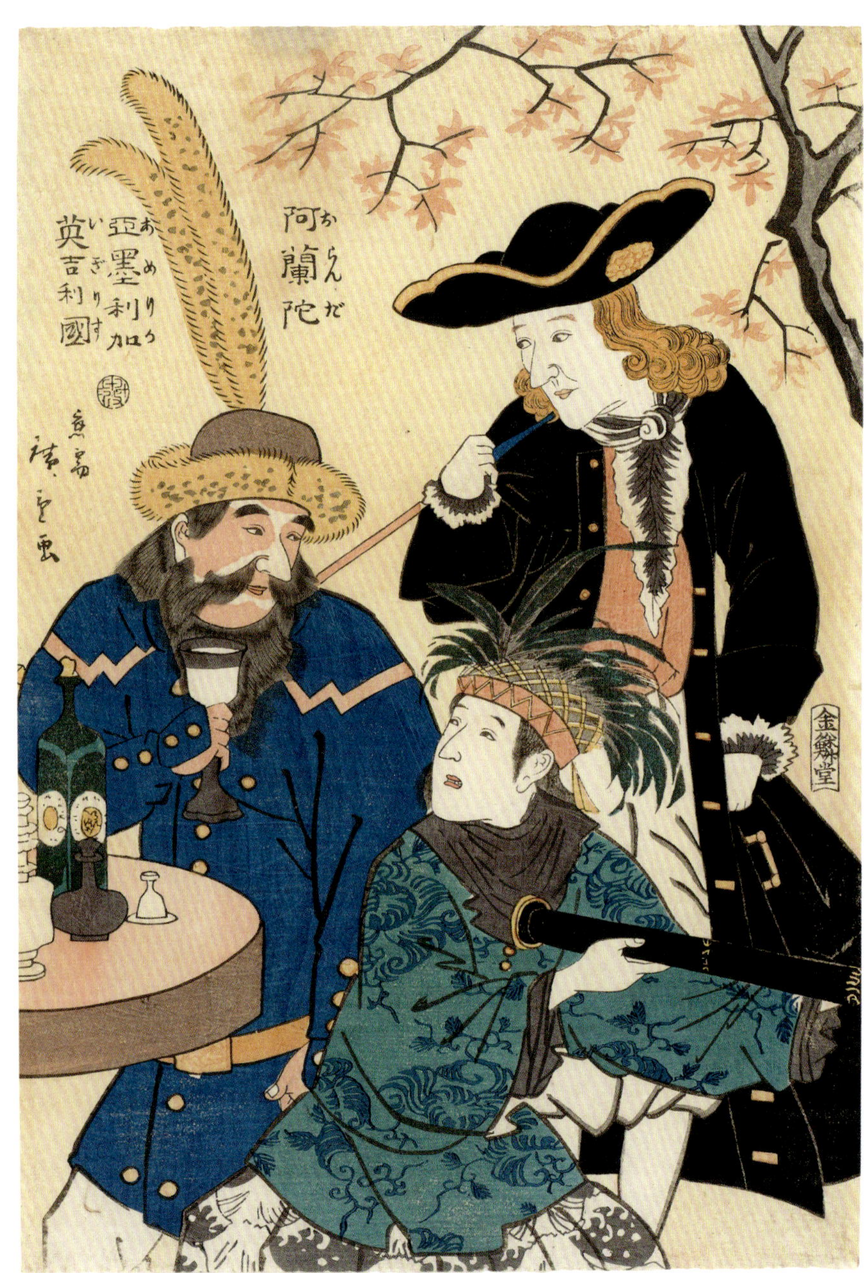

52
Utagawa Hiroshige II (1826–1869)
Holland America England, 1860

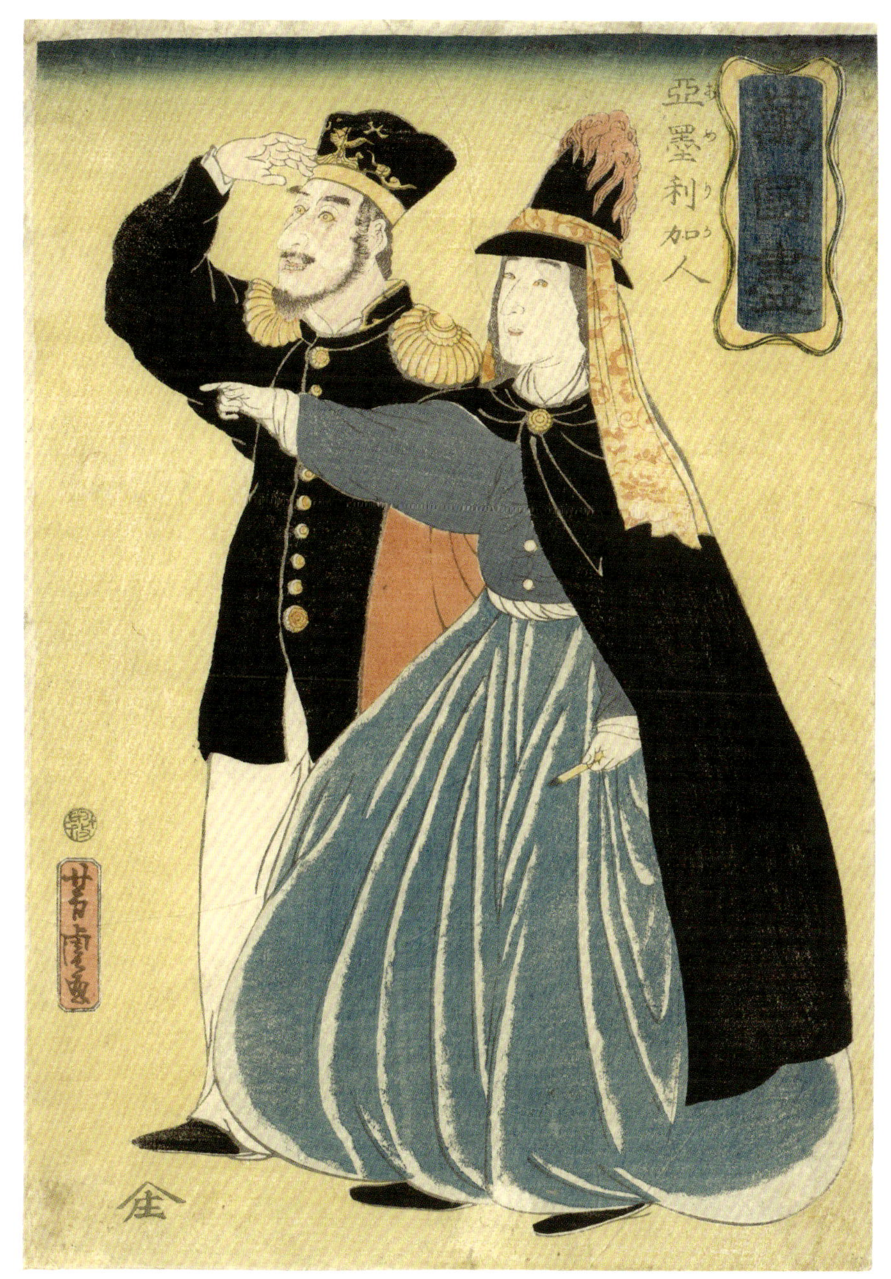

53
Utagawa Yoshitora (active 1850–1880)
Americans, from the series *A Collection of
Various Countries*, 1860

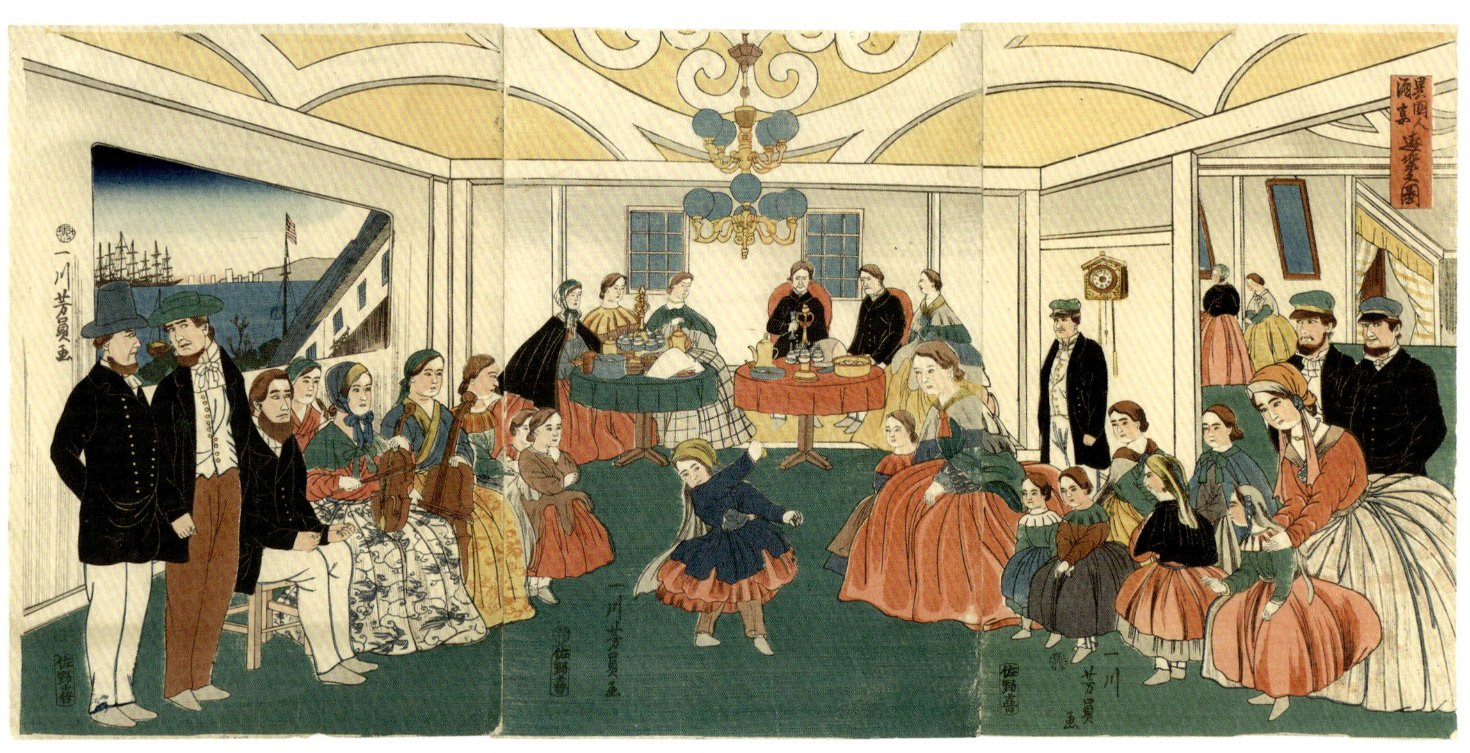

54

Utagawa Yoshikazu (active 1850–1870)

Banquet and Musicale in a Foreigner's Home, 1860

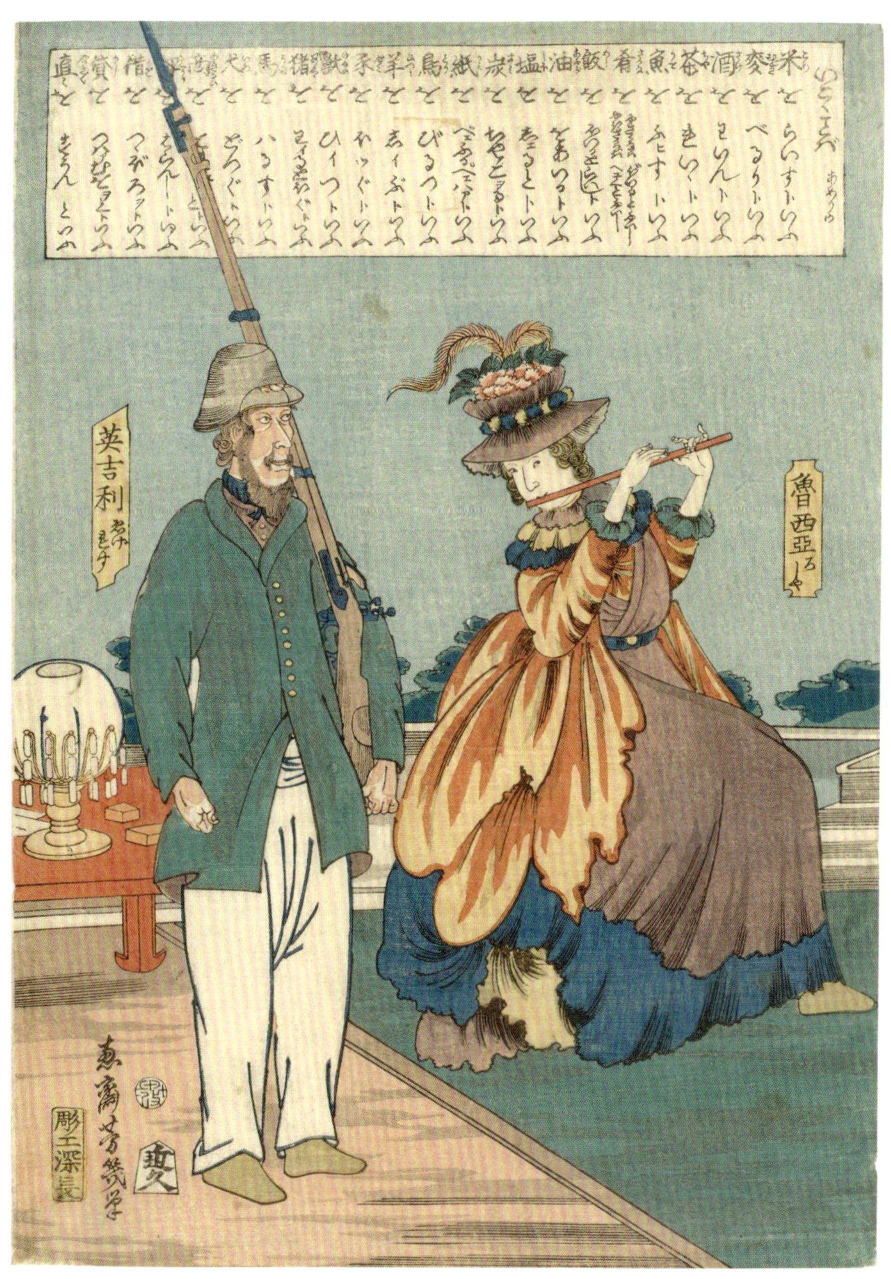

55
Utagawa Yoshiiku (1853–1904)
An Englishman and a Russian Woman, 1860

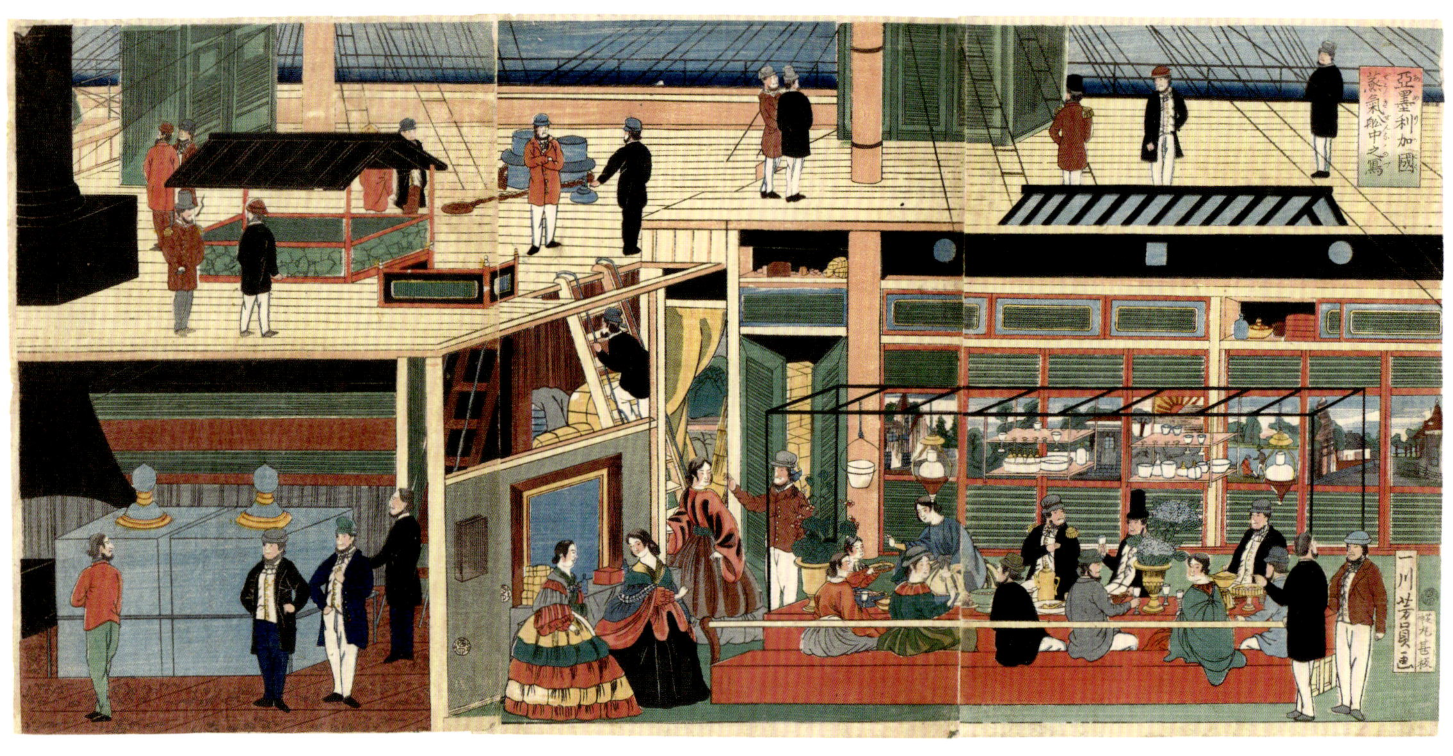

56

Utagawa Yoshikazu (active 1850–1870)

Interior of an American Steamship, 1861

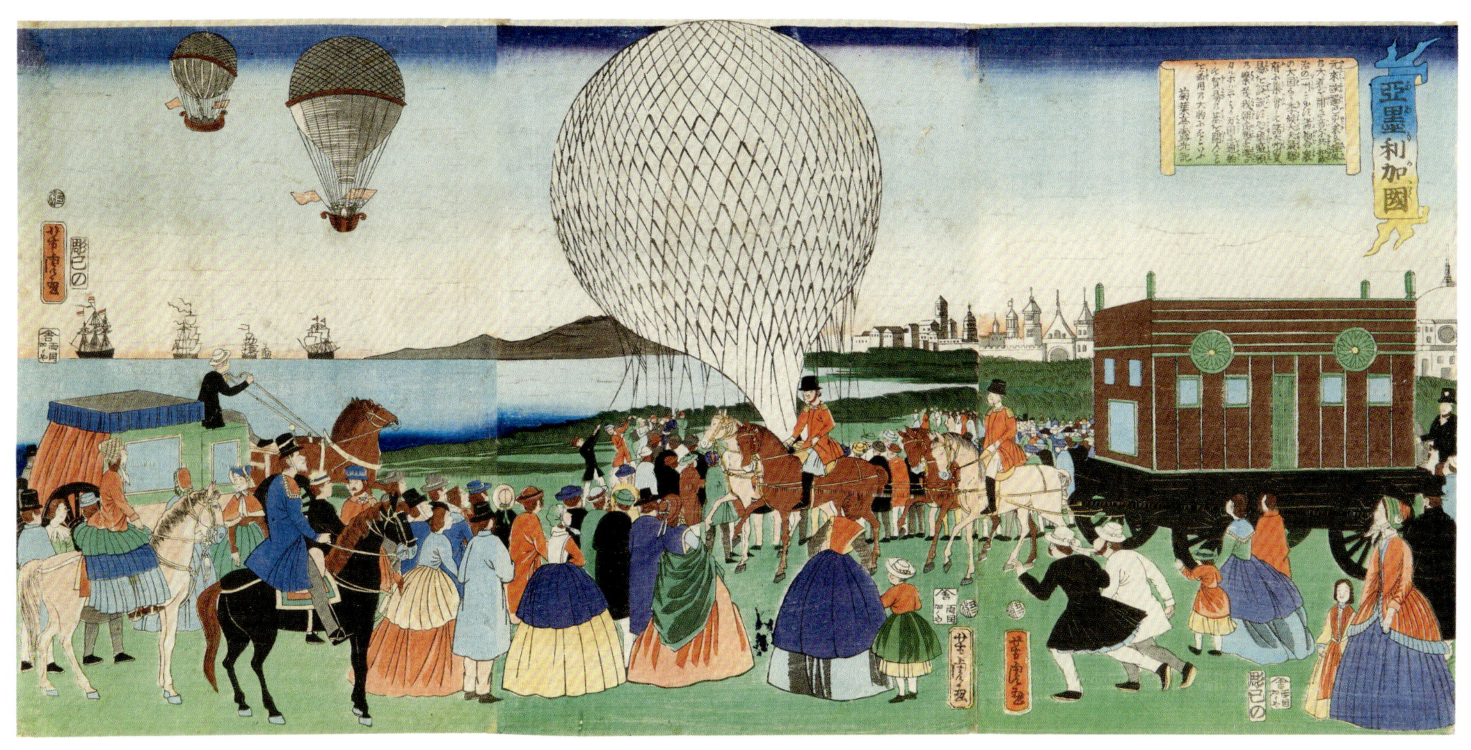

57
Utagawa Yoshitora (active 1850–1880)
Balloon Ascension in America, 1865

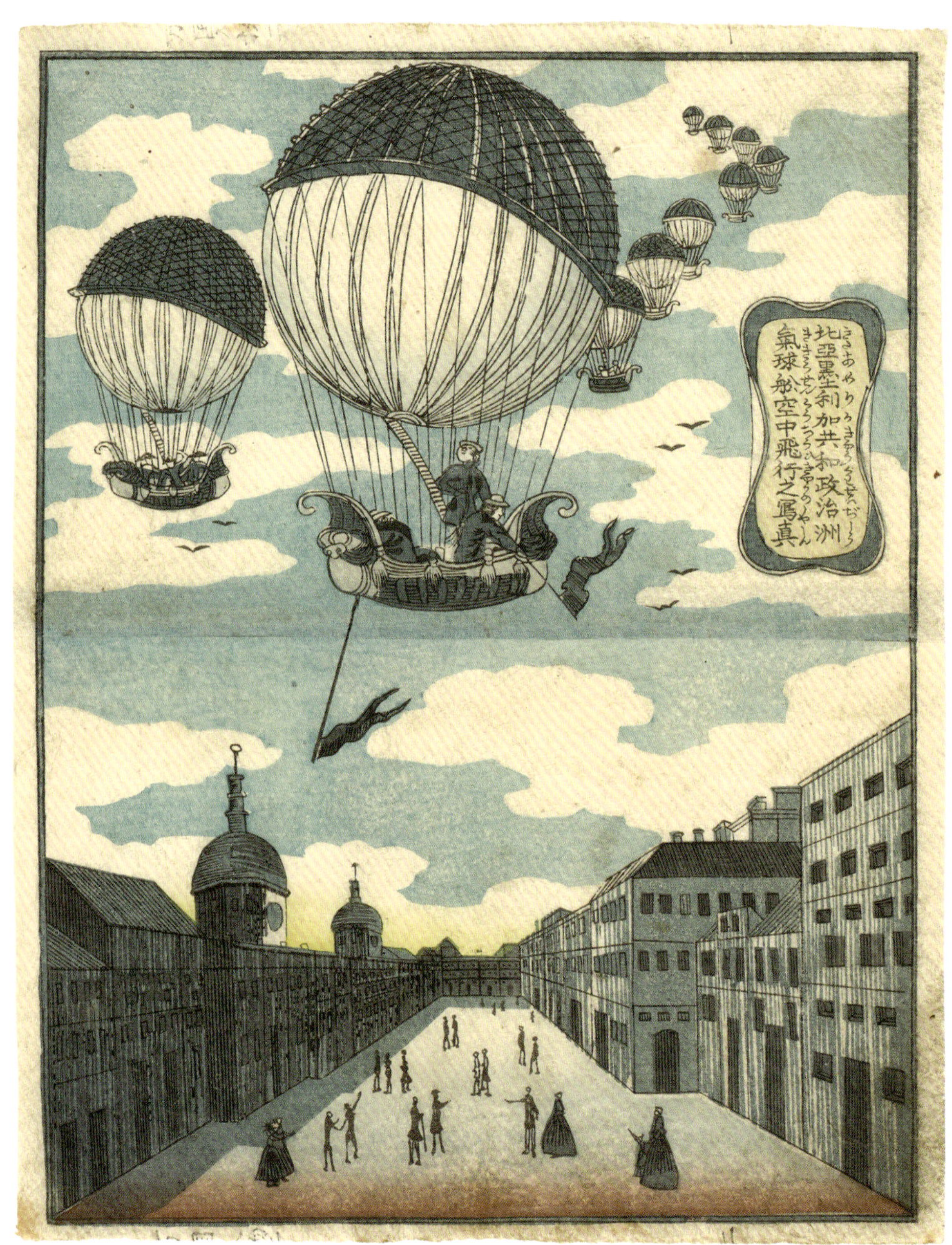

58

Utagawa Yoshitora (active 1850–1880)
Balloons in Flight in the United States of North America, from the series *People of Foreign Lands*, 1861

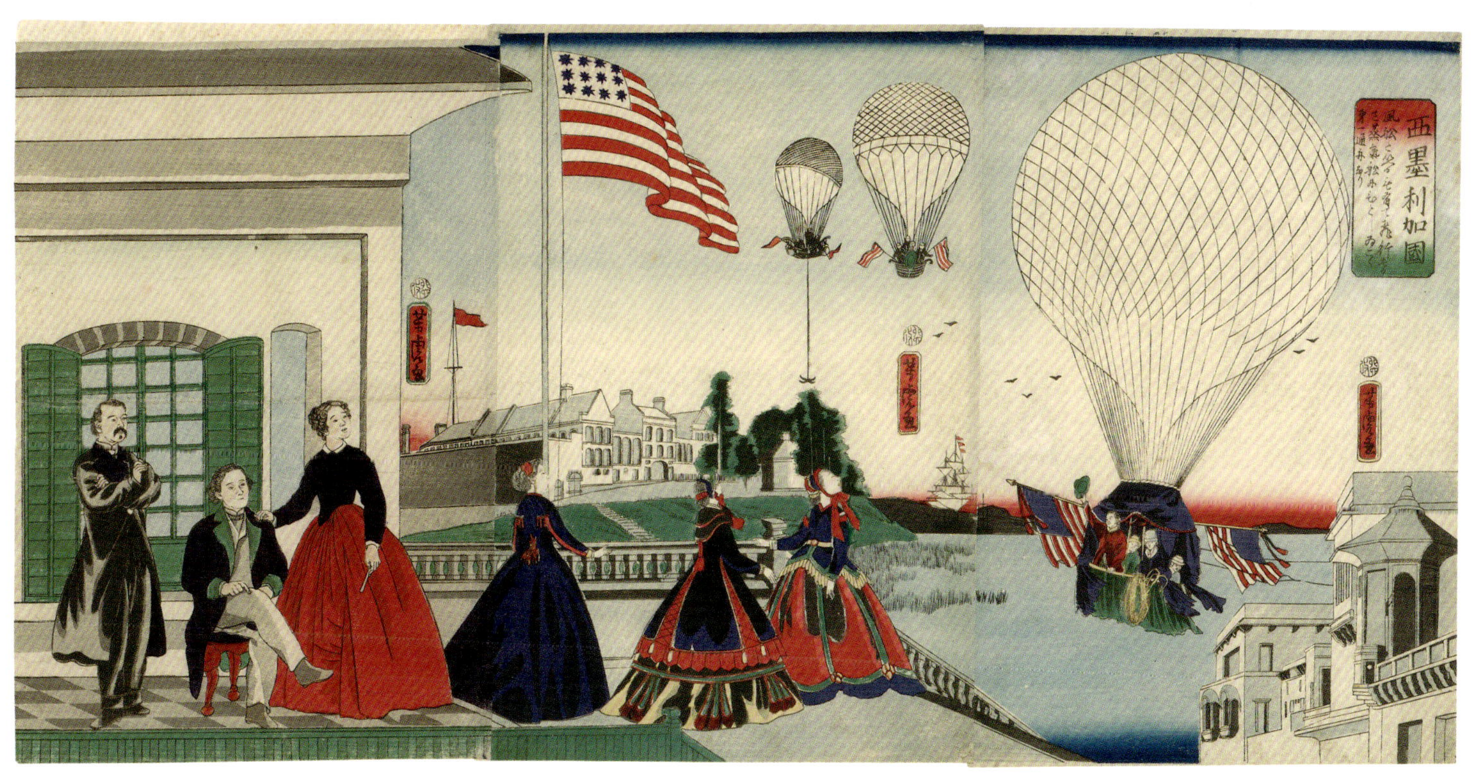

59
Utagawa Yoshitora (active 1850–1880)
The Country of America, 1867

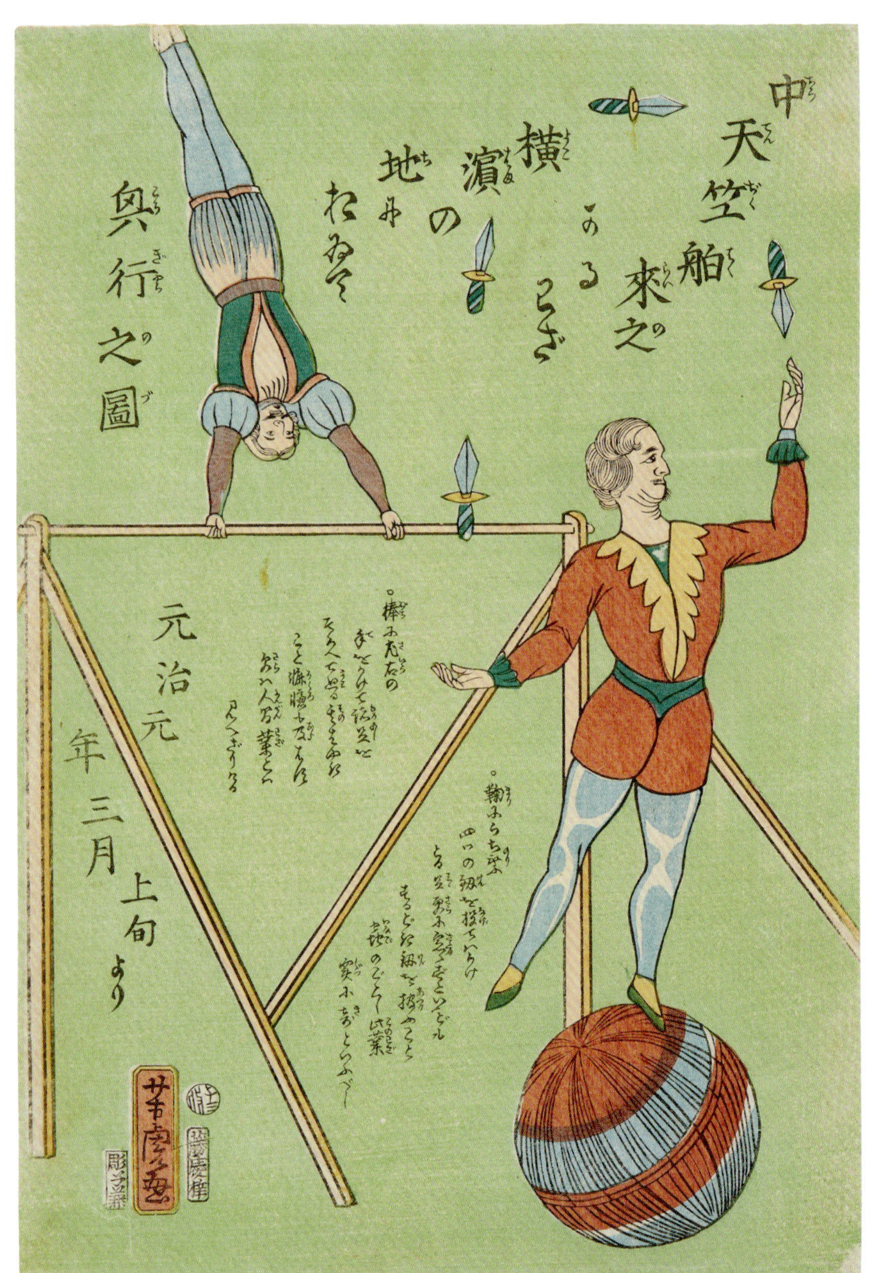

60

Utagawa Yoshitora (active 1850–1880)
Acrobats from Central India Performing at Yokohama, 1864

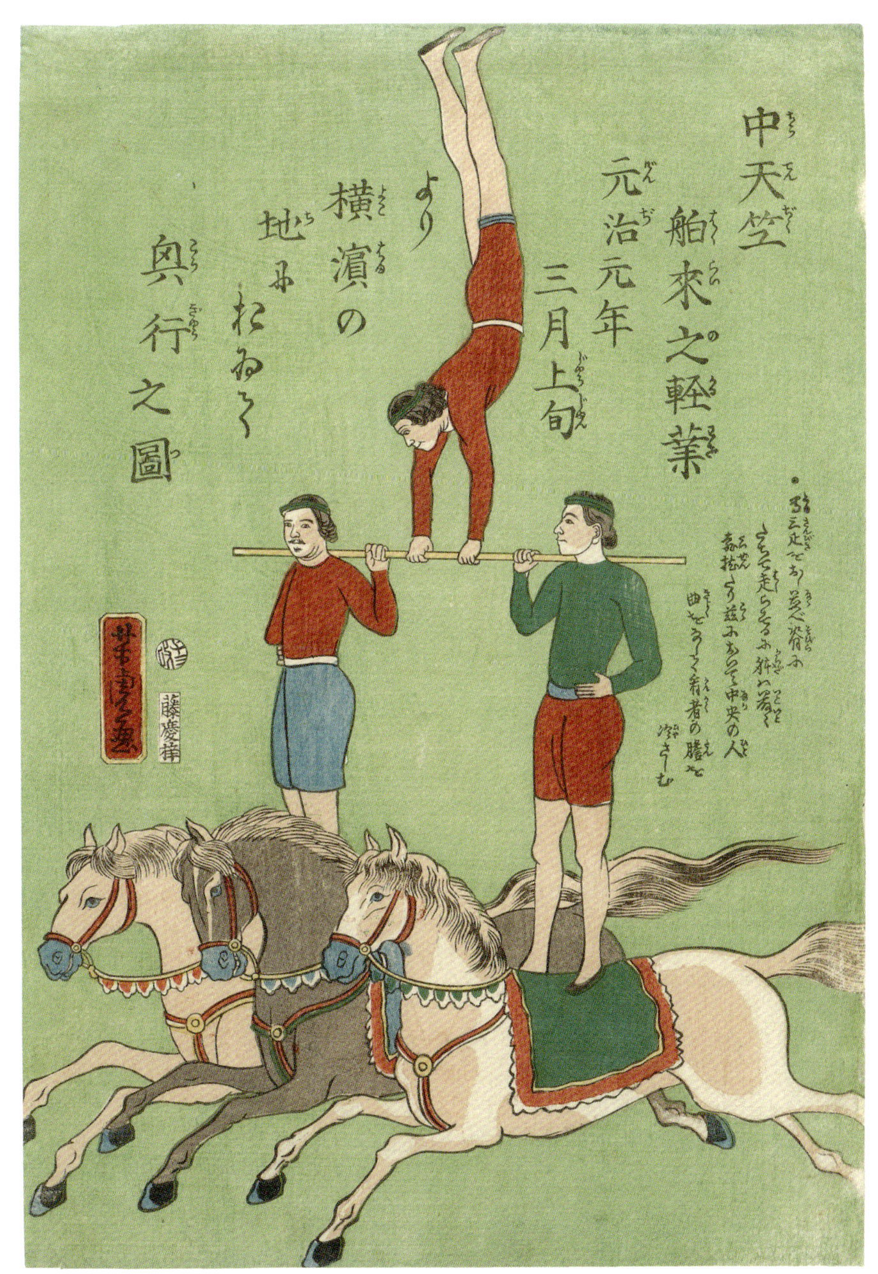

61

Utagawa Yoshitora (active 1850–1880)

Acrobats from Central India Performing at Yokohama, 1864

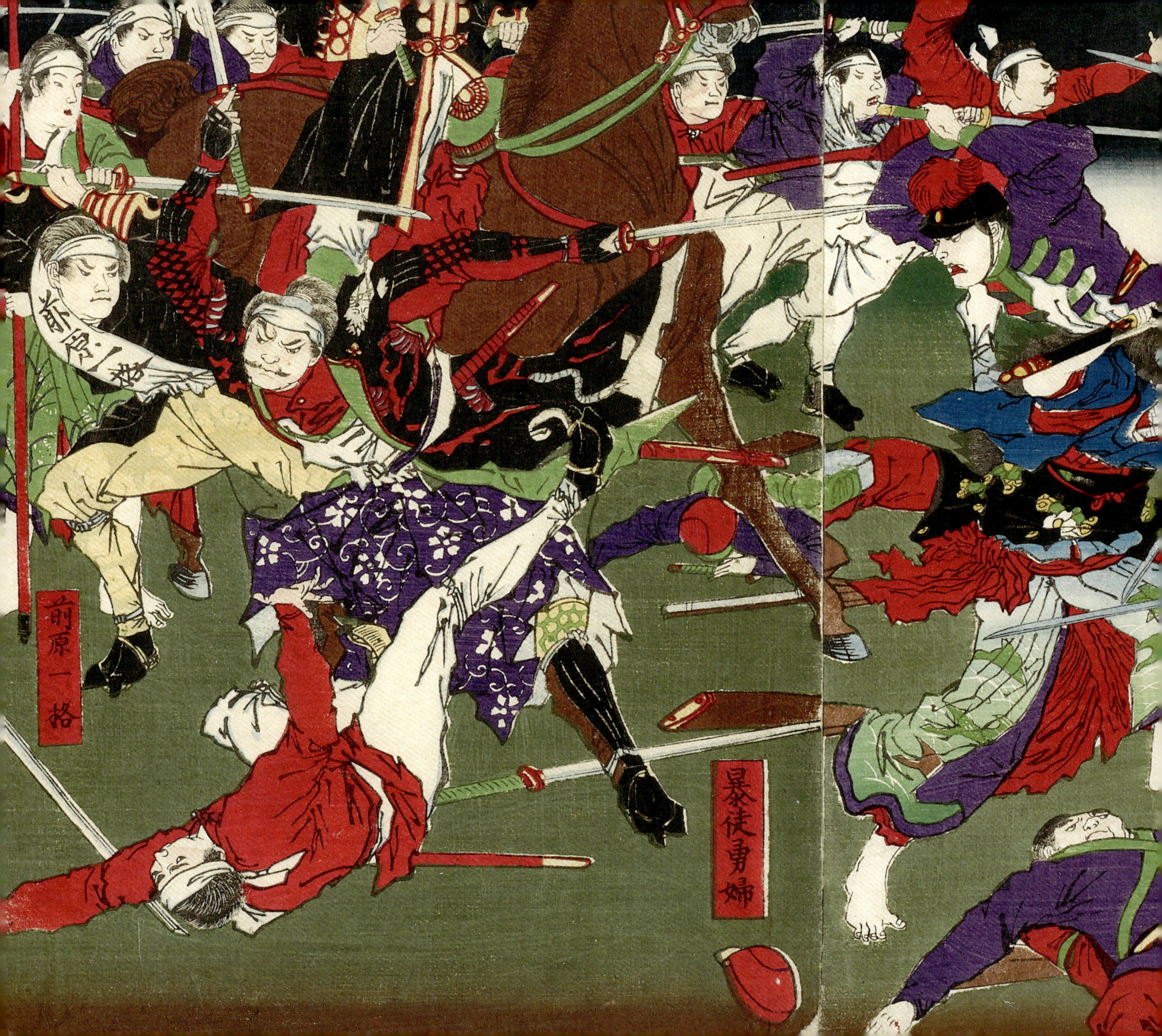
前原一格
暴徒勇婦

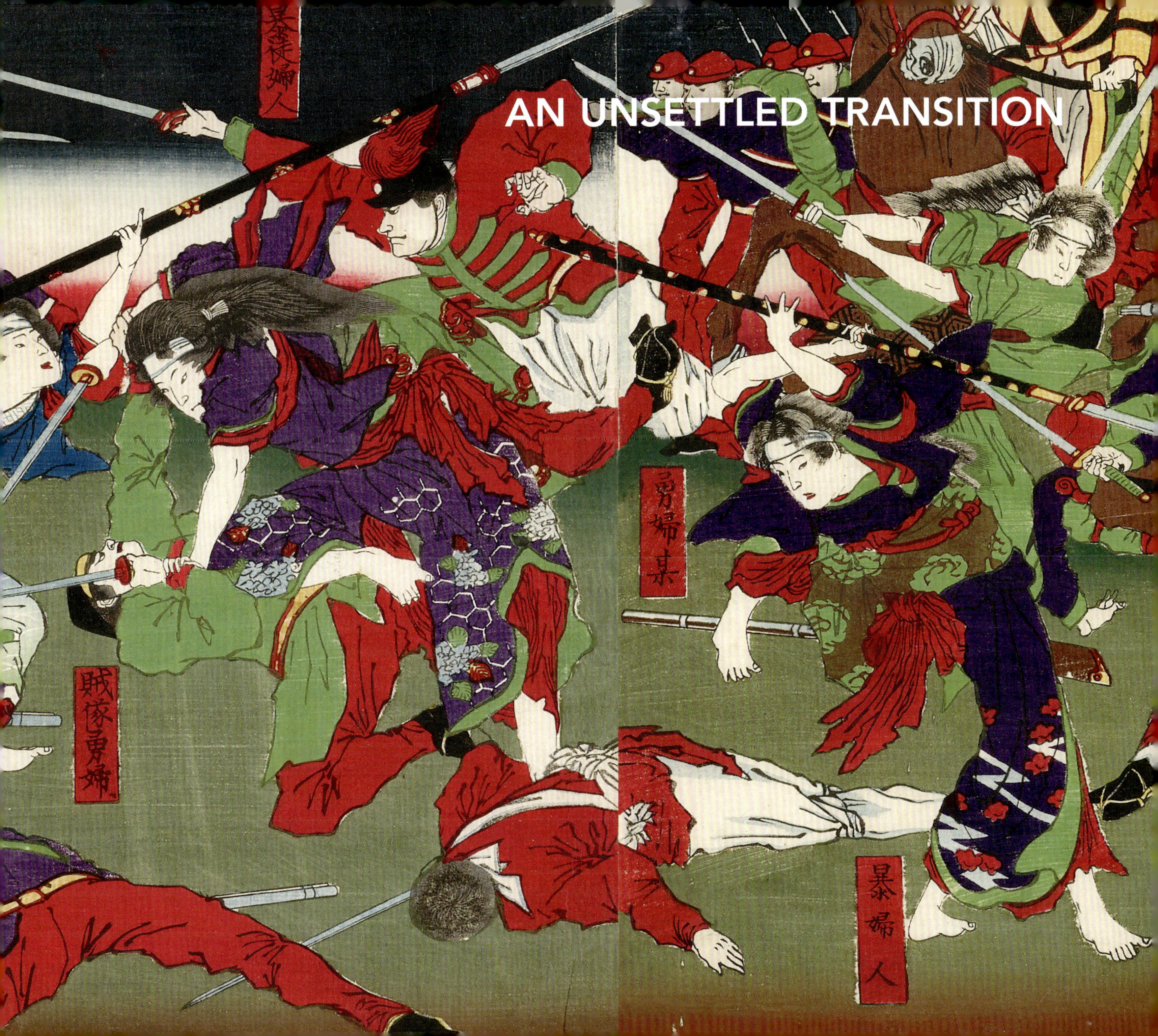
AN UNSETTLED TRANSITION
暴徒婦人
賊傔勇婦
勇婦某
暴婦人

62
Tsukioka Yoshitoshi (1839–1892)
Battle of the Sannō Shrine, 1874

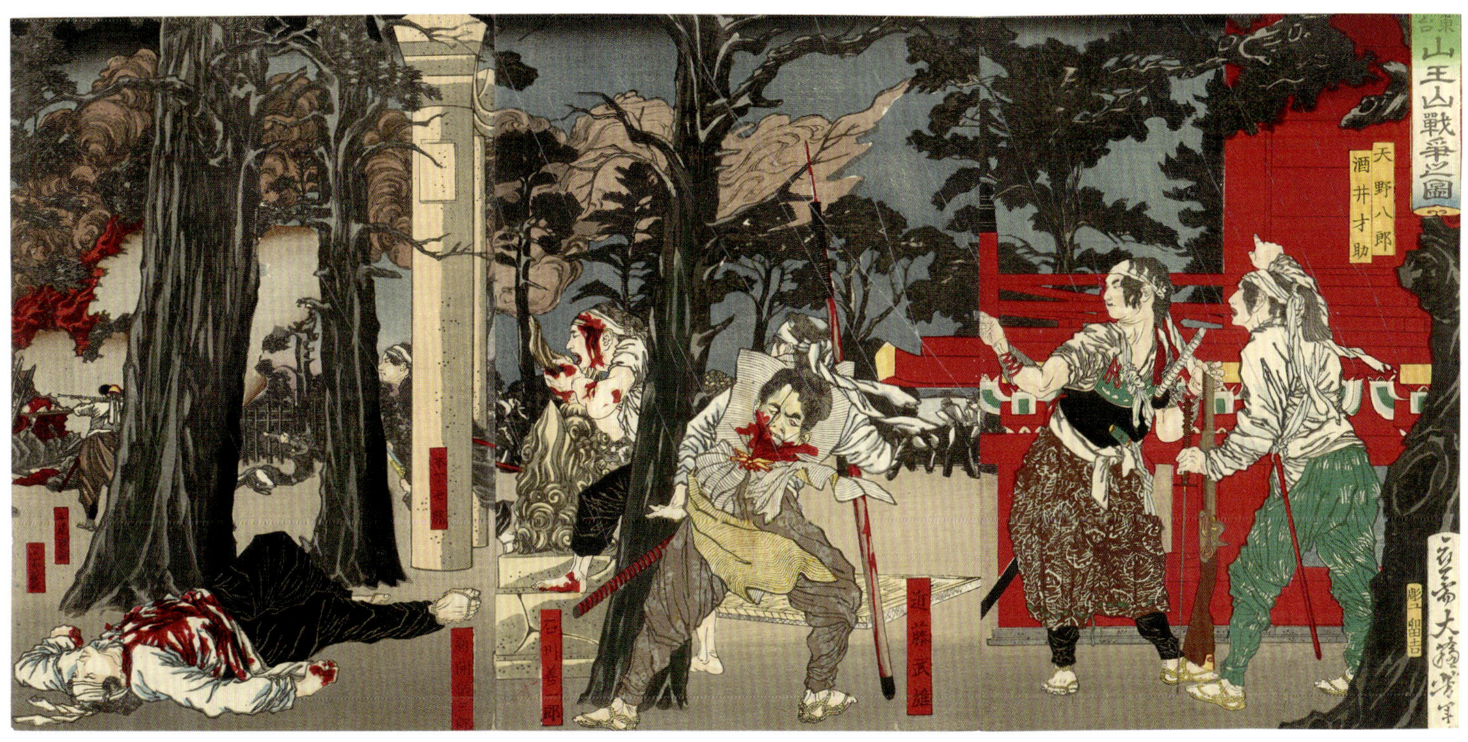
東台山王山戦争之図
天野八郎
酒井才助
近藤武雄
石川善一郎
大蘇芳年筆
彫留吉

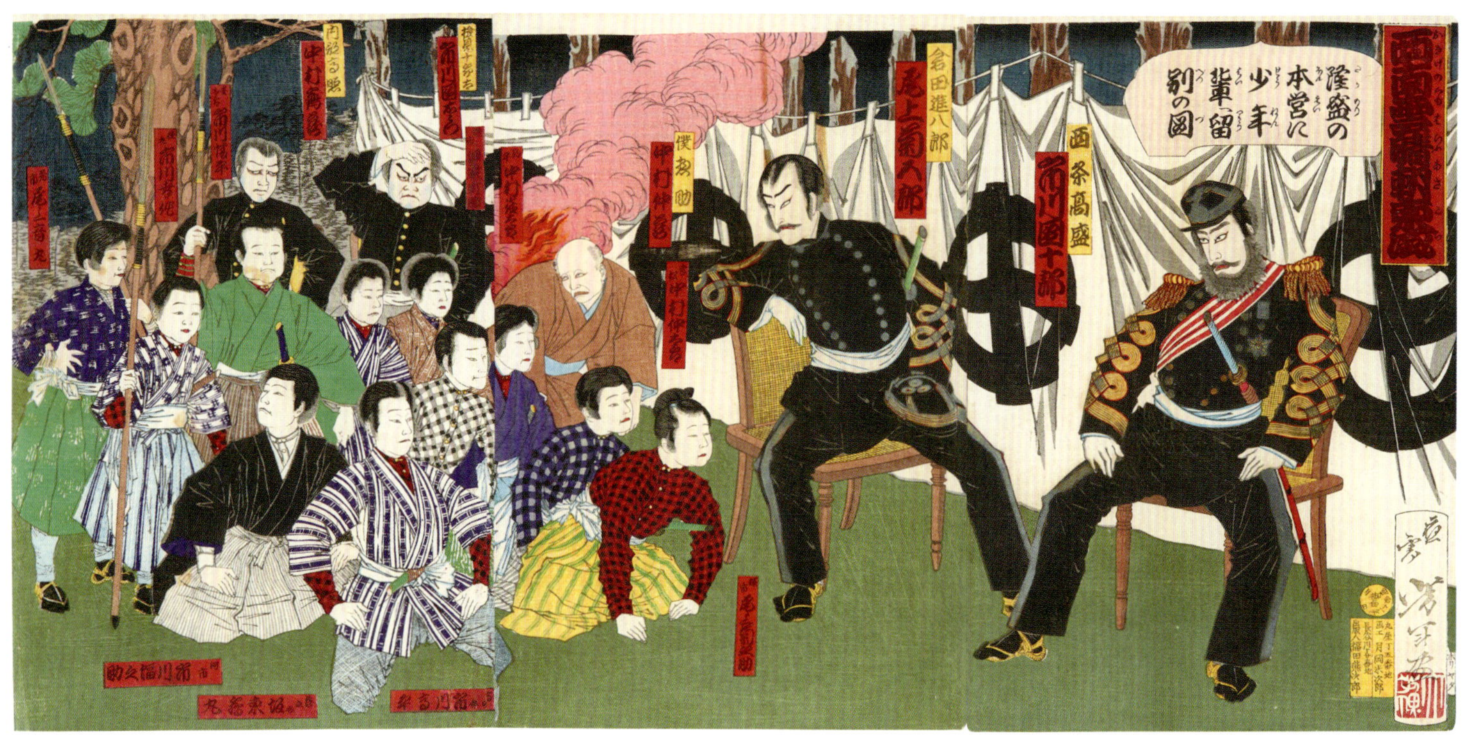

63

Tsukioka Yoshitoshi (1839–1892)

The Eastern Wind Clears Away the Clouds in the South West, 1878

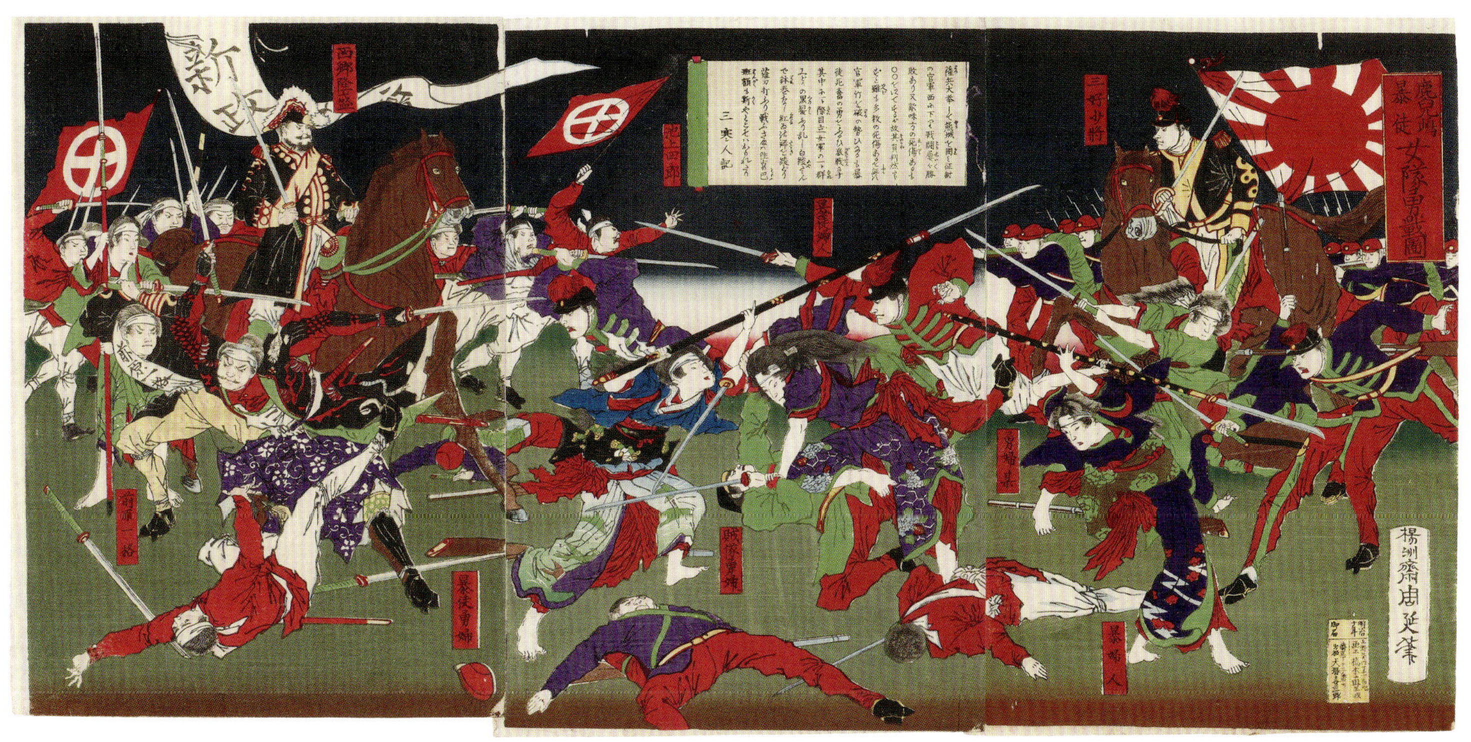

64
Yōshū Chikanobu (1838–1912)
The Women's Brigade of the Kagoshima Rebels in Brave Battle, 1877

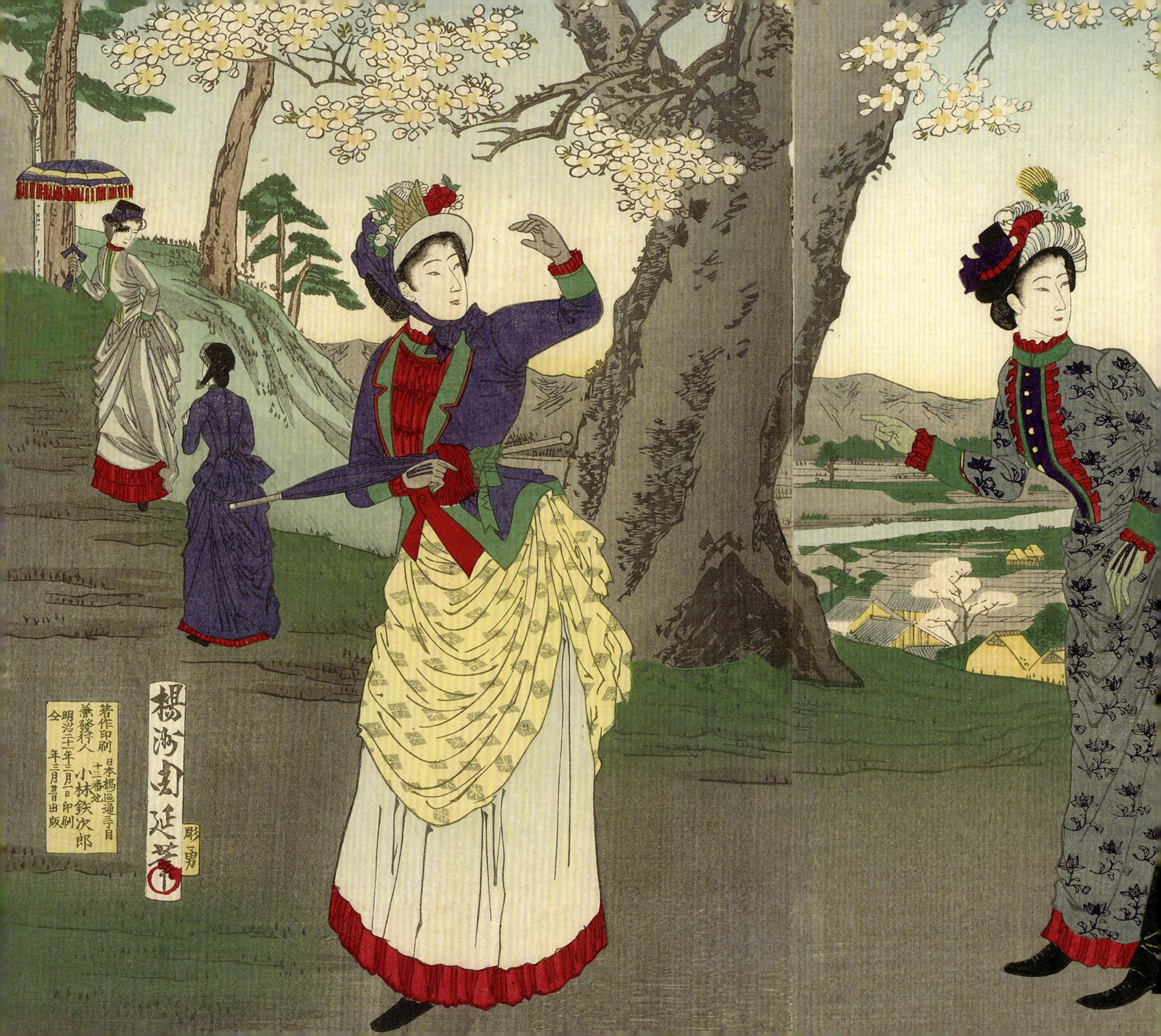

楊洲周延筆
彫勇
著作印刷
兼發行人　小林鉄次郎
日本橋區通三丁目十三番地
明治三十一年三月一日印刷
全年三月三日出版

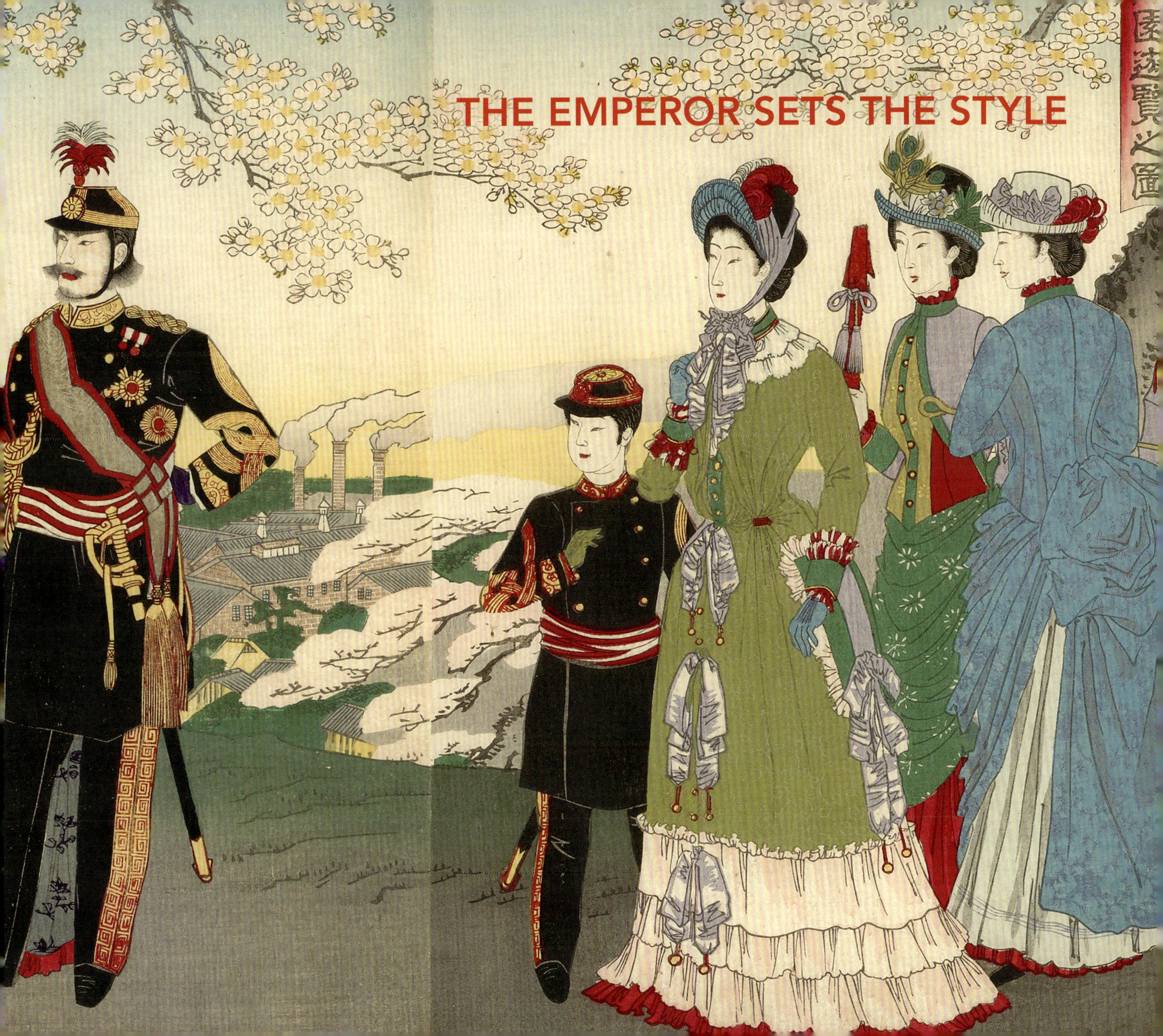

THE EMPEROR SETS THE STYLE

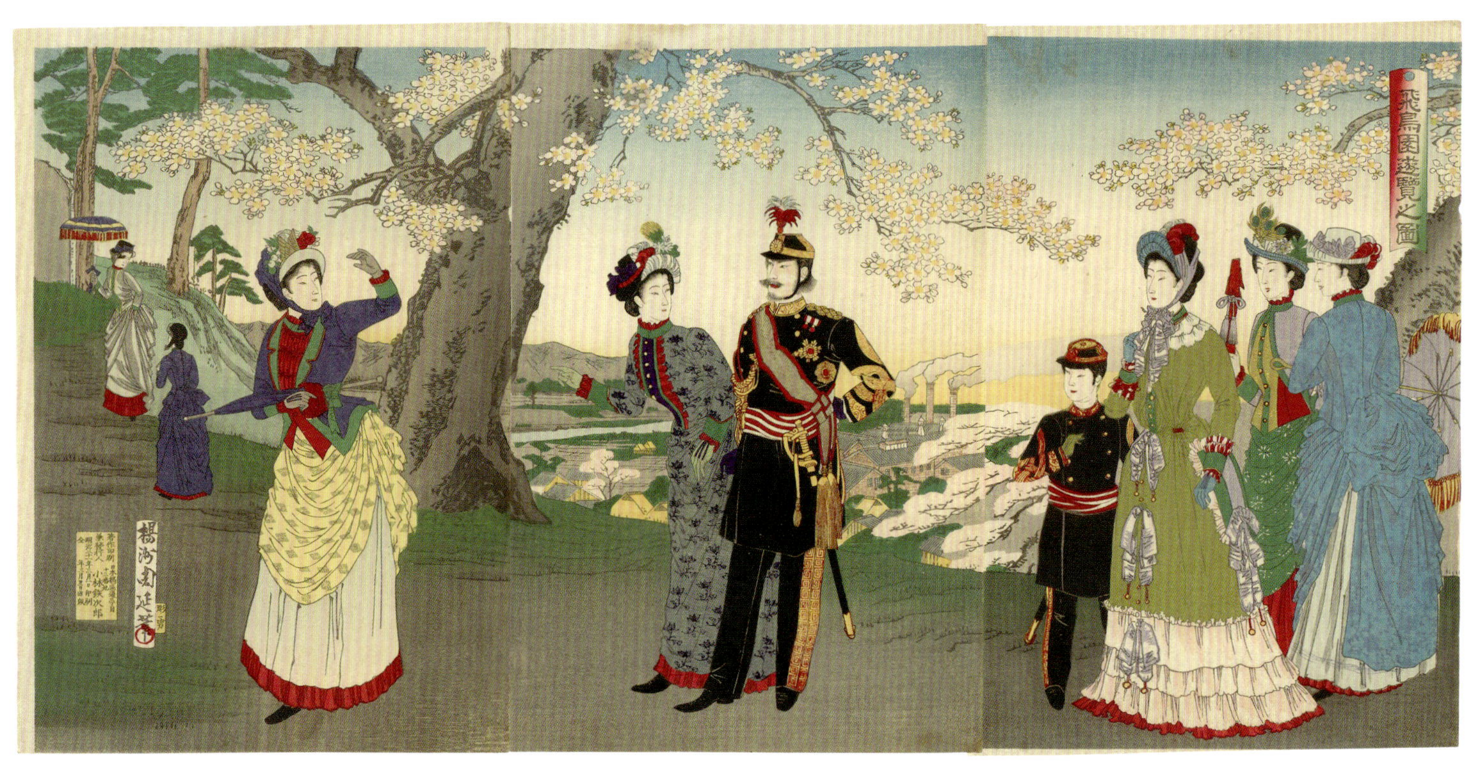

65

Yōshū Chikanobu (1838–1912)

Imperial Party Visits the Park at Asuka, 1888

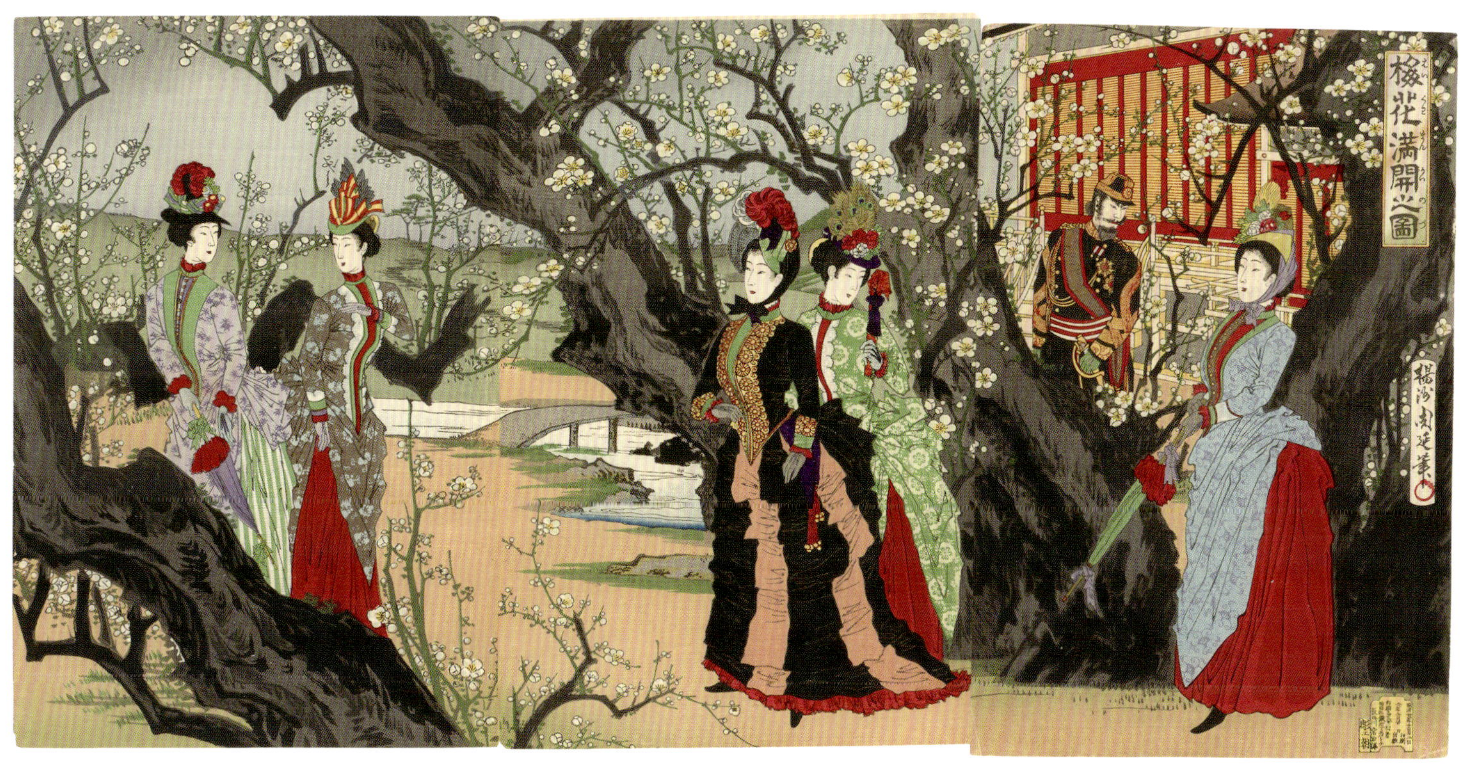

66

Yōshū Chikanobu (1838–1912)

Plum Trees in Full Bloom, the Meiji Emperor, Empress, and Women of Nobility, 1888

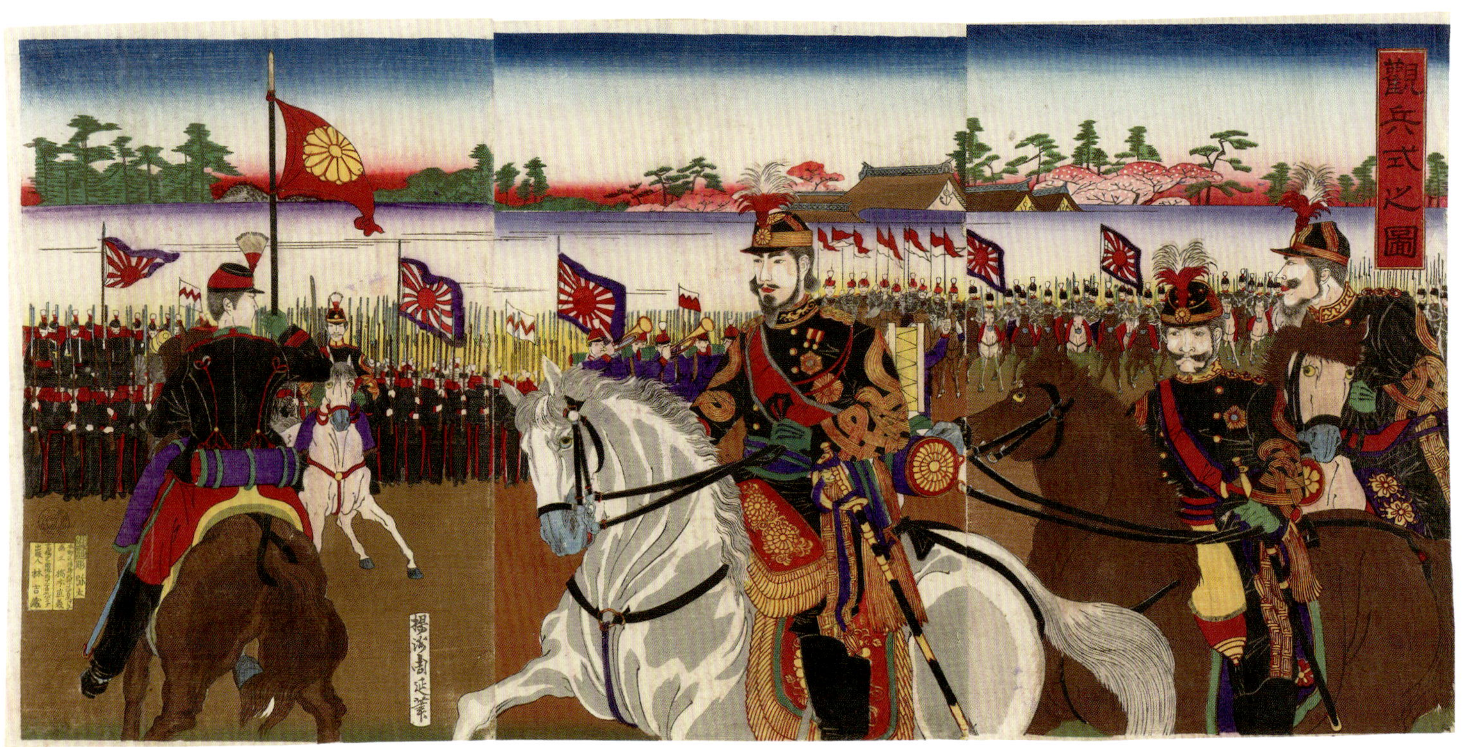

67

Yōshū Chikanobu (1838–1912)

The Meiji Emperor and His Officers Reviewing the Troops, 1887

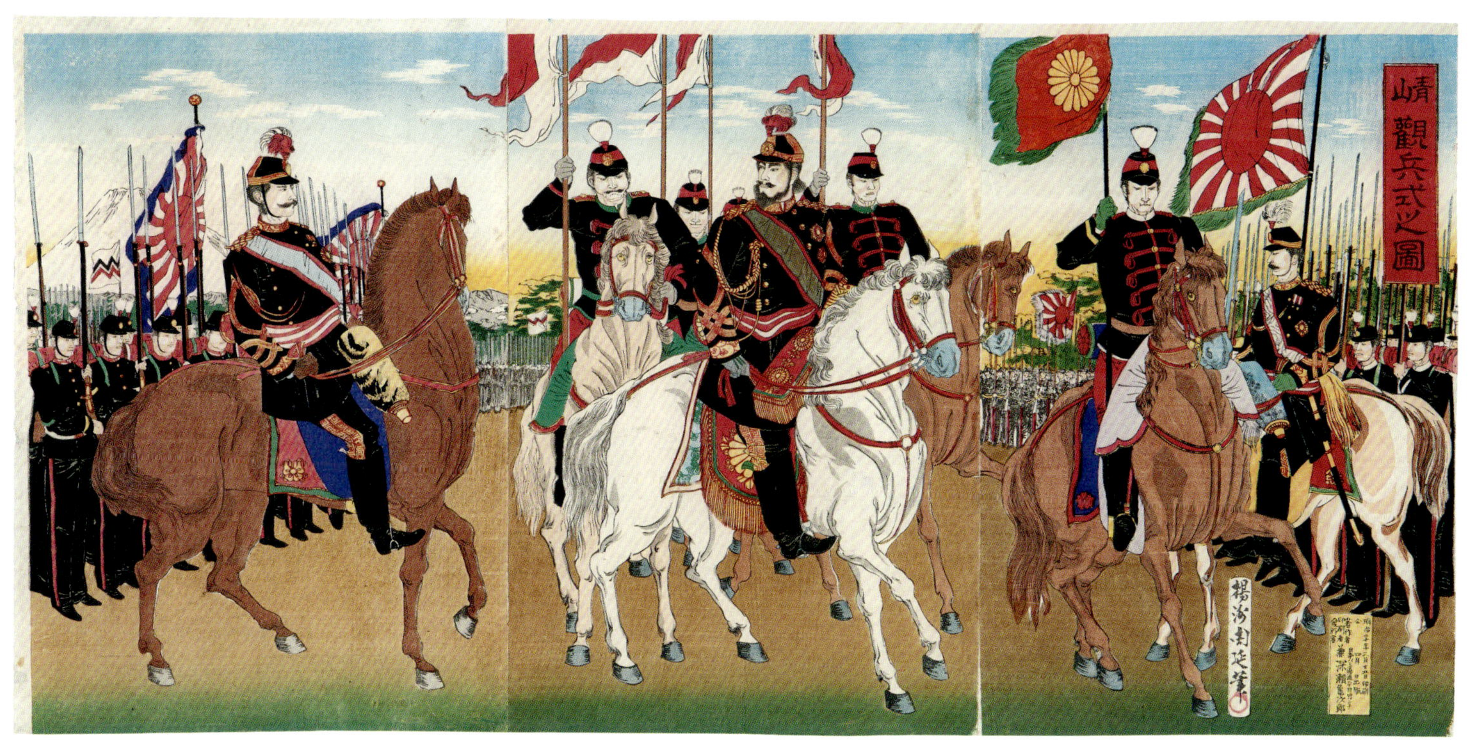

68

Yōshū Chikanobu (1838–1912)

A Military Parade at Aoyama, 1887

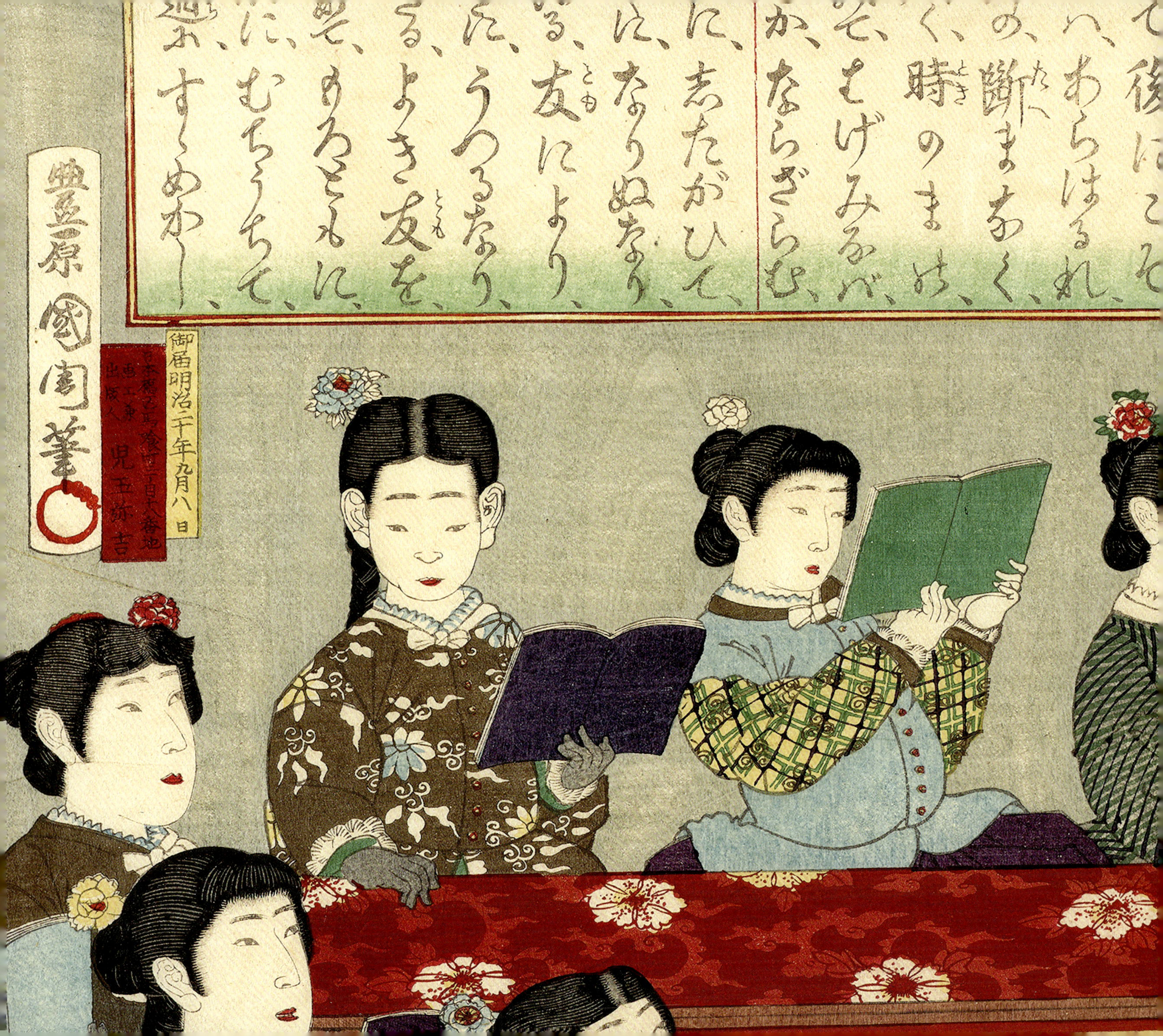

て後にて、へ、あらはるれ、の、たちまるべく、時のまゝは、そ、とげみるべ、か、ならざらむ、に、したがひに、なりぬなり、る、友により、うつるなり、よき友を、に、むちうちて、りろそれに、楽すゝめ！

豊原國周筆

御届明治二十年九月八日

日本橋区〇〇〇三十八番地
画工兼
出版人　兒玉又吉

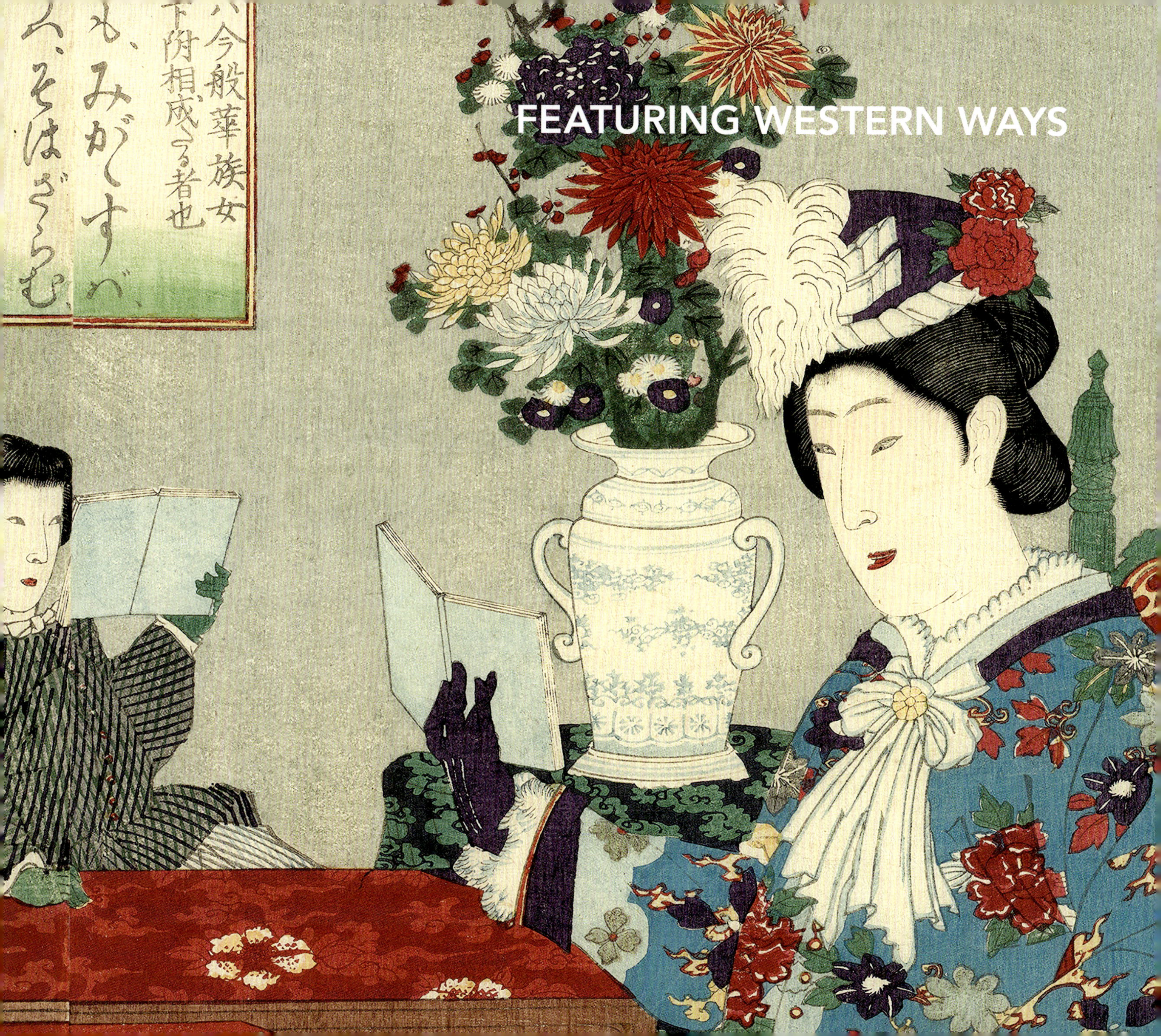
FEATURING WESTERN WAYS
八今般華族女
下阿相成る者也
み
、
も
が
、
す
そ
べ
は
ざ
ら
む
入

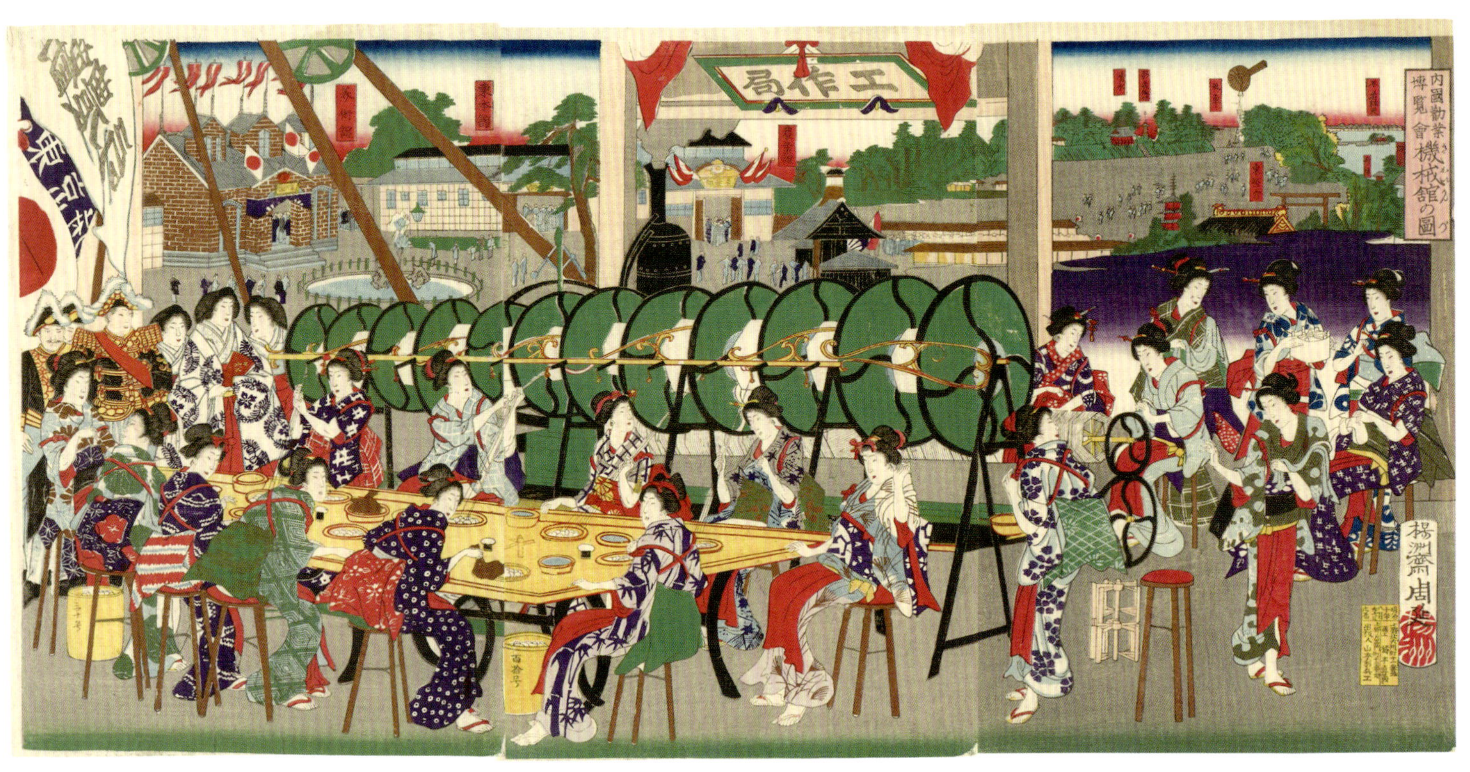

69

Yōshū Chikanobu (1838–1912)

The Hall of Machinery at the Exhibition for the Promotion of
Domestic Industry, 1877

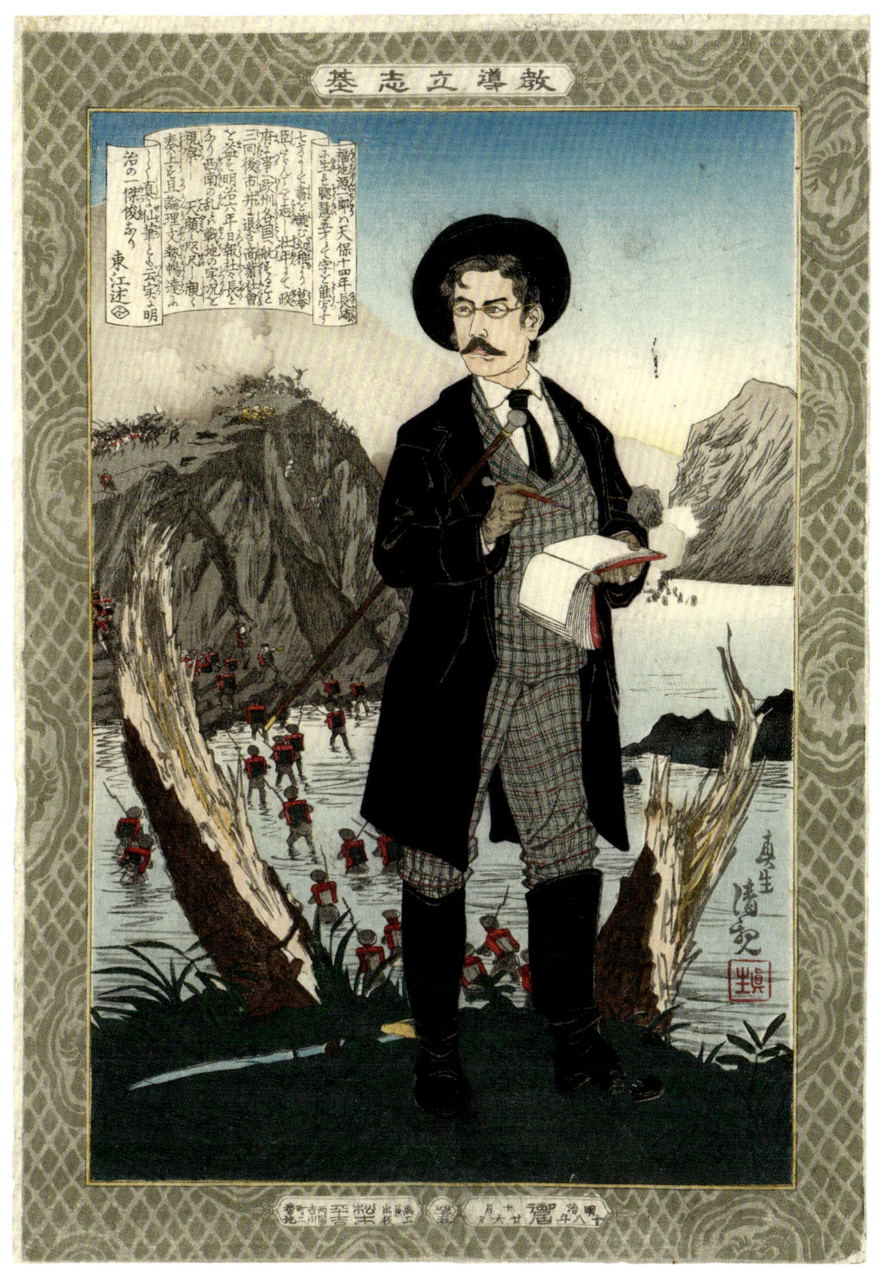

70

Kobayashi Kiyochika (1847–1915)

The Journalist Fukuchi Gen'ichirō, from the series *Instruction in the Fundamentals of Success*, 1885

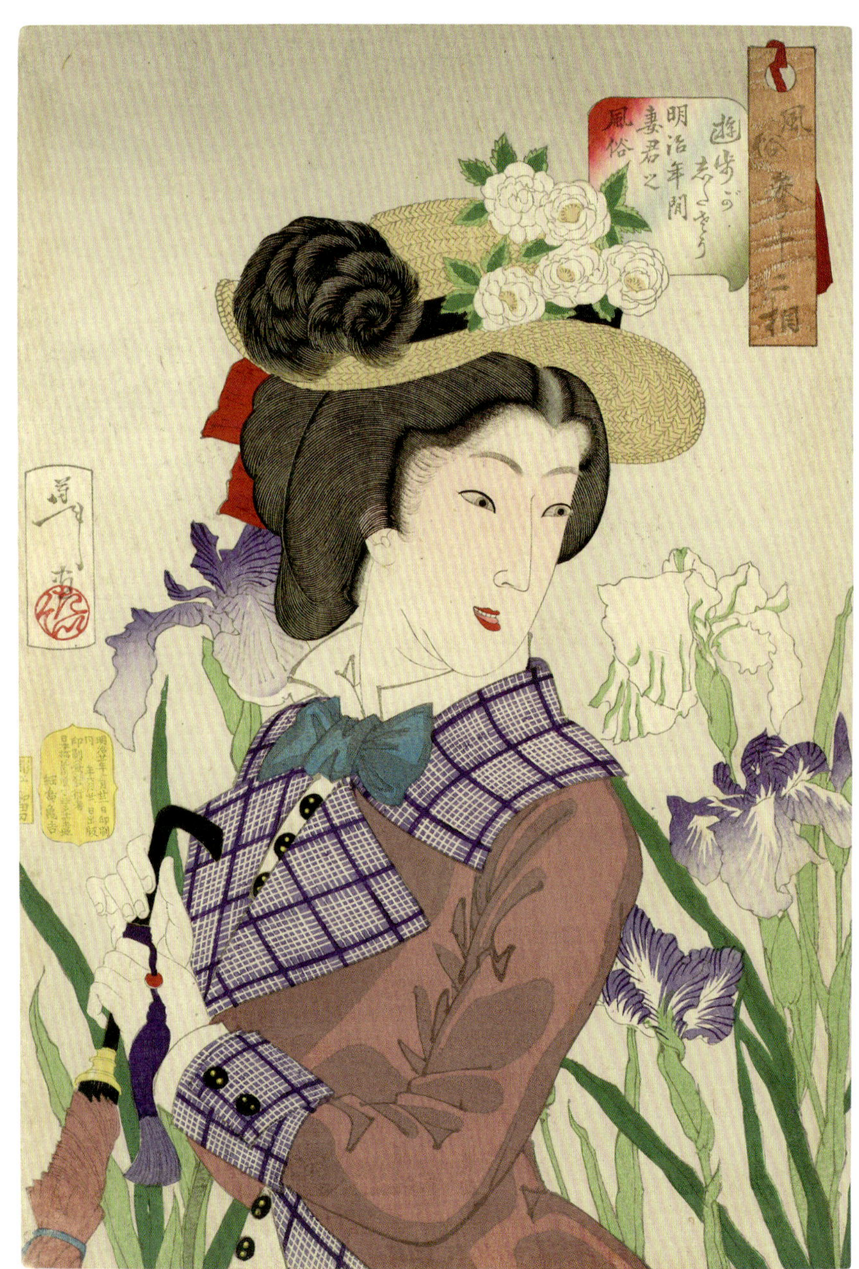

71

Tsukioka Yoshitoshi (1839–1892)

The Appearance of an Upper-Class Wife of the Meiji Era, from the series *Thirty-Two Customs and Manners*, 1888

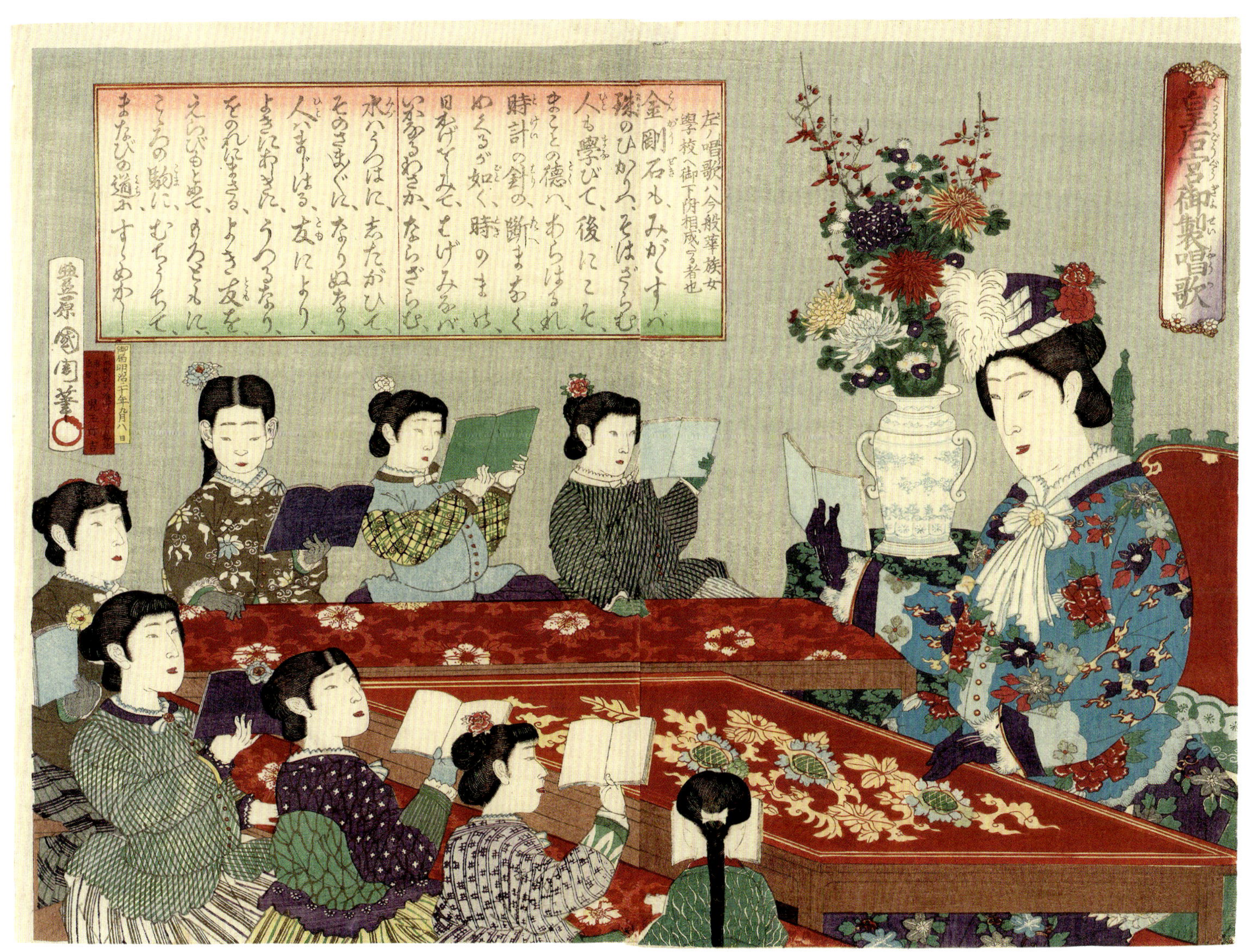

72

Toyohara Kunichika (1835–1900)

Song Composed by the Empress, 1887

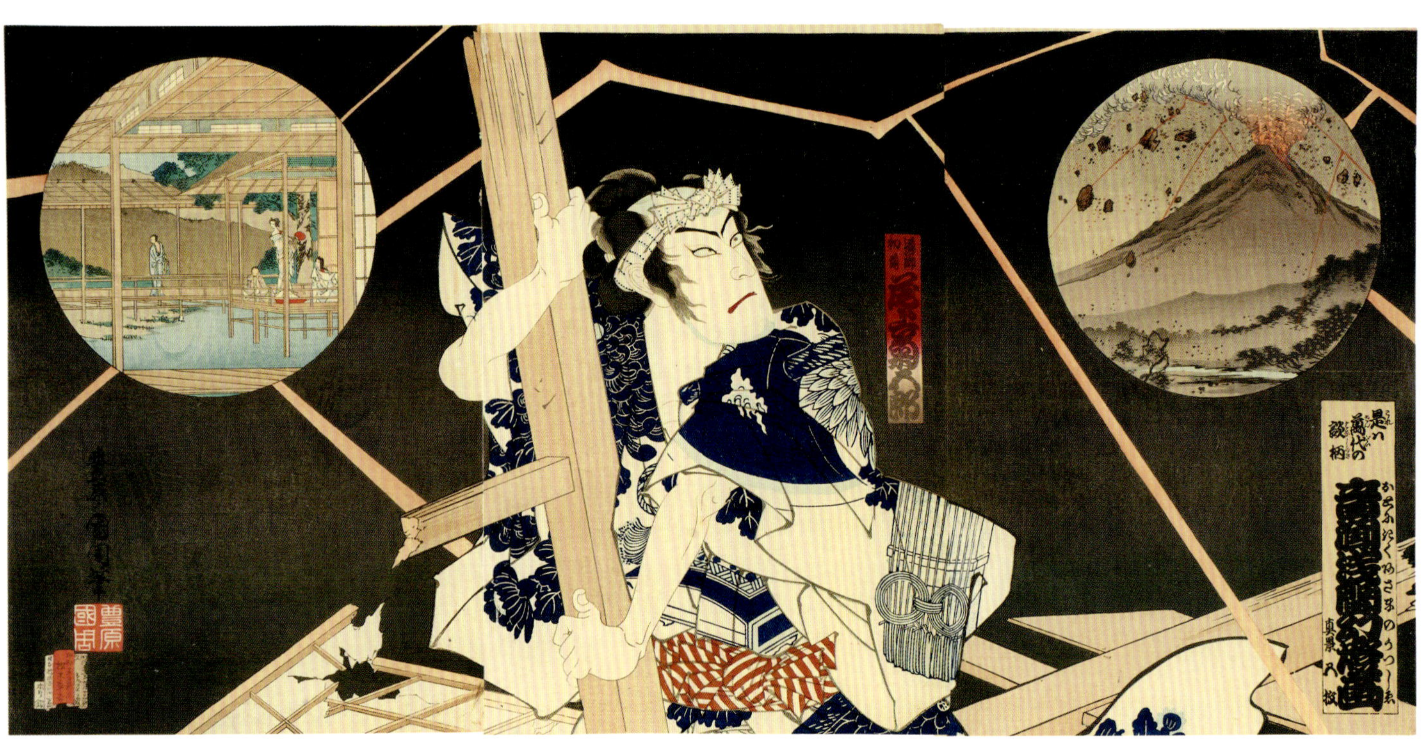

73
Toyohara Kunichika (1835–1900)
A Depiction of Mount Asama through Sounds, 1888

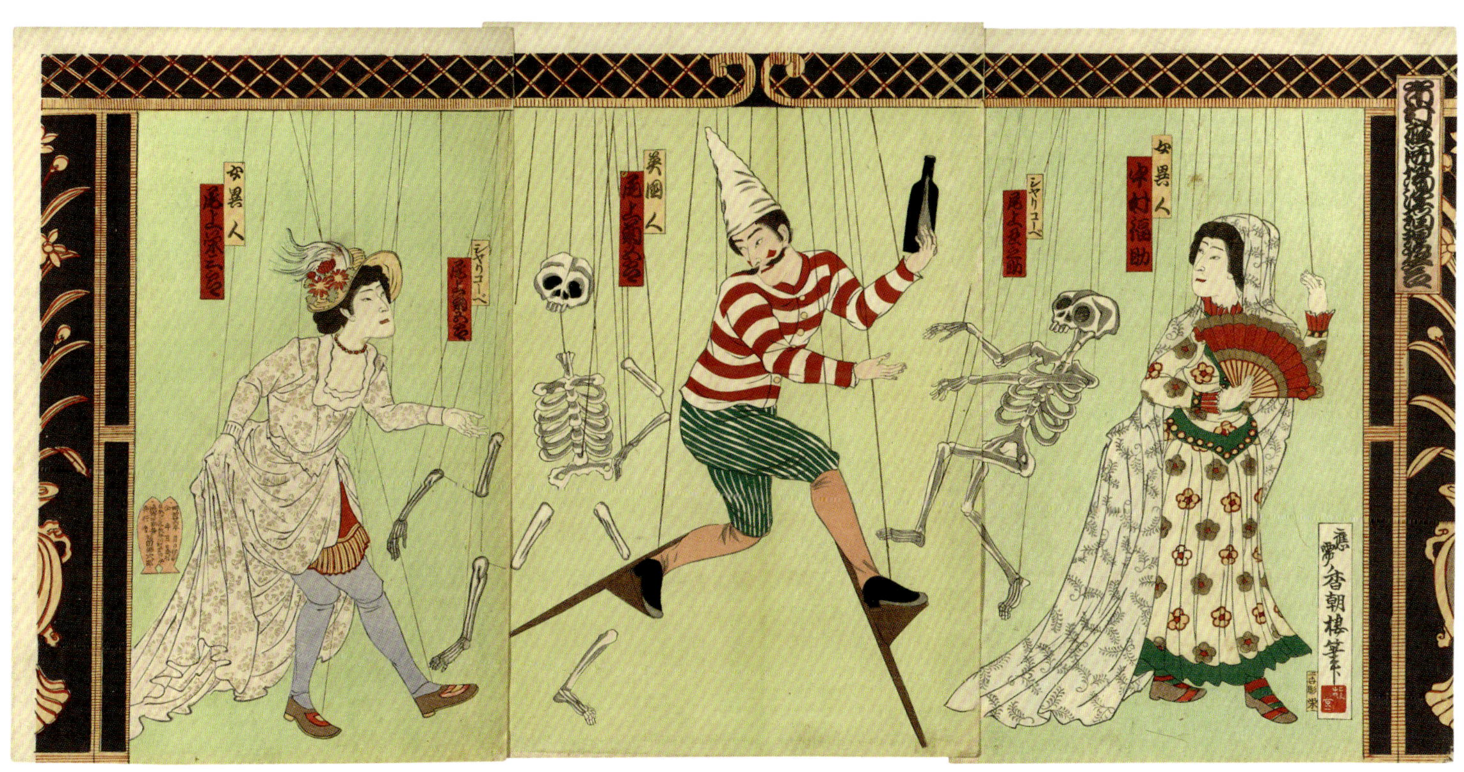

74
Utagawa Kunisada III (1848–1920)
Marionettes Imitating the Sound of a Bell Playing at Ichimura Theater, 1893

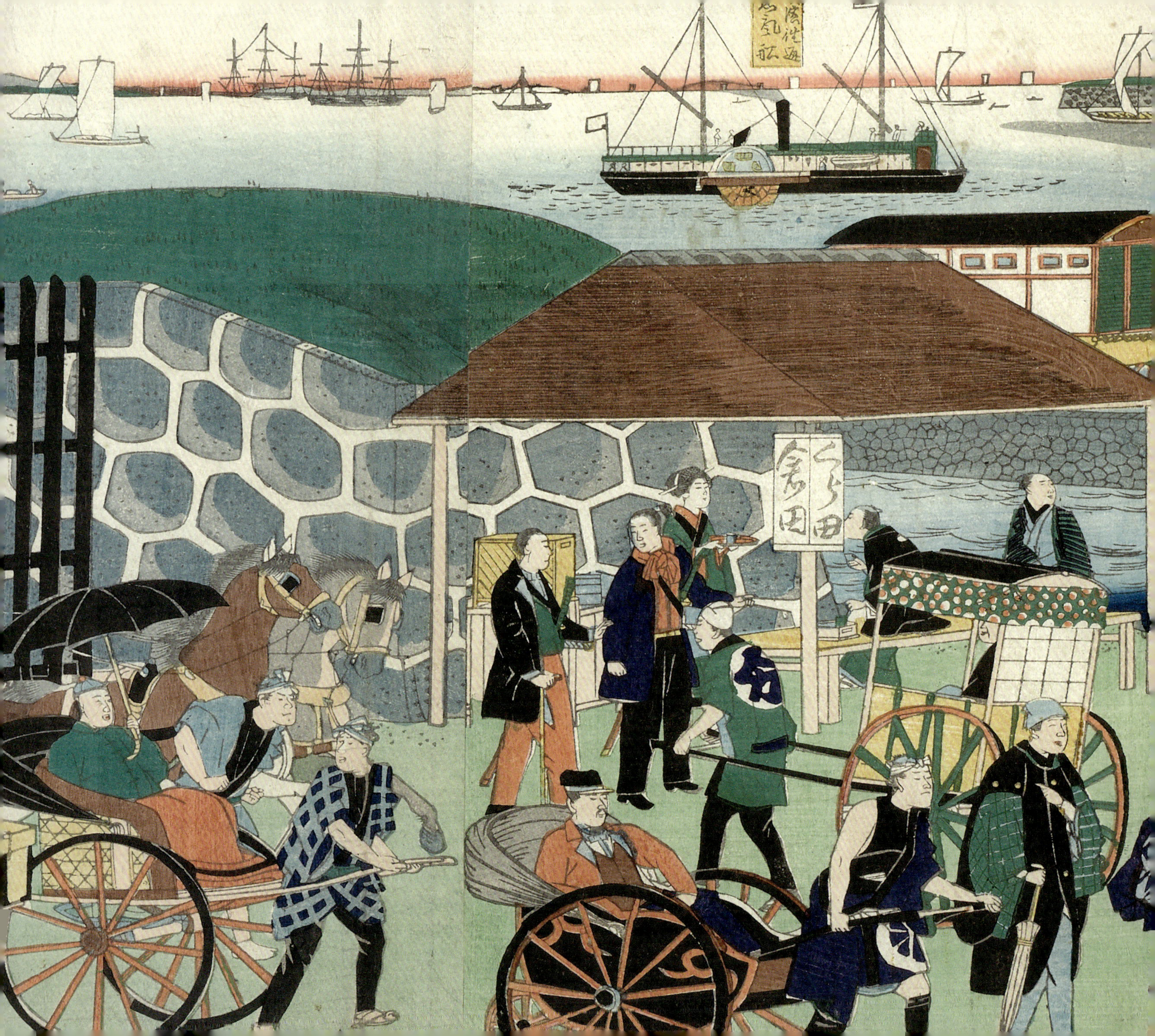

隅田堤遊歩
蒸気舩
くらゐ
金田

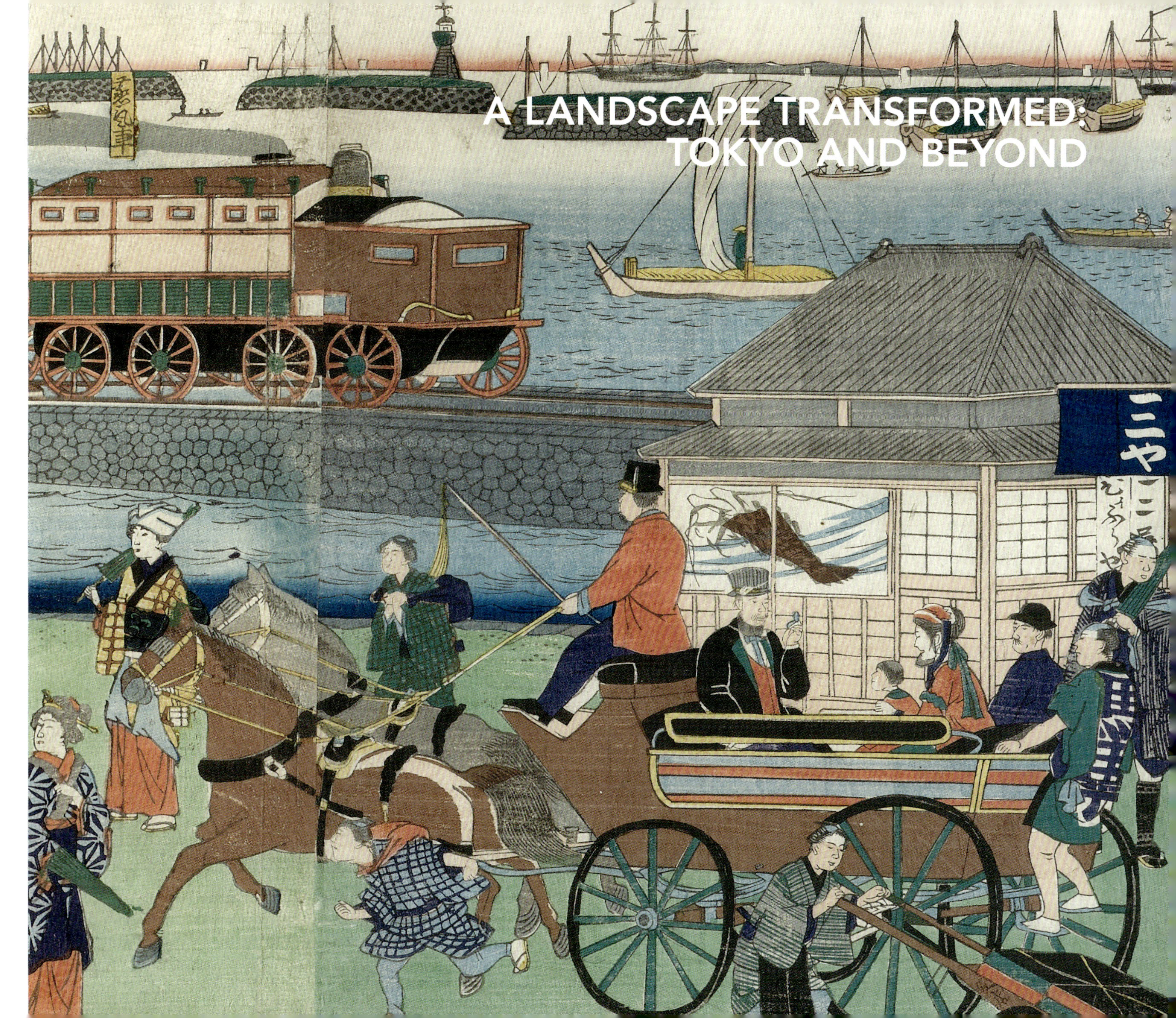
A LANDSCAPE TRANSFORMED:
TOKYO AND BEYOND

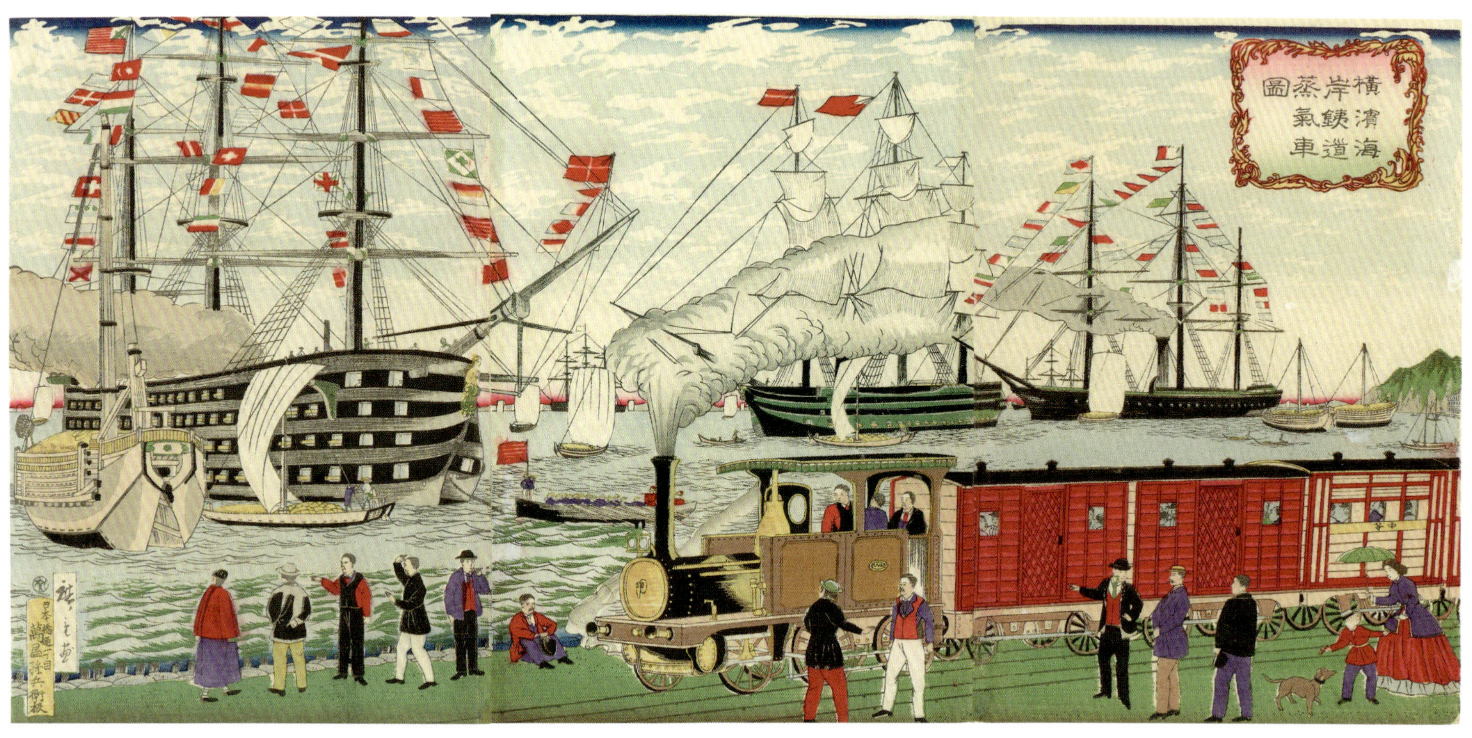

77

Utagawa Hiroshige III (1843–1894)

Railroad Along the Coast of Yokohama, 1874

122   A Landscape Transformed: Tokyo and Beyond

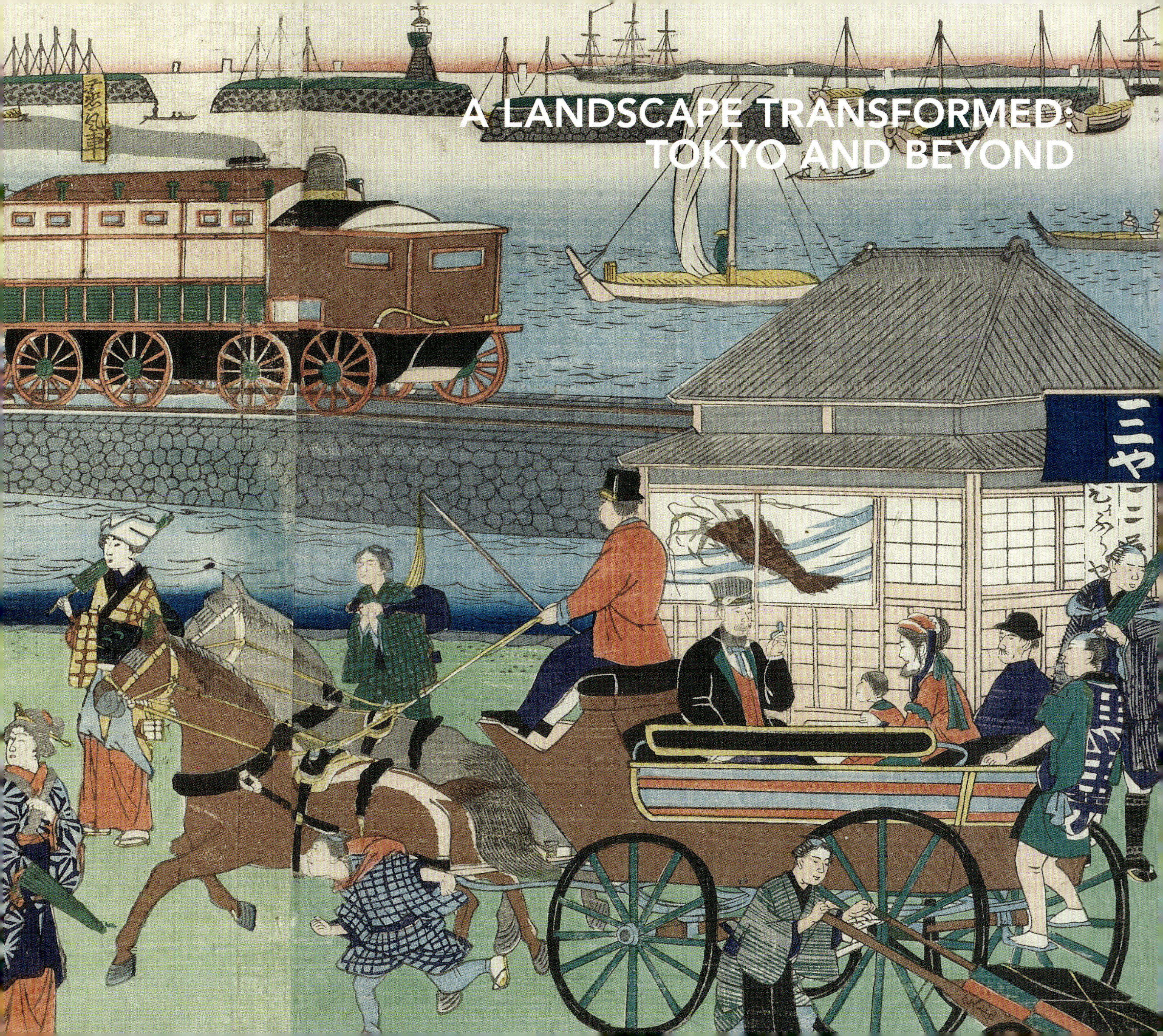

A LANDSCAPE TRANSFORMED:
TOKYO AND BEYOND

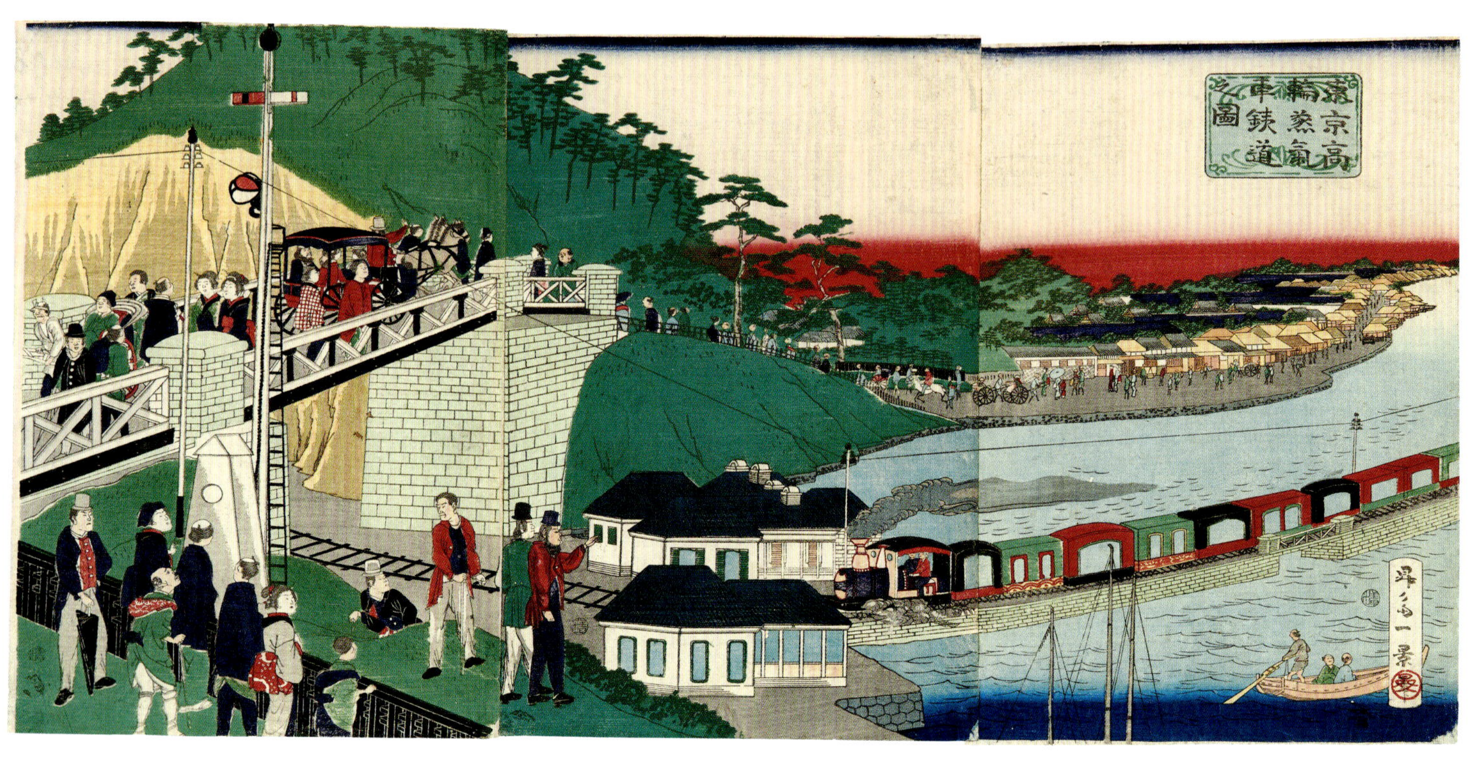

75
Shōsai Ikkei (active 1870s)

Steam Train at Takanawa in Tokyo, ca. 1872

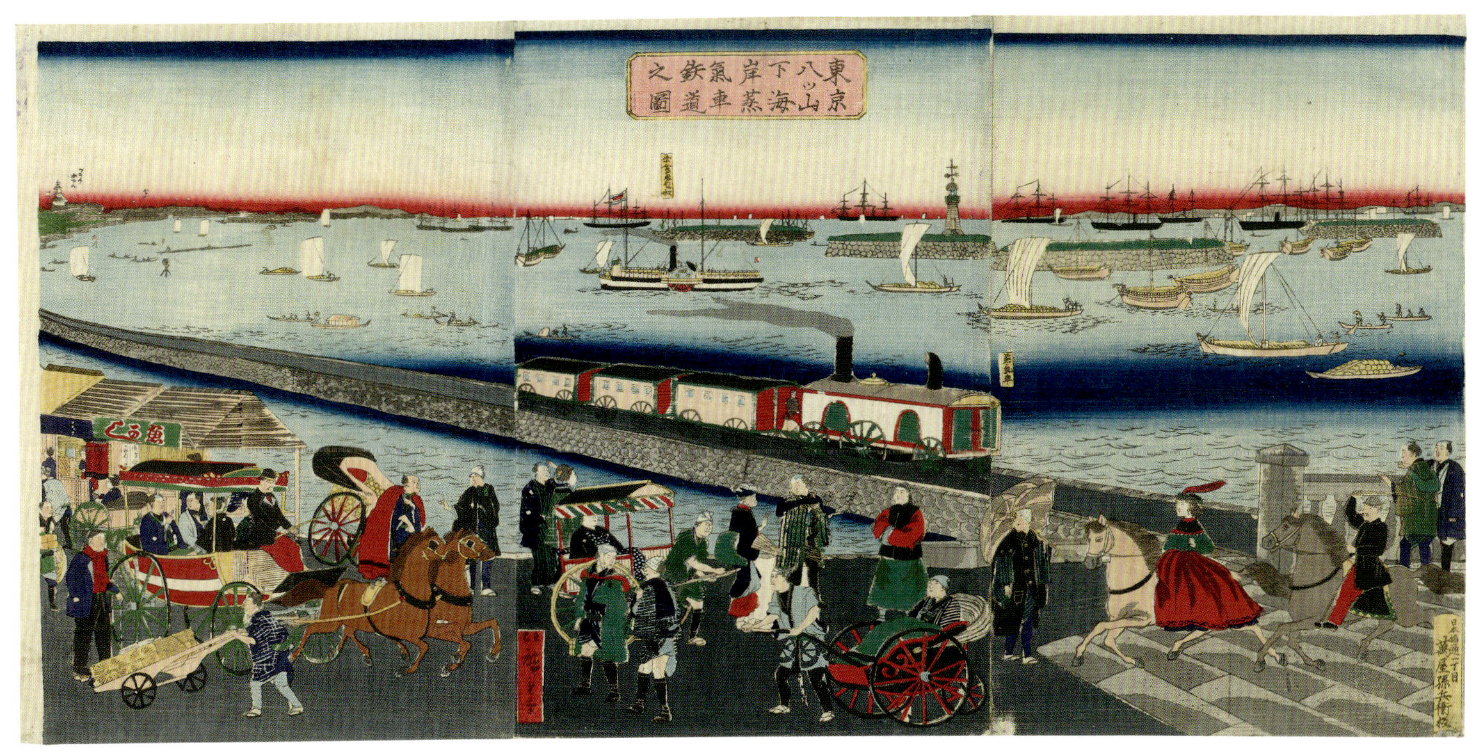

76
Utagawa Hiroshige III (1843–1894)
Steam Train at Yatsunoyama in Tokyo, ca. 1875

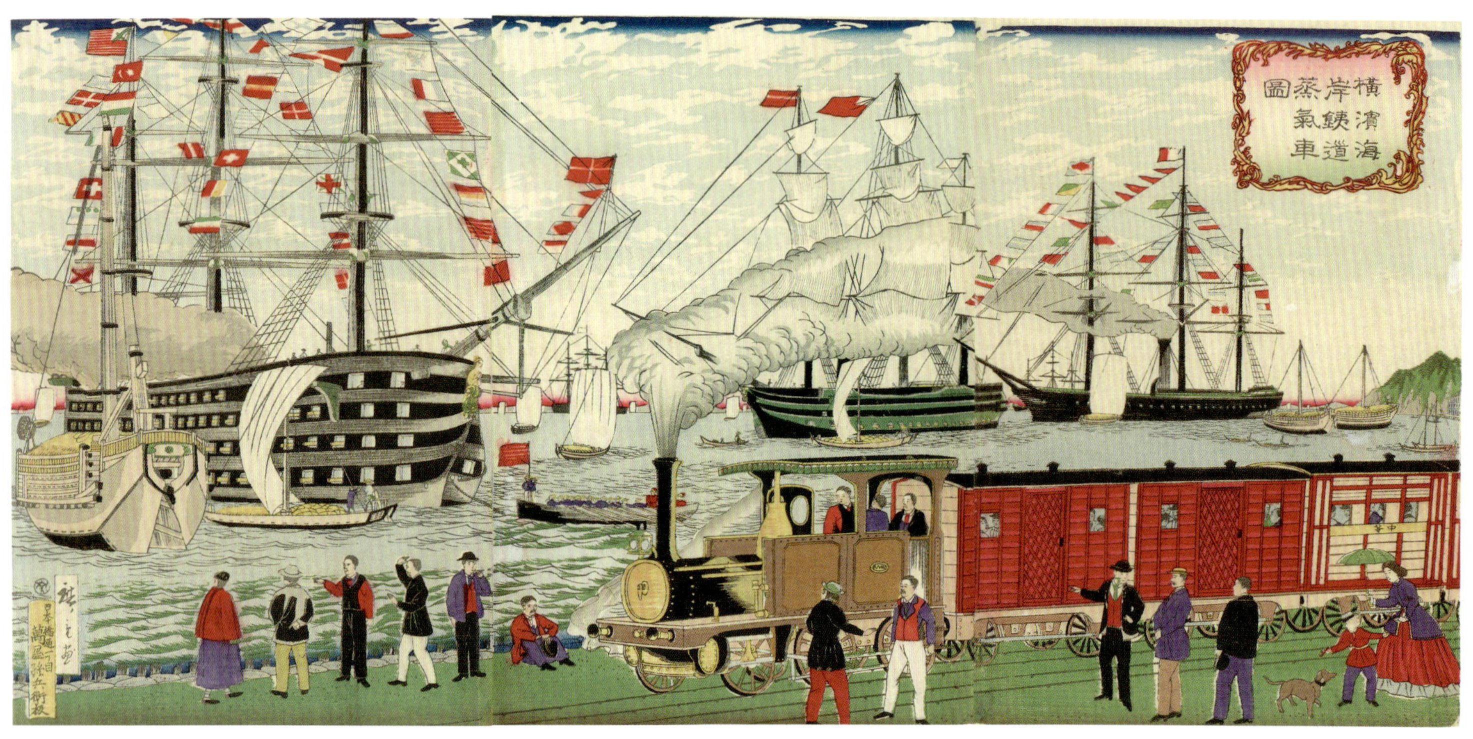

77

Utagawa Hiroshige III (1843–1894)

Railroad Along the Coast of Yokohama, 1874

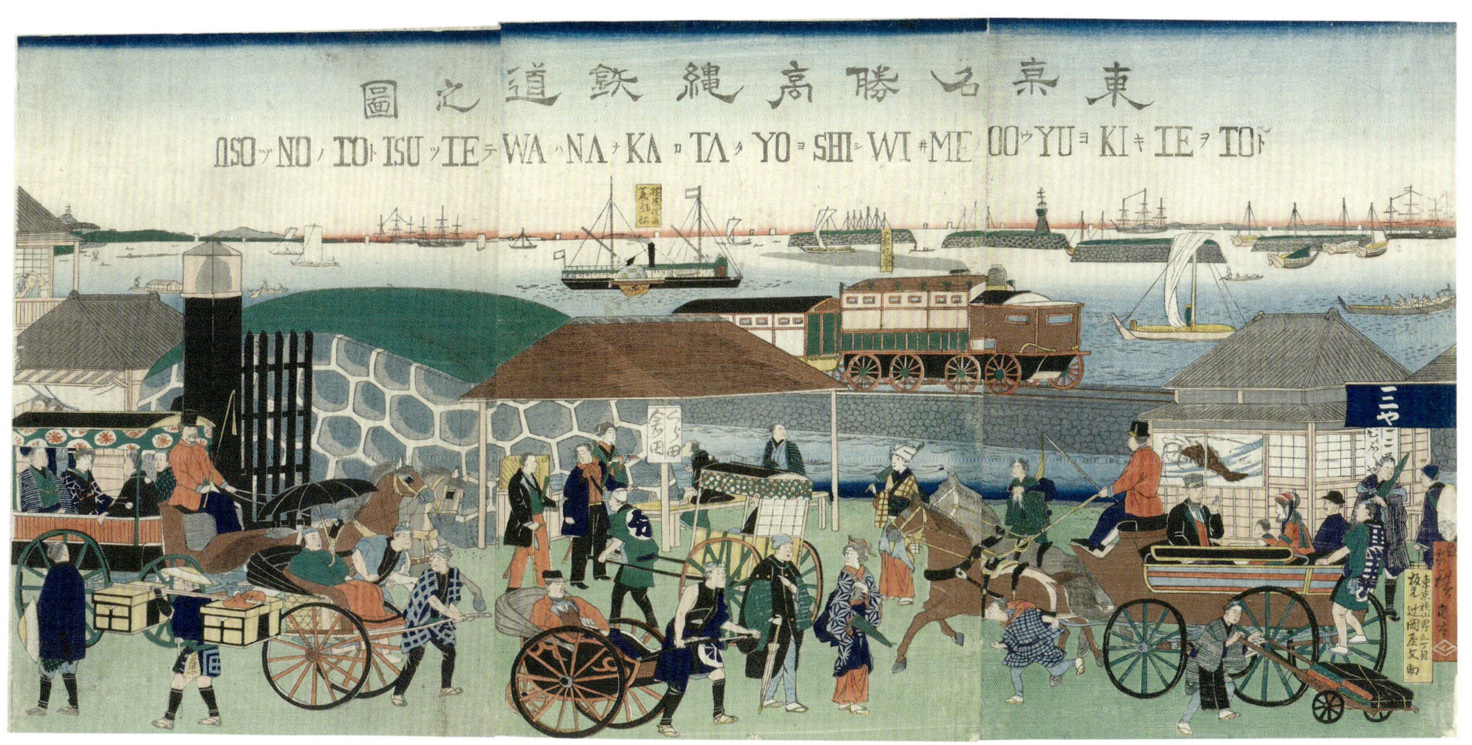

78

Utagawa Hiroshige III (1843–1894)

View of Tokyo with a Picture of the Railroad at Takanawa, ca. 1875

79
Utagawa Kunitoshi (active 1860–1890)
The National Diet Building of the Empire of Great Japan, 1889

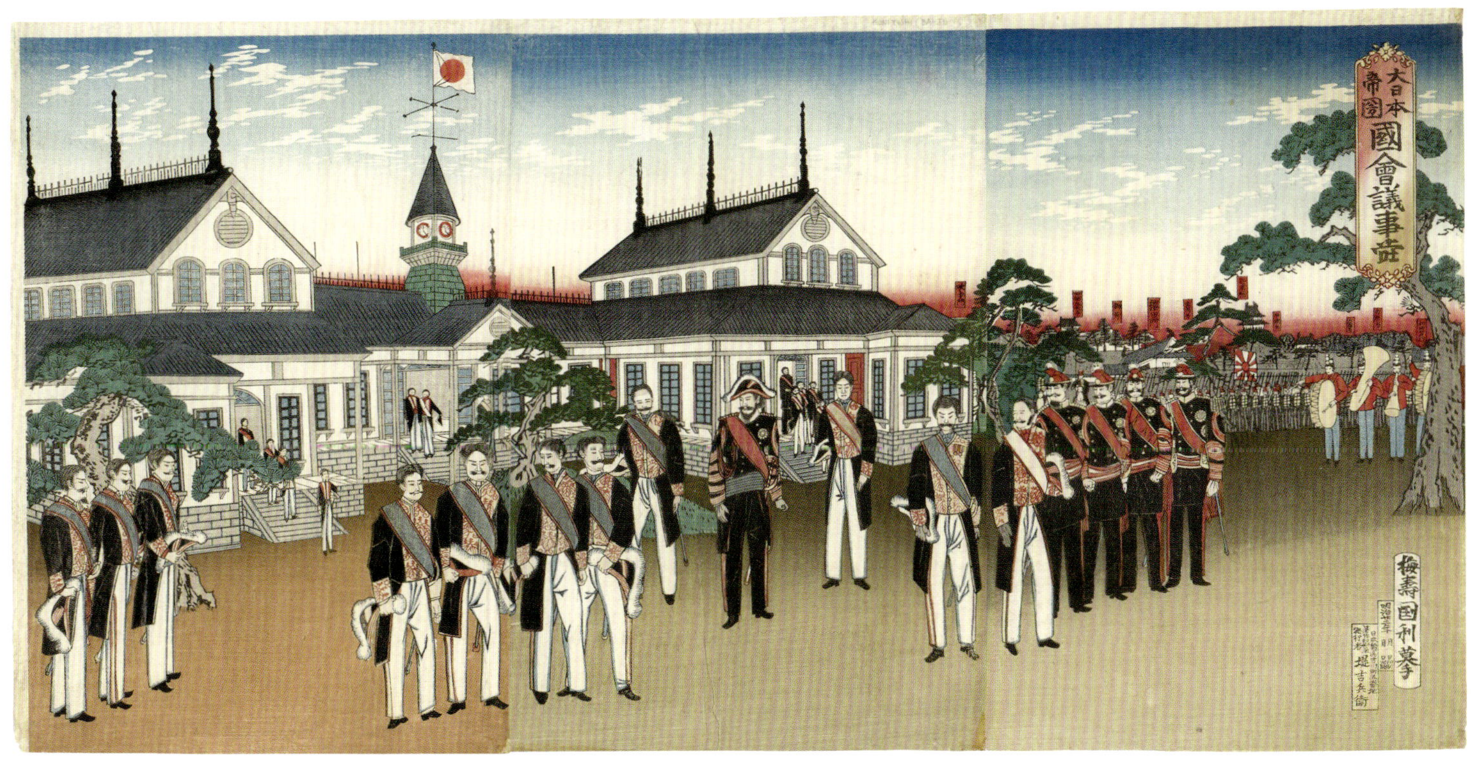

大日本帝國
國會議事堂
梅壽　國利筆
堀吉兵衛

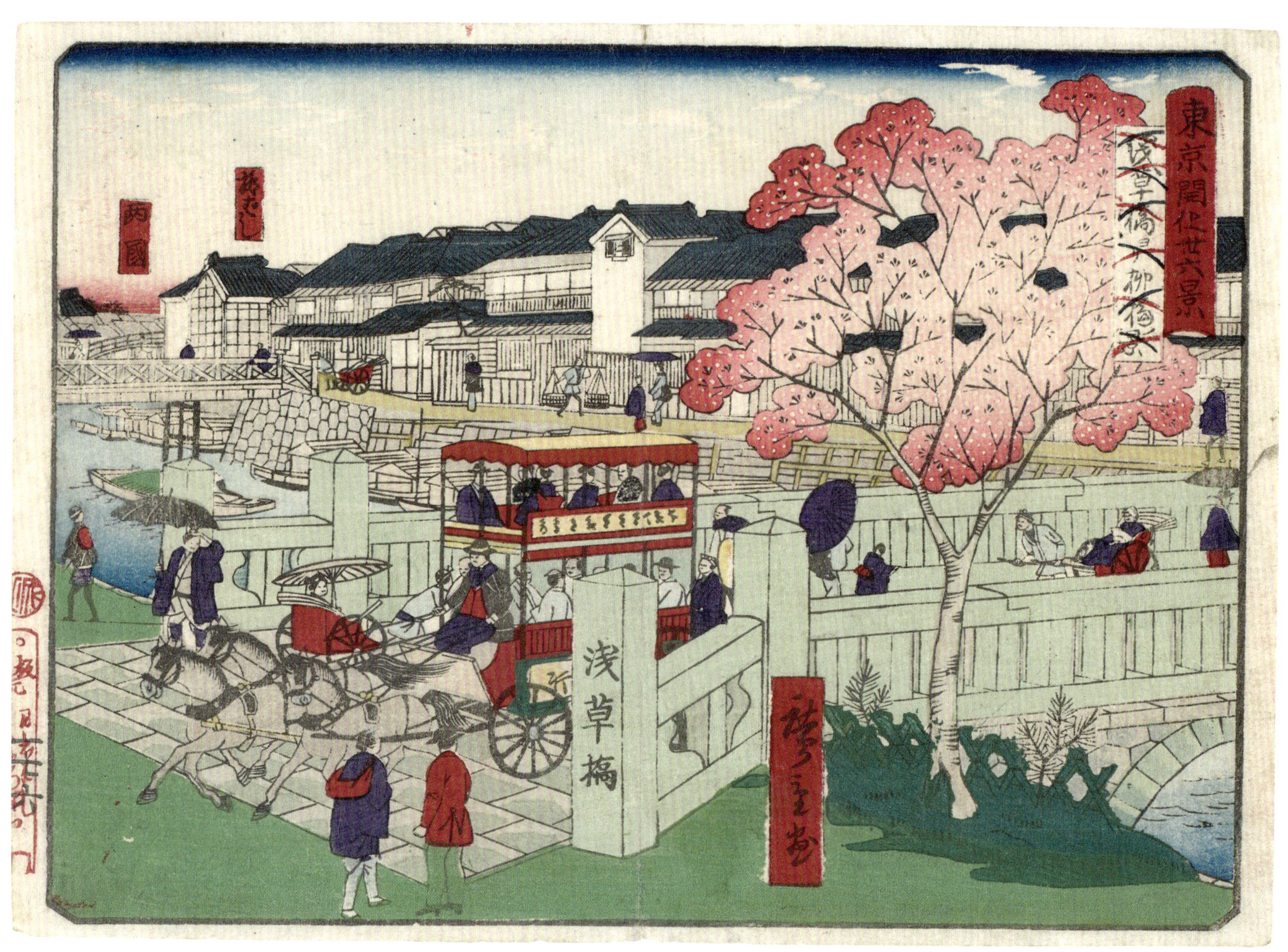

80

Utagawa Hiroshige III (1843–1894)

Yanagi Bridge from Asakusa Bridge, from the series
Thirty-Six Views of Modern Tokyo, 1874

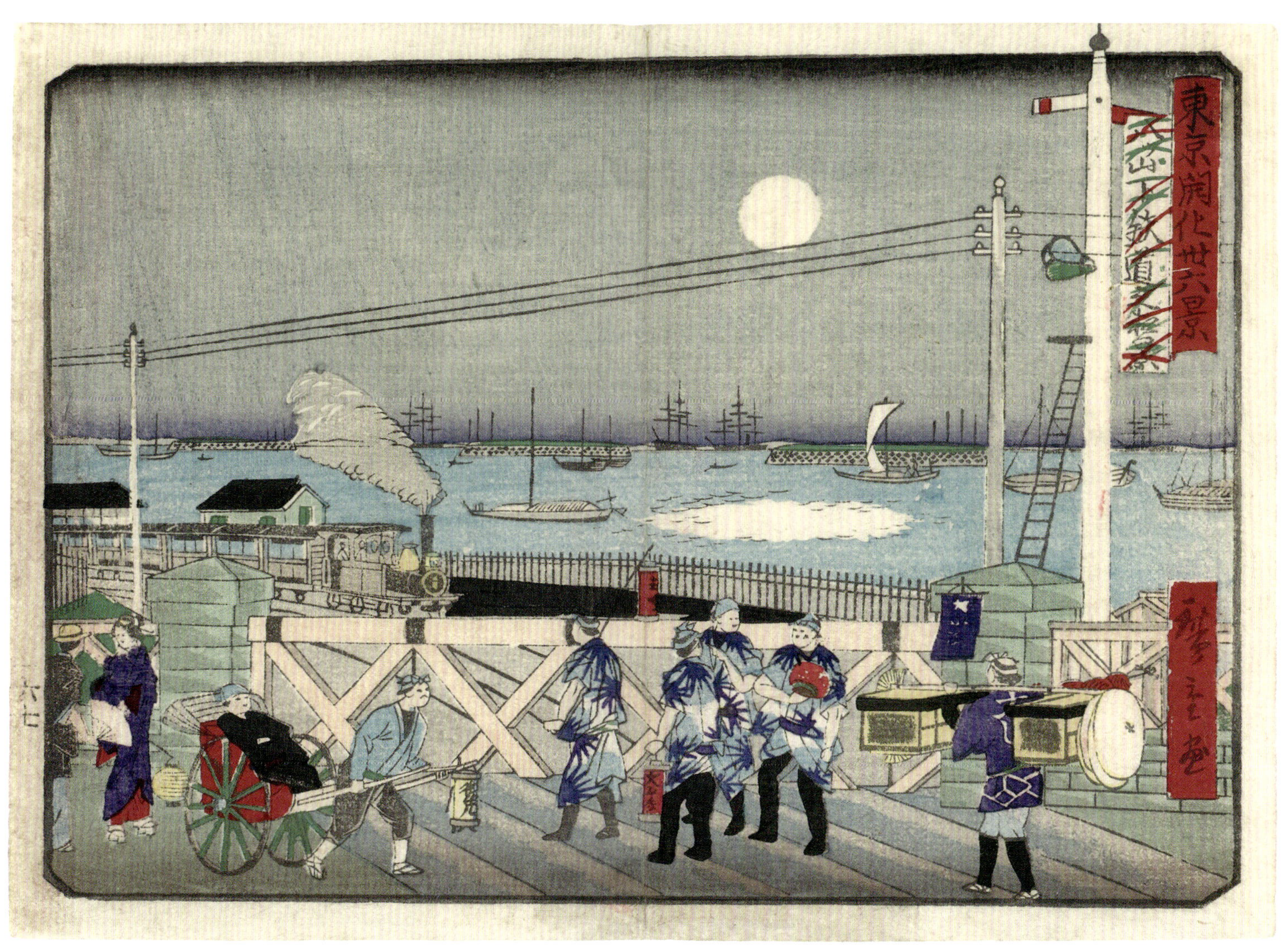

81

Utagawa Hiroshige III (1843–1894)

Night View of the Railroad at Yatsuyama, from the series
Thirty-Six Views of Modern Tokyo, 1874

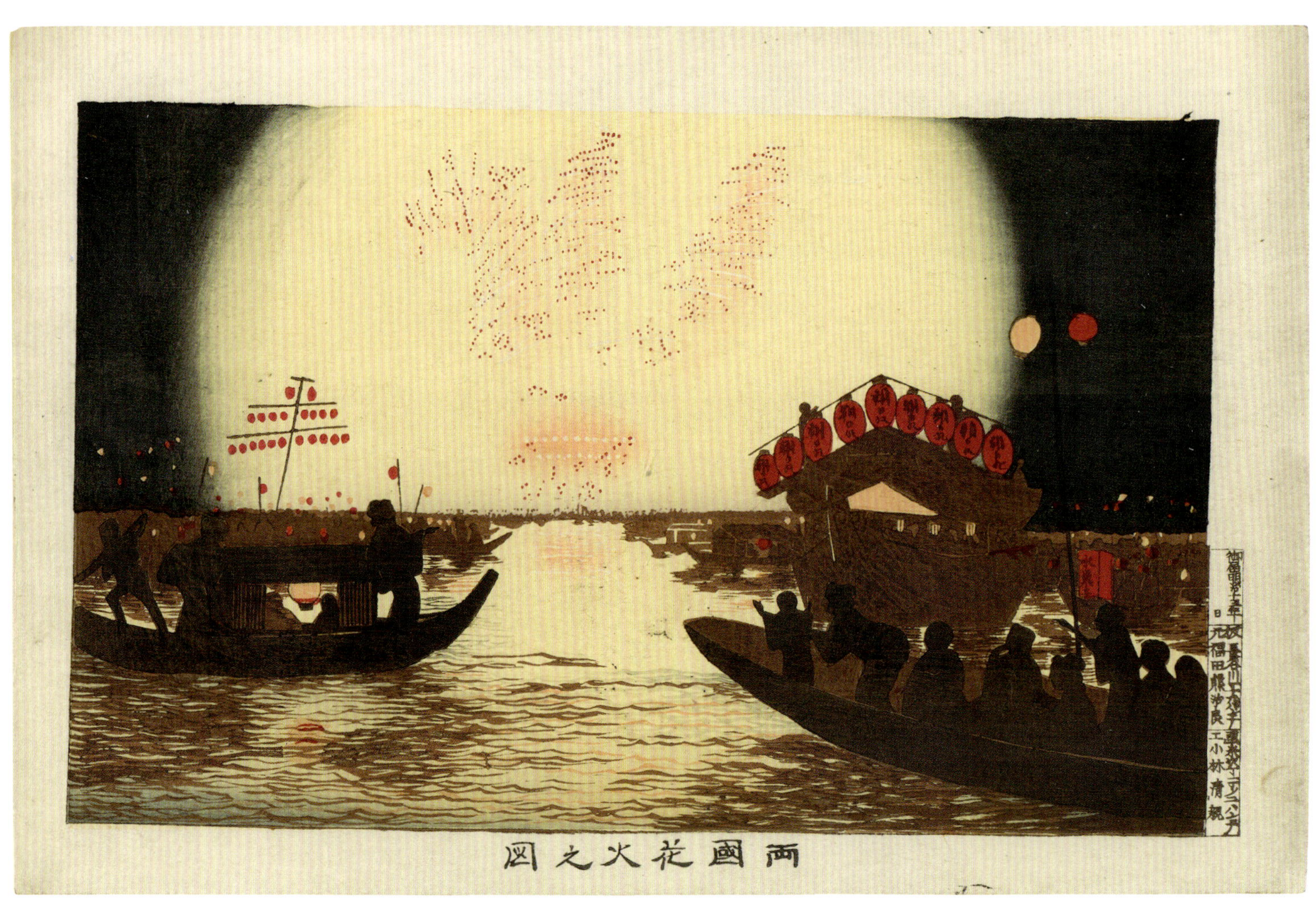

82

Kobayashi Kiyochika (1847–1915)

Fireworks at Ryōgoku, 1880

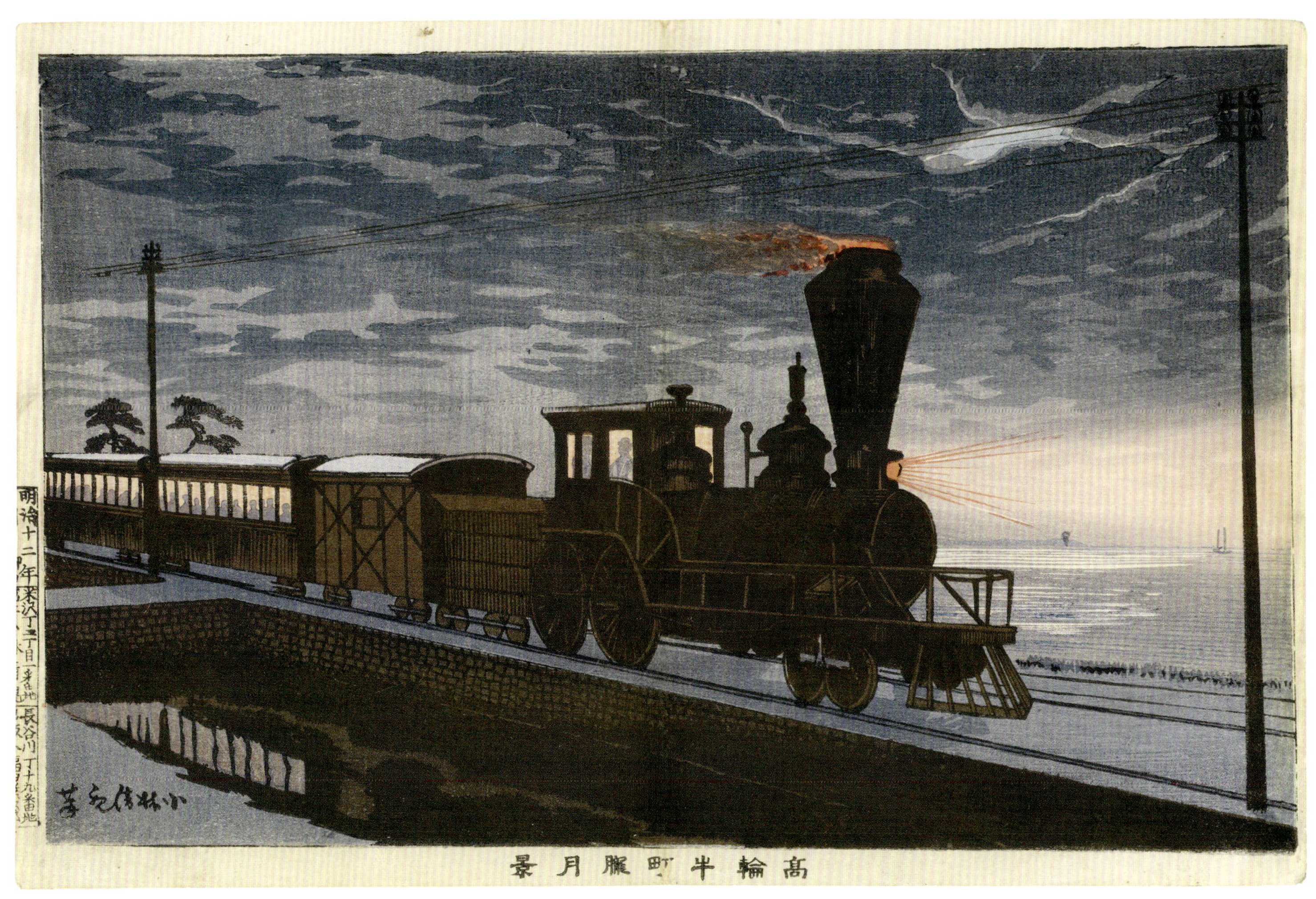

83
Kobayashi Kiyochika (1847–1915)

Hazy Moon at Ushimachi, Takanawa, 1879

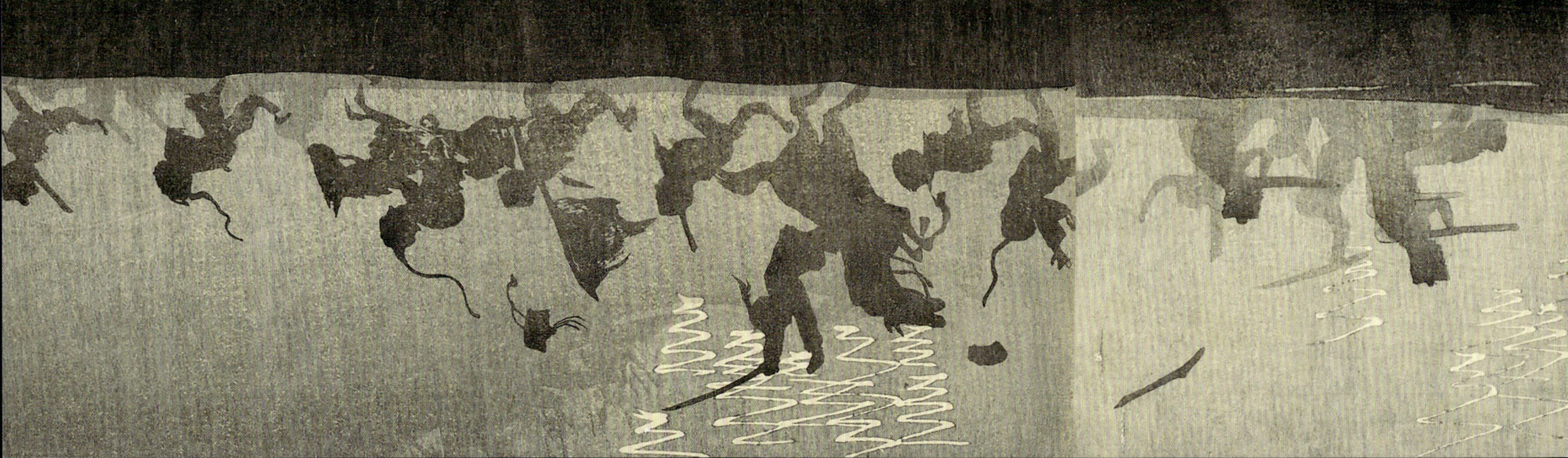

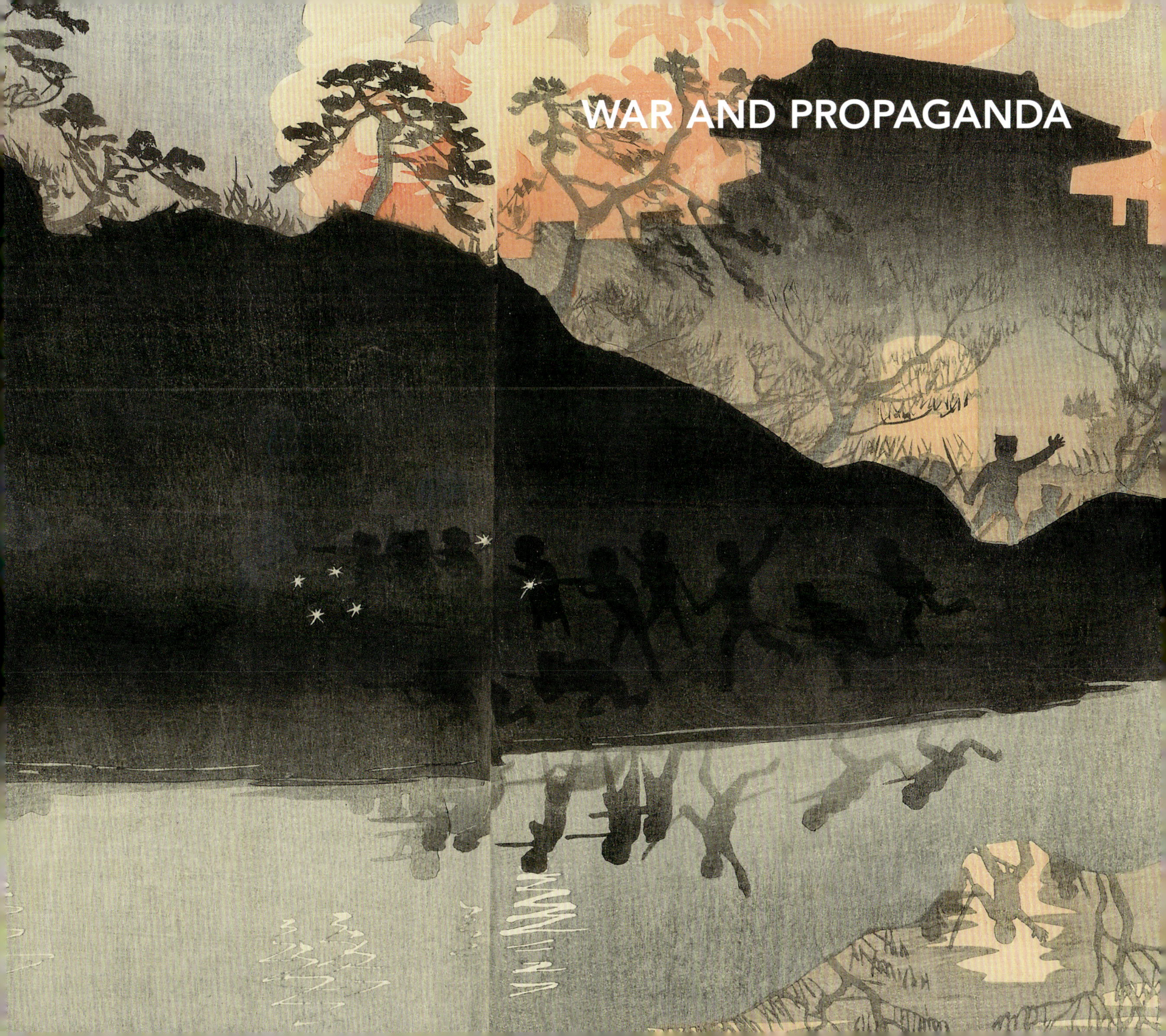
WAR AND PROPAGANDA

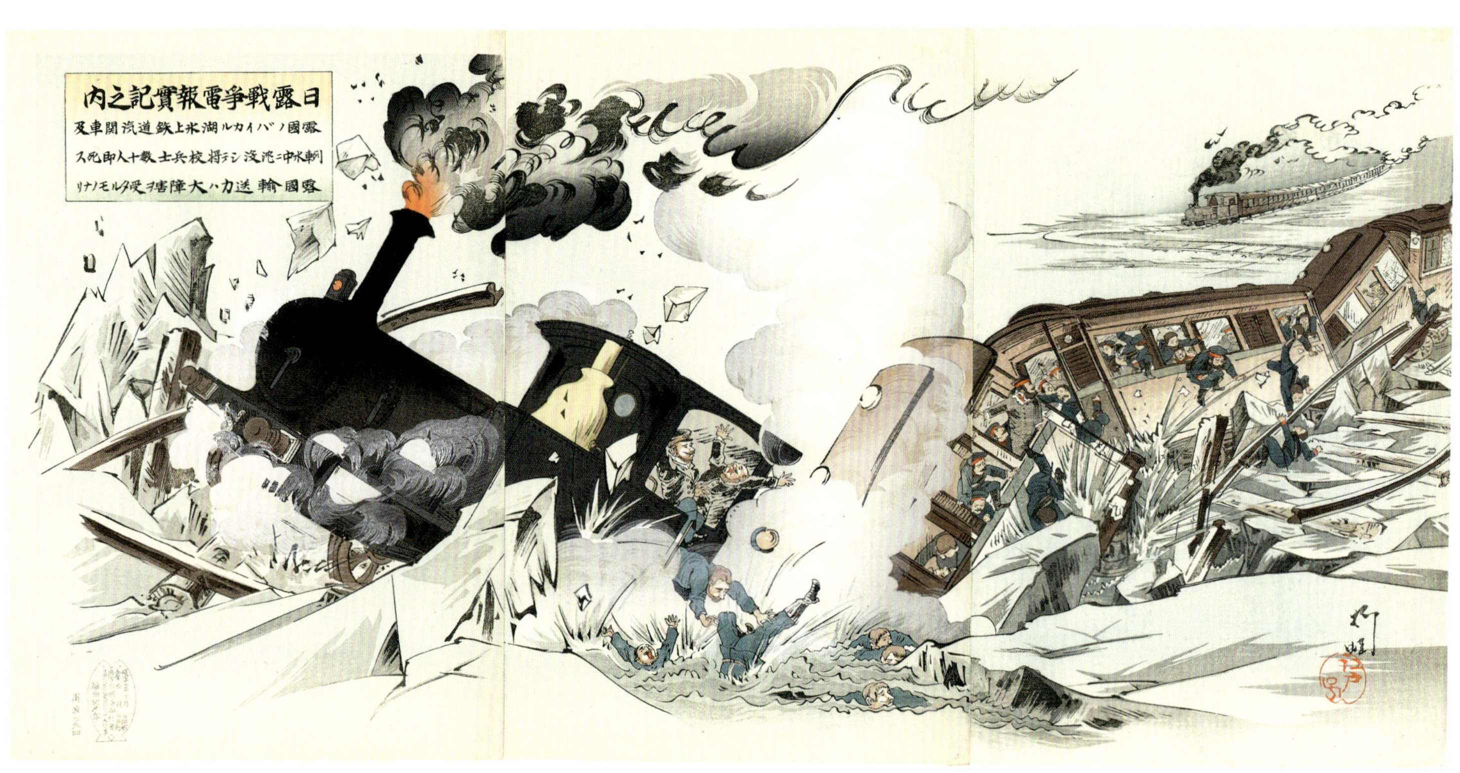

84

Yōshū Chikanobu (1838–1912)

An Enemy Troop Train Falling through the Ice of Lake Baikal, from
Telegraphed Reports of the Russo-Japanese War, 1904

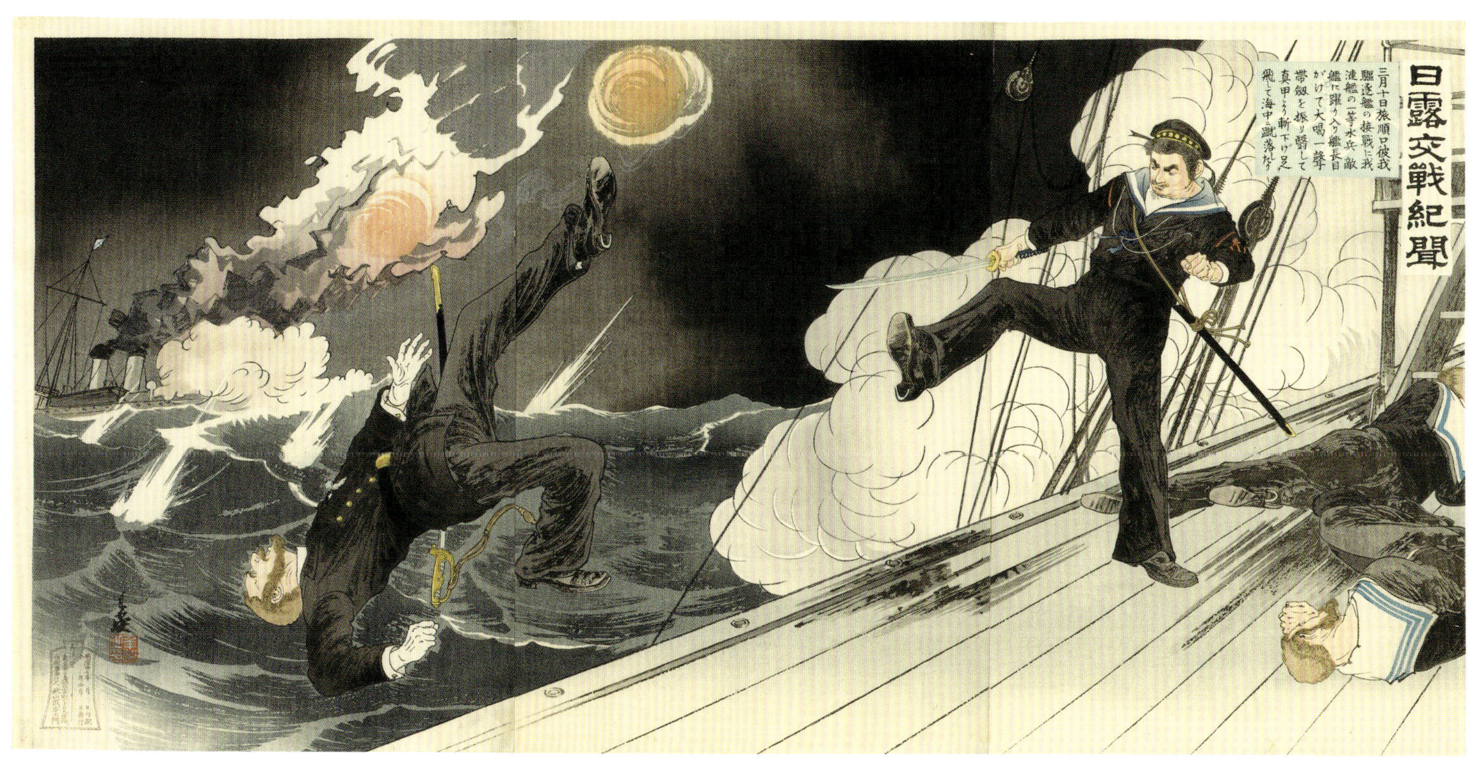

85

Migita Toshihide (1863–1925)

*Japanese Sailor Leaps Onboard a Russian Warship and Kicks Its Captain
Overboard*, from *Records of the Russo-Japanese War*, 1904

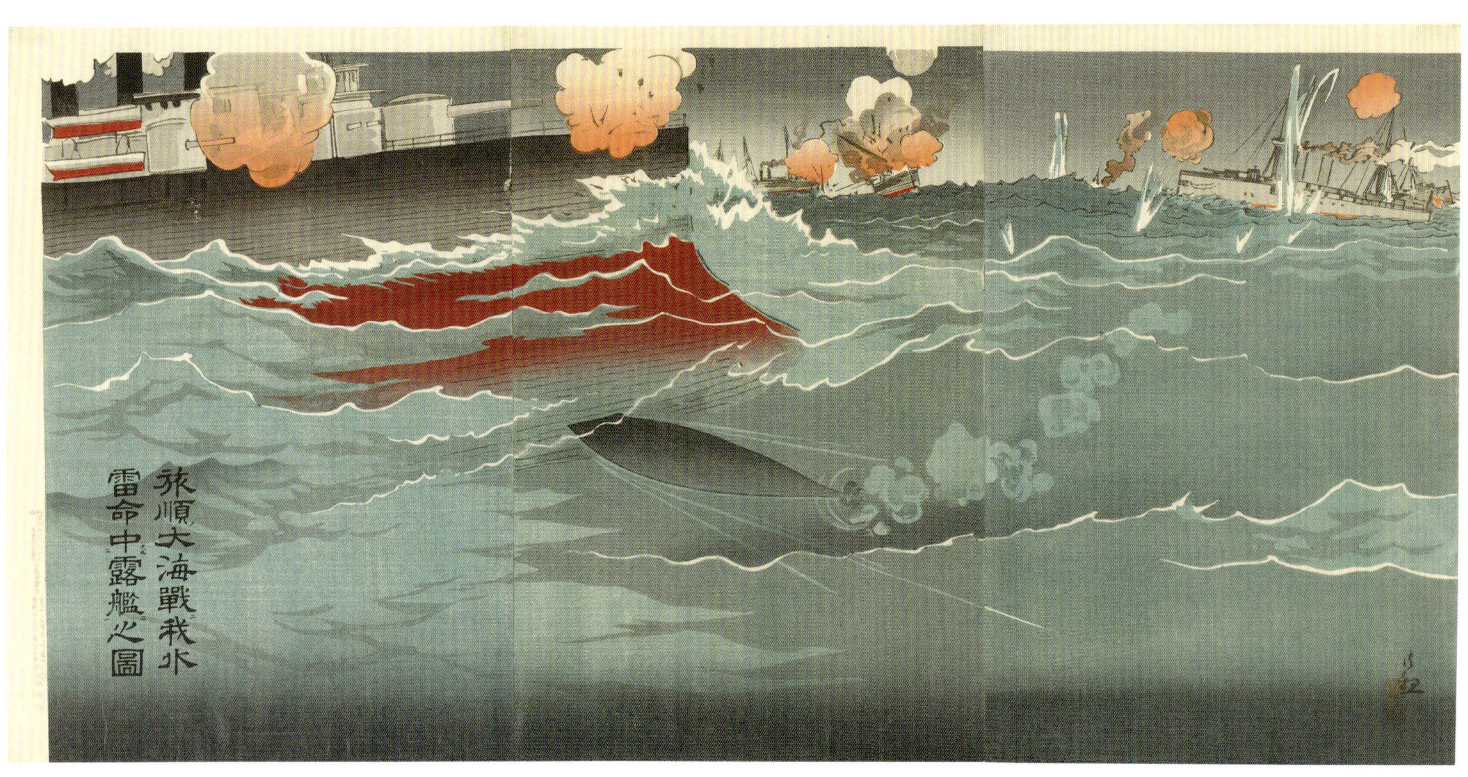

86

Kobayashi Kiyochika (1847–1915)

A Torpedo Hitting a Russian Warship at Port Arthur, February 1904, 1904

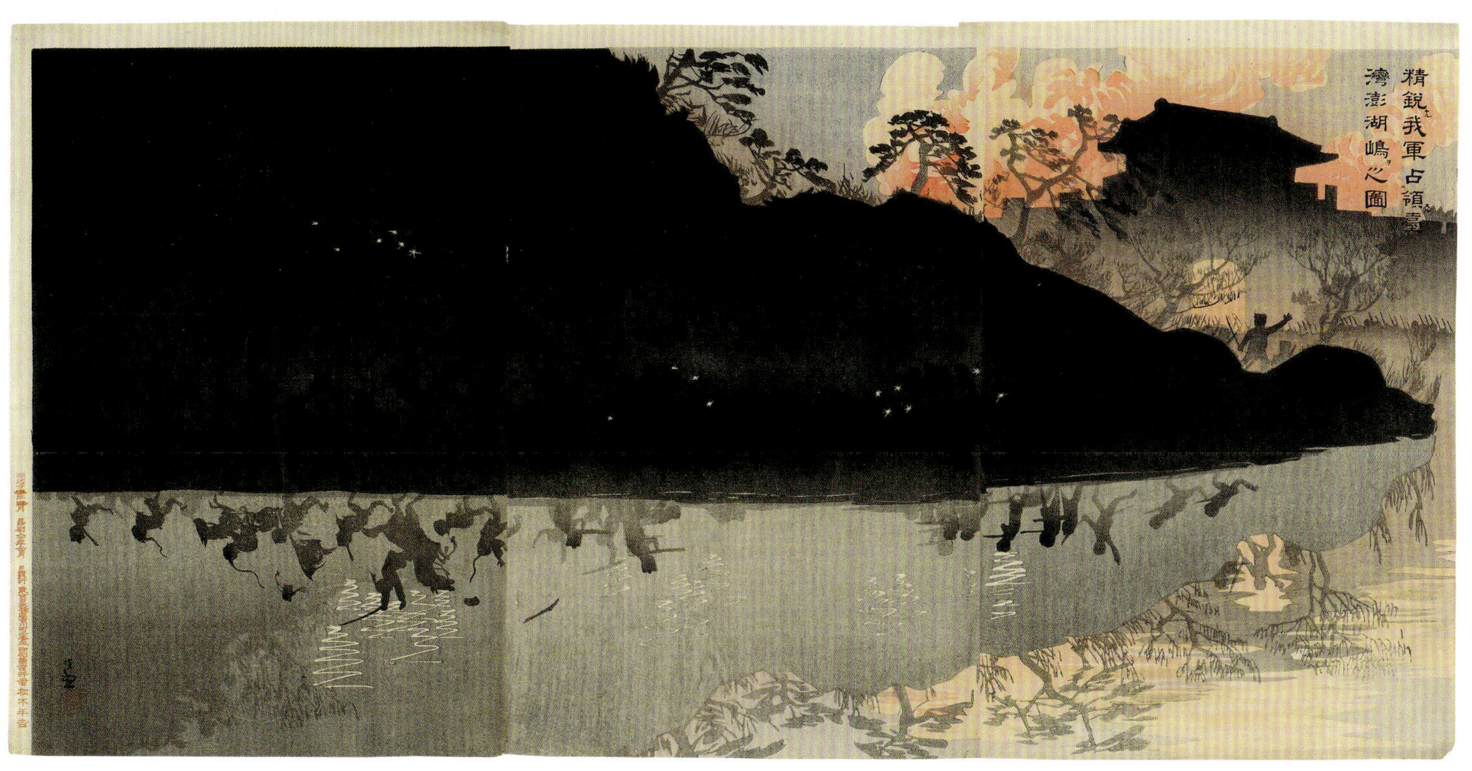

87
Kobayashi Kiyochika (1847–1915)
Our Elite Forces Occupying the Pescadores Islands of Taiwan, 1894

88

Utagawa Kokunimasa (1874–1944)

Red Cross Field Hospital of Great Japan Treating the Wounded during the Russo-Japanese War,
with inset vignette *Barbarian Russian Soldiers*, 1904

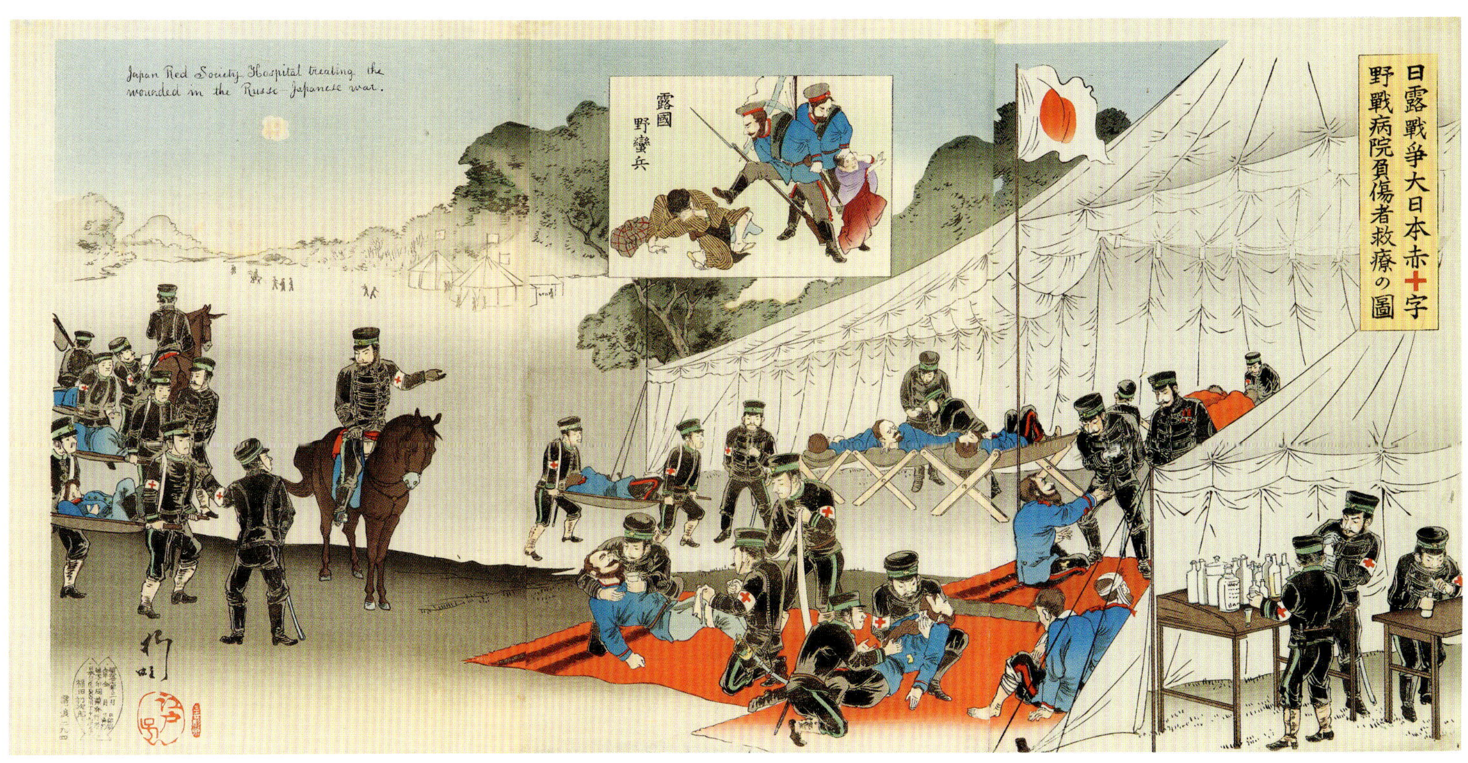

Japan Red Society Hospital treating the wounded in the Russo-Japanese war.
露國
野蠻兵
日露戰爭大日本赤十字
野戰病院負傷者救療の圖

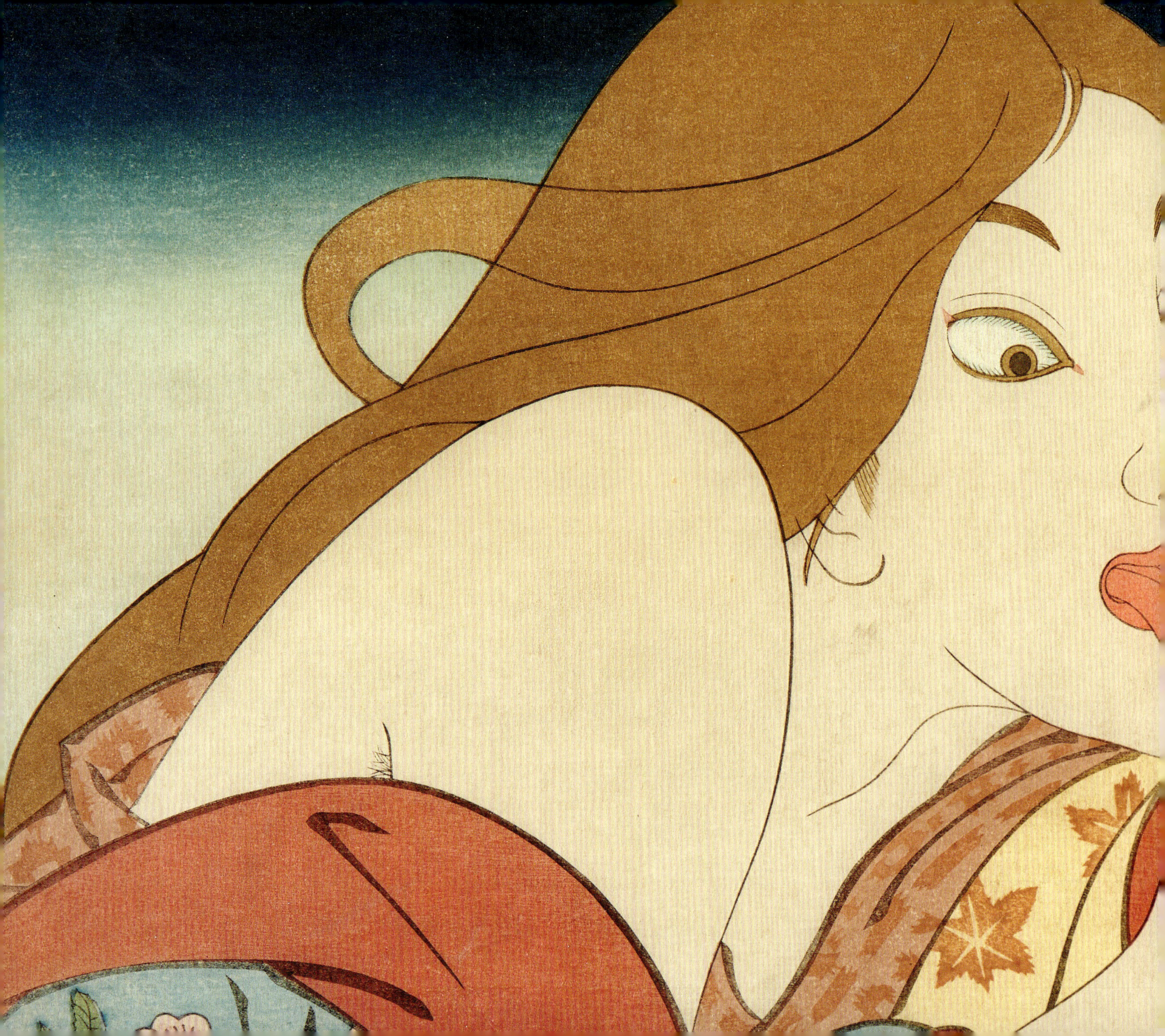

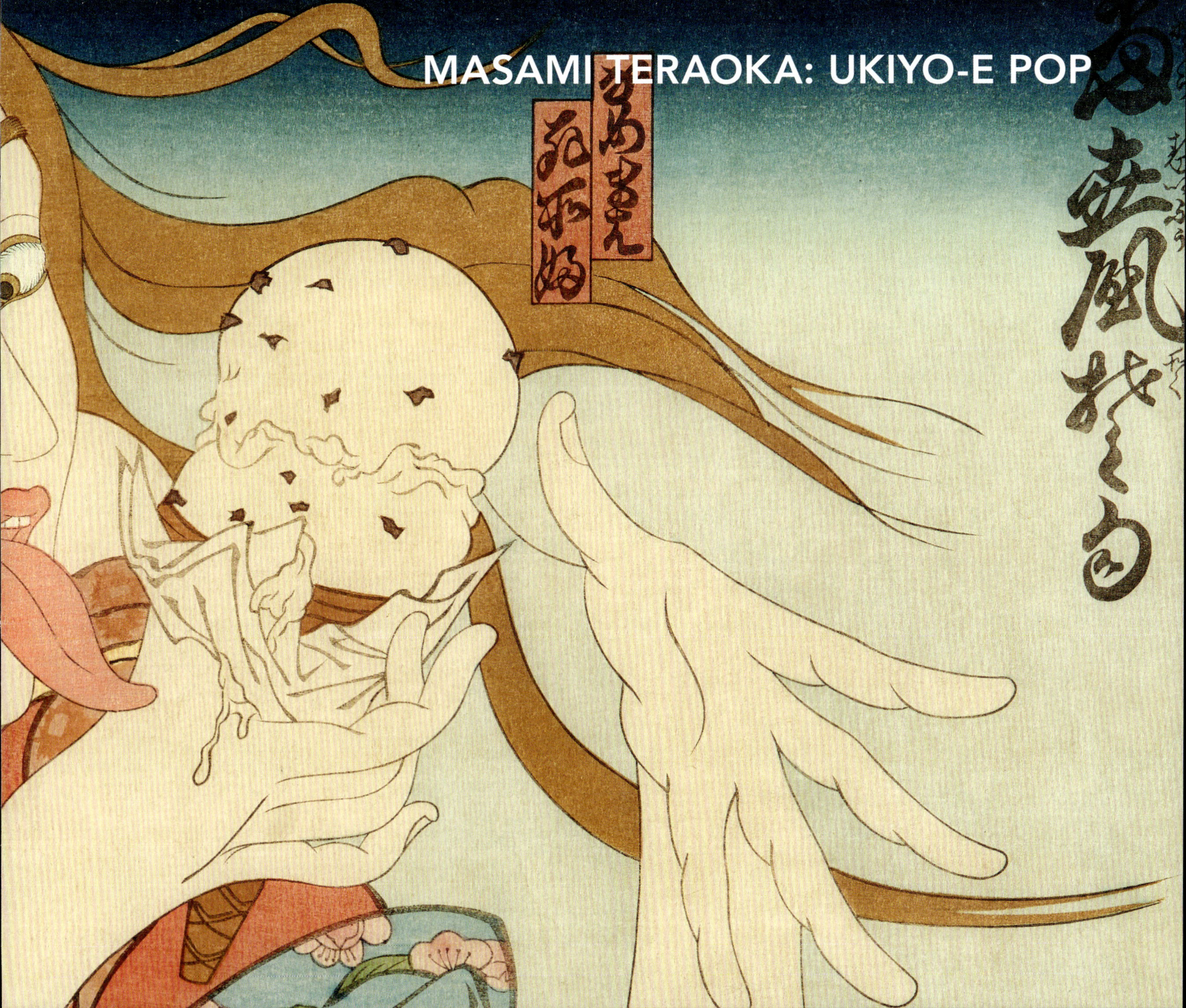

MASAMI TERAOKA: UKIYO-E POP

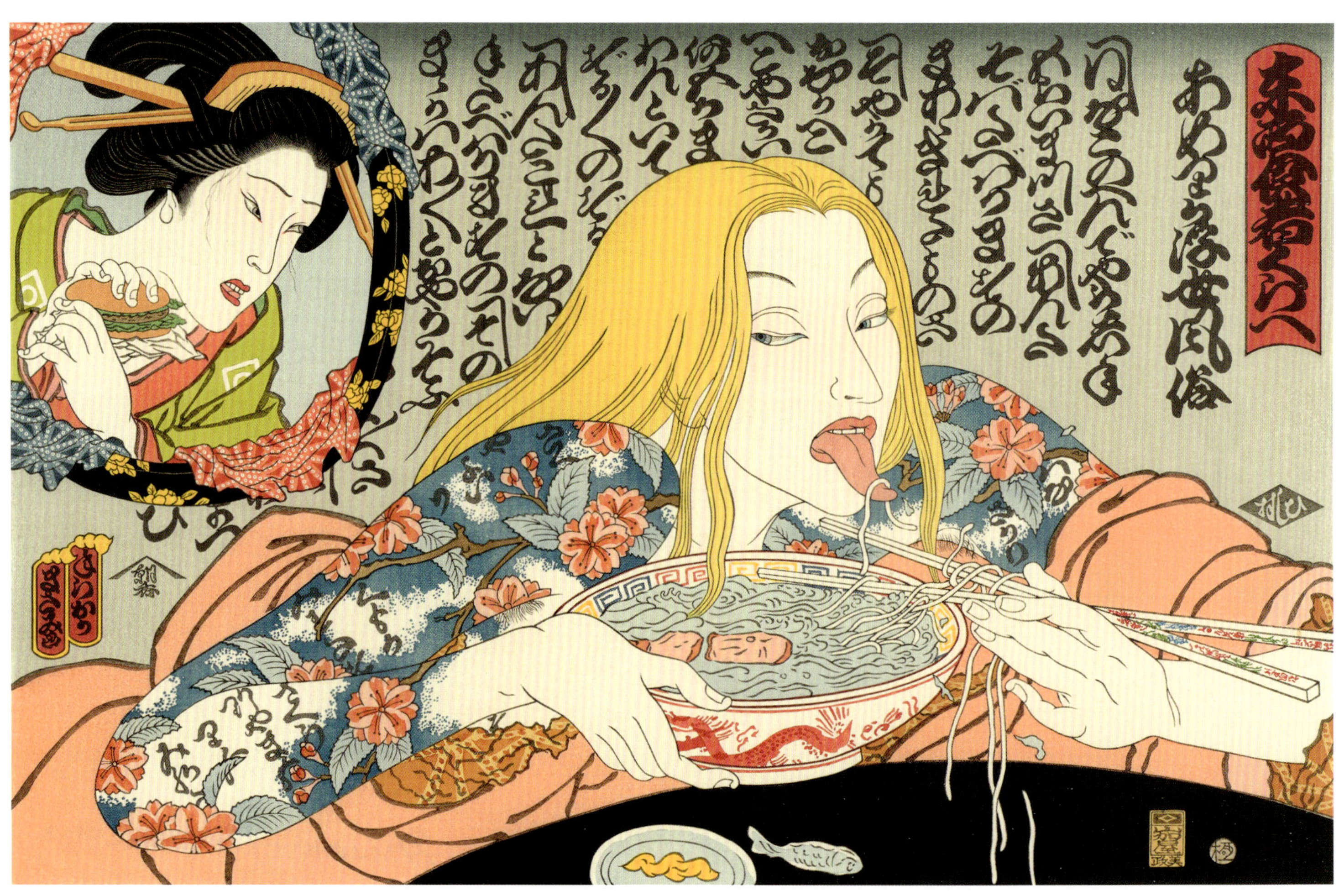

89

Masami Teraoka (American, b. Japan 1936)

Tattooed Woman and Geisha III, from the series
McDonald's Hamburgers Invading Japan, 2018

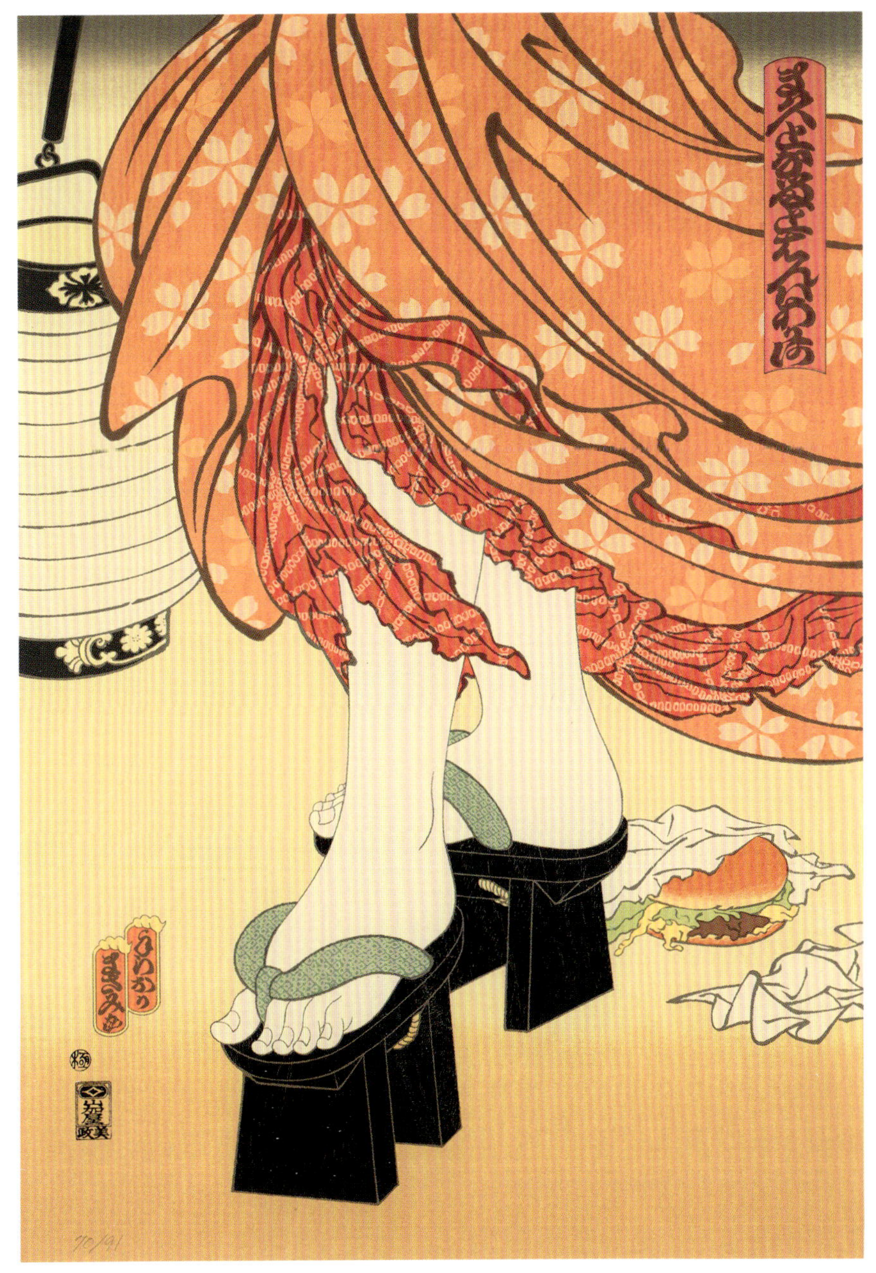

90
Masami Teraoka (American, b. Japan 1936)
Chochin-Me, from the series *McDonald's Hamburgers Invading Japan*, 1982

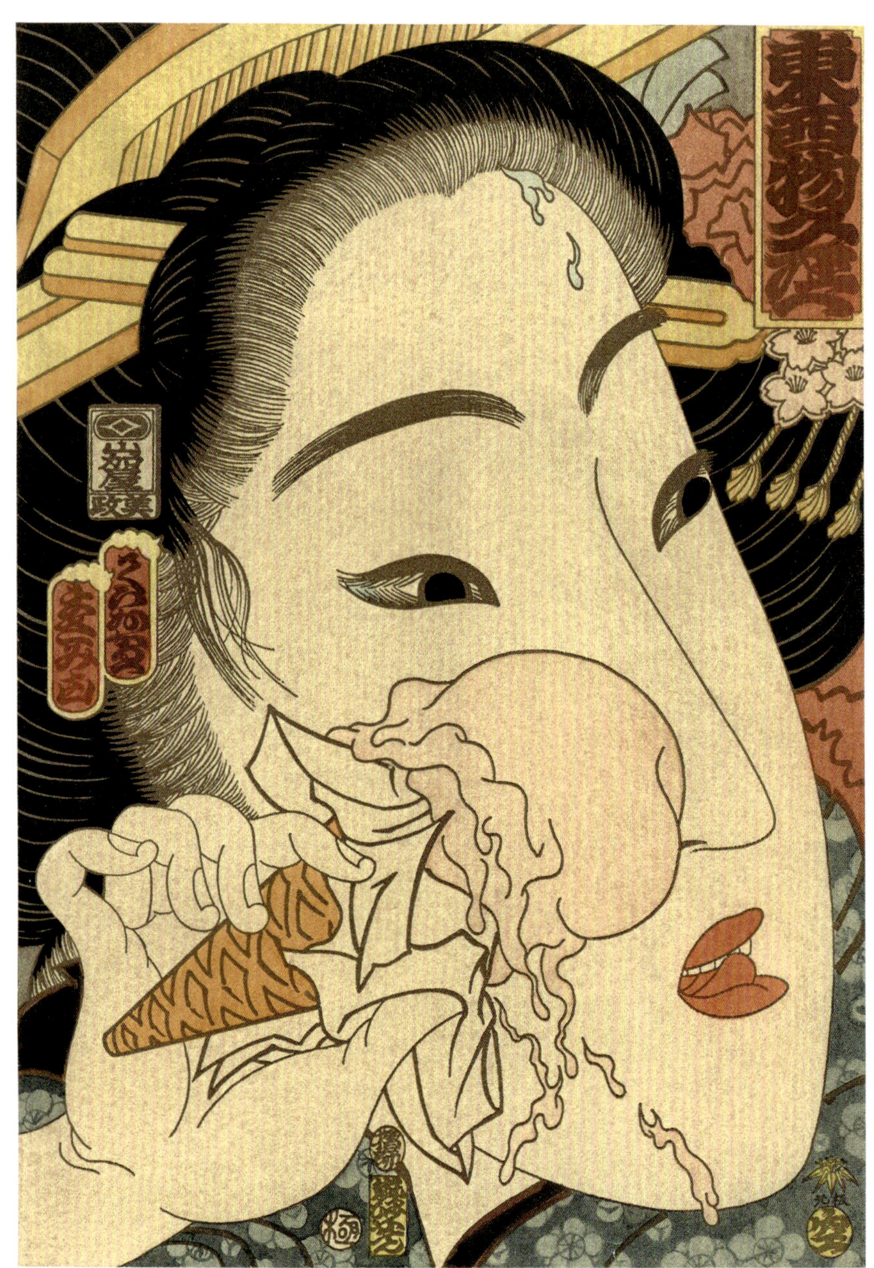

91
Masami Teraoka (American, b. Japan 1936)
Geisha with Ice-Cream Cone (Cherry), from the series *31 Flavors Invading Japan*, 1977

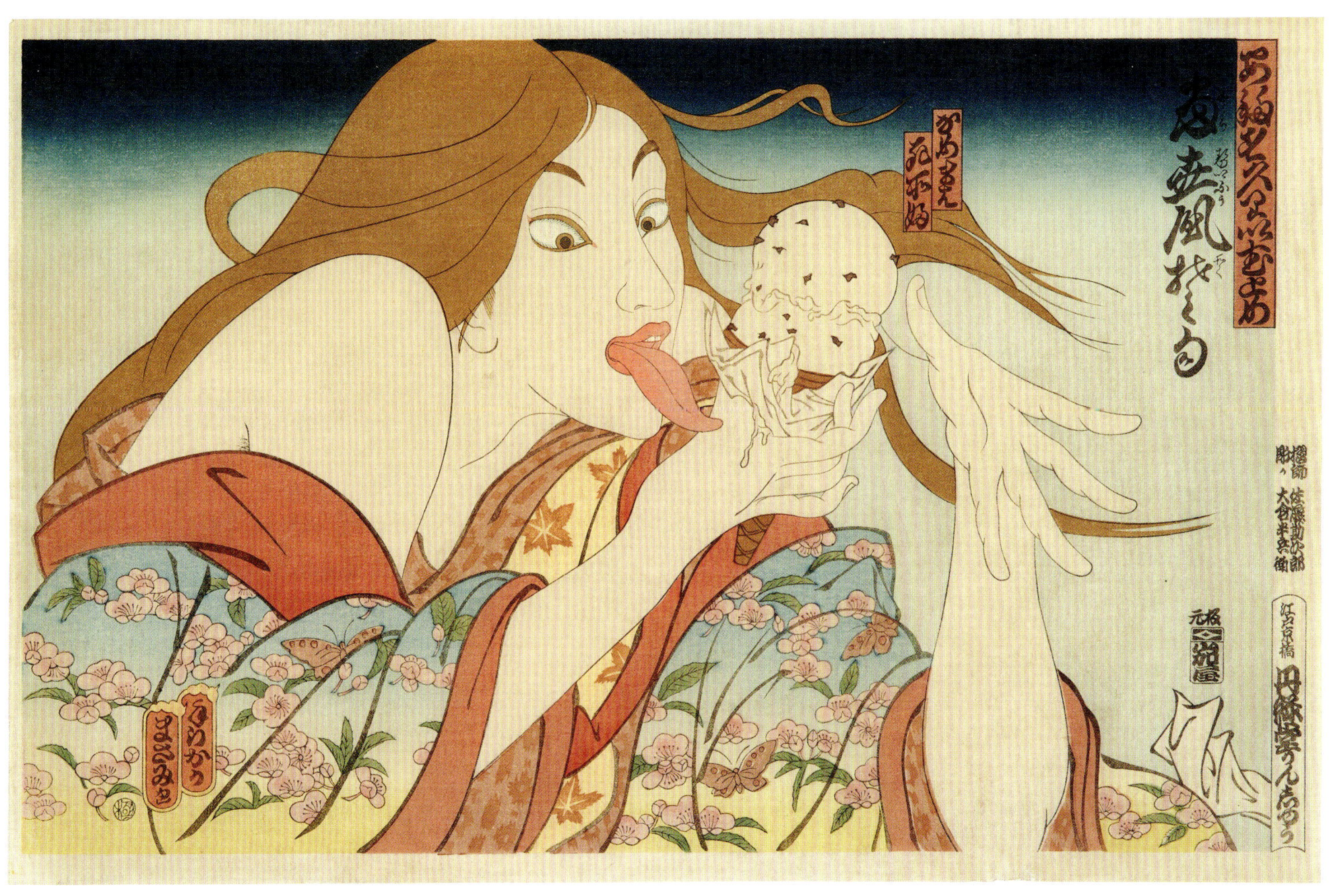

92

Masami Teraoka (American, b. Japan 1936)

Today's Special, from the series *31 Flavors Invading Japan*, 1977

NOTES

INTRODUCTION

1   The de Young and Legion of Honor would not merge to form the Fine Arts Museums of San Francisco until 1972. However, with the prospect (achieved in 1966) of a new Asian art wing housing the major art donations from noted collector Avery Brundage, the de Young's Japanese prints were permanently transferred to the Achenbach in 1964.

JAPANESE PRINTS IN TRANSITION

1   Asai Ryōi (1612–1691), a priest and an author of popular fiction, summarized this new meaning in his book *Tales of the Floating World* (*Ukiyo monogatari*, 1666): "[L]iving only for the moment, savoring the moon, the snow, the cherry blossoms, and the maple leaves, singing songs, drinking sake, and diverting oneself just in floating, unconcerned by the prospect of imminent poverty, buoyant and carefree, like a gourd carried along with the river current: this is what we call *ukiyo*."

2   The term "ukiyo-e" can also include paintings and book illustrations. The earliest reliably dateable single-sheet print is an actor print by Torii Kiyonobu I (1664–1729), *Sawamura Kodenji as Tsuya-no-Mae*, depicting a performance that took place in 1698. The only known extant impression of this print is in the collection of Worcester Art Museum, Massachusetts.

3   For a discussion of the development of color printing, see Allen Hockley, "Suzuki Harunobu: The Cult and Culture of Color," in *Designed for Pleasure: The World of Edo Japan in Prints and Paintings, 1680–1860*, ed. Julia Meech and Jane Oliver (New York: Asia Society, 2008), 83–99.

4   Melinda Takeuchi, "Shini-e," in *The Hotei Encyclopedia of Japanese Prints*, ed. Amy Newland (Leiden: Brill, 2005), 1:234.

5   The original Yoshiwara was established in Nihonbashi in 1618, but it was relocated after being destroyed by fire in 1657.

6   The Tokugawa government regulated the content of prints and how they were made throughout their history. The Tenpō Reforms, a set of sumptuary laws issued 1841–1843, targeted images of actors and prostitutes as well as elaborate printing effects. On the relationship between Hiroshige's prints and the Tenpō Reforms, see Henry D. Smith II, "Hiroshige in History," in *Hiroshige: Prints and Drawings*, ed. Matthi Forrer et al. (Munich: Prestel 2011), 41–42.

7   Post stations, spaced at regular intervals along the highways of premodern Japan, were villages managed by regional authorities to provide lodging and other services to traveling officials.

8   For an overview of the sites depicted in this series, see Melanie Trede, "Edo: Images of a City between Visual Poetry and Idealized Reality," in *Hiroshige*, ed. Trede and Bichler (Cologne: Taschen, 2008), 8–16.

9   Takahashi Seiichirō, "Meiji hanga to Yoshitoshi," in *Yoshitoshi no zenbōten*, ed. Segi Shin'ichi (Tokyo: Seibu Museum of Art, 1977). The blood was printed in combinations of safflower red (*Carthamus tinctorius L.*, *benihana*), vermilion (*shu*), and iron oxide (*bengara*). Shimoyama Susumu, "Tsukioka Yoshitoshi ga egaita hizan na chi no hyōgen," in *Tsukioka Yoshitoshi: botsugo 120-nen kinen*, ed. Ukiyo-e Ōta Memorial Museum (Tokyo: Ukiyo-e Ōta Memorial Museum of Art, 2012), 170–173.

10 The painting was once owned by Yoshitoshi's friend, the actor Ichikawa Danjūrō IX, and it inspired him to create a dance performance. It is now in the collection of Worcester Art Museum, Massachusetts.

11 According to the *Ukiyo-e daijiten*, more than eight hundred unique designs by fifty artists were produced by fifty or so publishers between 1860 and 1872. Around half of these were issued from 1860 to 1862.

12 Most figures are Europeans, with occasional glimpses of Chinese merchants and dark-skinned servants or slaves.

13 A possible source for these images is an engraving of the first hydrogen balloon voyage by Jacques Alexandre César Charles and Marie-Noël Robert in 1783.

14 After the show ended, Carlisle opened a dairy business and later assembled a company of Japanese acrobats that toured internationally as the Imperial Japanese Troupe. Frederik L. Schodt, *Professor Risley and the Imperial Japanese Troupe: How an American Acrobat Introduced Circus to Japan — and Japan to the West* (Berkeley: Stone Bridge Press, 2012), 113–143.

15 Julia Meech, *The World of the Meiji Print: Impressions of a New Civilization* (New York and Tokyo: Weatherhill, 1986), 114, 133–134.

16 Ibid., 118–119.

17 Ibid., 138–139.

18 With the opening of Japan to global markets in 1859, imported reds began to replace vegetable and mineral pigments: cochineal carmine from 1869, and the synthetic colorants eosin from 1877 and naphthol reds from 1889. See Anna Cesaratto et al., "A timeline for the introduction of synthetic dyestuffs in Japan during the late Edo and Meiji periods," *Heritage Science* 6:22 (2018). https://doi.org/10.1186/s40494-018-0187-0. Accessed December 30, 2021.

19 The "magic lantern" was a candlelit slide projector, imported by the Dutch in the eighteenth century and adapted for local use. Magic-lantern shows, in which a narrative sequence of images was projected onto a screen to a spoken and/or musical accompaniment, were popular for teaching and entertainment in Meiji Japan. Elaborate visual effects, including moving images, were possible by employing multiple devices and shadow puppets. The magic-lantern show was one of a series of public events organized by the theologian turned journalist Tanaka Chigaku to raise money for victims of the disaster. The slides Tanaka showed were derived from etchings based on the photographs of Tanaka's colleague Yoshihara Hideo. Ōkubo Ryō, "Bandaisan funka no shikakuka wo megutte 19 seikimatsu ni okeru eizō no ryūtsū," *Engeki eizō gaku* (2011), 10–13.

20 Kikugorō's play was based on the D'Arc family troupe's show in the summer of 1894. The date stamp of Meiji 24 (1893) in the margin of the print predates the D'Arc performance; given the singularity of the subject matter, a likely explanation for the disparity is that the publisher misdated the print.

21 Andreas Marks documented 939 designs produced by more than one hundred different publishers during the Sino-Japanese War, and about three hundred during the Russo-Japanese War. See Marks, "Meiji Period War Prints and Their Publishers," in *Conflicts of Interest: Art and War in Modern Japan*, ed. Philip K. Hu (Saint Louis: Saint Louis Art Museum, in association with University of Washington Press, 2016), 29–30, 32.

22 Kiyochika produced at least 181 battle-print designs for the Sino-Japanese War. Ibid., 26.

23 An impression of this design as it was first issued is in the collection of the Museum of Fine Arts, Boston, accession number RES.23.264-6. See Rhiannon Paget, entry for catalog #57, in *Conflicts of Interest: Art and War in Modern Japan*, ed. Philip K. Hu (Saint Louis: Saint Louis Art Museum, in association with University of Washington Press, 2016), 154.

PLATE LIST

A NOTE TO THE READER: Height precedes width in all dimensions, and measurements are for the size of the image. Reproductions of the works in the plates section of this volume include the original paper borders and edges; triptych panels have been placed together to illustrate each composition in full and reflect some of the uneven joinings in the artists' work.

KABUKI STARS

1

Torii Kiyoshige (active 1724–1764)
Somekawa Kozōshi and Ichikawa Danjūrō II as a Merchant Trying to Seduce a Young Girl, ca. 1720–1729
Woodcut with hand-coloring, metallic pigments, and "lacquer," 11⅛ × 5⅞ in. (28.3 × 14.9 cm)
Gift of Miss Carlotta Mabury
54755.24

2

Torii Kiyomasu II (1706–1763)
The Actors Matsushima Heitarō and Kamakura Chōkurō as Oiso no Tora and Meido no Kohachi, 1725
Woodcut with hand-coloring and metallic pigments, 13⅜ × 6¼ in. (33.9 × 15.9 cm)
Museum purchase, Achenbach Foundation for Graphic Arts Endowment Fund
1970.25.58

3

Utagawa Toyokuni (1769–1825)
The Actor Ichikawa Danjūrō VI as a Nobleman, from an untitled series of half-length portraits of actors, 1796
Color woodcut with mica, 12⁹⁄₁₆ × 10⅛ in. (31.9 × 25.7 cm)
Katherine Ball Collection
41.42.116

4

Utagawa Kunimasa I (ca. 1773–1810)
The Actor Nakamura Nakazō II as Matsuomaru in the "Carriage-Stopping" Scene in the Play "Sugawara's Secret" at the Miyako Theater, 1796
Color woodcut with hand-coloring, mica, and "lacquer," 15⁵⁄₁₆ × 10¼ in. (38.9 × 26 cm)
Museum purchase, Achenbach Foundation for Graphic Arts Endowment Fund
1970.25.52

5

Shunkōsai Hokushū (active 1808–1832)
The Actor Nakamura Utaemon III as Ishikawa Goemon, Disguised as the Farmer Gosaku, 1830
Color woodcut with metallic pigments, 15⅛ × 10¹⁄₁₆ in. (38.4 × 25.5 cm)
Museum purchase, Achenbach Foundation for Graphic Arts Endowment Fund
1978.1.10

6

Unidentified Edo artist (active mid-19th century)
Female Admirers Weeping before a Large Memorial Portrait of the Actor Ichikawa Danjūrō VIII, 1856
Color woodcut, 14¹⁵⁄₁₆ × 9¹⁵⁄₁₆ in. (37.9 × 25.3 cm)
Museum purchase, Achenbach Foundation for Graphic Arts Art Trust Fund
1984.1.87

BEAUTIES

7

Suzuki Harunobu (1725–1770)
The Descending Geese of the Koto Bridge, from the series *Eight Parlor Views*, 1766
Color woodcut, 11⅛ × 8⅜ in. (28.2 × 21.2 cm)
Museum purchase, Achenbach Foundation for Graphic Arts Endowment Fund
1970.25.31

8

Suzuki Harunobu (1725–1770)
Osen Playing with a Cat Held by a Visitor to Her Tea Shop, ca. 1768–1770
Color woodcut, 11⅛ × 8⅜ in. (28.2 × 21.3 cm)
Katherine Ball Collection
41.42.112

9

Isoda Koryūsai (active 1764–1788)
Night Rain, from the series *Eight Elegant Views
of Nagauta Performances*, ca. 1772–1776
Color woodcut, 10⅝ × 7½ in. (26.2 × 19 cm)
Gift of Miss Carlotta Mabury
54755.150

10

Isoda Koryūsai (active 1764–1788)
The Chrysanthemum Festival (Ninth Month),
from the series *Modern Amusements for the
Five Seasonal Festivals*, ca. 1775–1780
Color woodcut, 10¼ × 7⅞ in. (26.1 × 20 cm)
Gift of Miss Carlotta Mabury
54755.154

11

Kitagawa Utamaro (ca. 1754–1806)
Two Women with Fans beside a Stream, from
the series *The Six Elegant Tama Rivers*,
ca. 1802–1805
Color woodcut, 14⅛ × 9⁹⁄₁₆ in. (35.9 × 24.3 cm)
Gift of Miss Carlotta Mabury
54755.1077.6

12

Kitagawa Utamaro (ca. 1754–1806)
The Chiyozuru Teahouse–Orise, from an
untitled series of teahouses and waitresses,
ca. 1794–1795
Color woodcut, 15¹⁄₁₆ × 9¹⁵⁄₁₆ in. (38.1 × 25 cm)
Museum purchase, Achenbach Foundation
for Graphic Arts Endowment Fund
2010.11

13

**Kitagawa Tsukimaro (active ca. 1800–1818,
d. 1830)**
*The Courtesan Takao Entertaining the Actors
Sawamura Gennosuke and Iwai Kiyotarō at the
Miuraya*, ca. 1805
Color woodcut triptych, 15⅛ × 10⅜ in.
(38.4 × 26.4 cm)
Achenbach Foundation for Graphic Arts
1963.30.5648

14

Kitagawa Utamaro (ca. 1754–1806)
Wife of a Virtuous Man, from the series
Ten Beautiful Faces, ca. 1797–1800
Color woodcut, 13 × 8⅞ in. (33 × 22.5 cm)
Gift of Miss Carlotta Mabury
54755.201

15

Kitagawa Utamaro (ca. 1754–1806)
*Tama River at Mount Kōya (Courtesan
Smoking a Pipe)*, from an untitled series of the
six Tama rivers, ca. 1795–1796
Color woodcut with embossing, 14½ × 10 in.
(36.9 × 25.4 cm)
Katherine Ball Collection
41.42.117

16

Kitagawa Utamaro (ca. 1754–1806)
Woman Blowing a Pinwheel, from the series
Physiognomies of Ten Women, 1792–1793
Color woodcut, 14¾ × 10 in. (37.4 × 25.4 cm)
Achenbach Foundation for Graphic Arts
1963.30.5610

17

Kitagawa Utamaro (ca. 1754–1806)
A Woman of Character, from the series *Moral
Instruction Seen through a Parent's Eyes*,
ca. 1798–1802
Color woodcut, 15³⁄₁₆ × 10⅛ in. (38.5 × 25.7 cm)
Katherine Ball Collection
41.42.118

18

Utagawa Kuniyoshi (1798–1861)
Snowy Morning, from the series *Among Snow,
Moon, and Flowers*, one sheet from a triptych,
ca. 1847–1848
Color woodcut, 14⅞ × 10 in. (37.8 × 25.4 cm)
Achenbach Foundation for Graphic Arts
1963.30.5504

19

Kikukawa Eizan (1787–1867)
Yosooi of the Matsubaya, from the series *Three
Wine Cups in the New Yoshiwara*, ca. 1815–1825
Color woodcut, 14⅞ × 10¹⁄₁₆ in. (37.8 × 25.6 cm)
Gift of the Heisler Family in memory of
Ivan Heisler
1978.1.76

THE VIEW FROM EDO

20

Katsushika Hokusai (1760–1849)
Storm below the Mountain, from the series
Thirty-Six Views of Mount Fuji, ca. 1830–1832
Color woodcut, 10³⁄₁₆ × 14⅝ in. (25.9 × 37.1 cm)
Gift of Patricia Brown McNamara, Jane Brown
Dunaway, and Helen Brown Jarman in memory
of Mary Wattis Brown
64.47.17

21

Katsushika Hokusai (1760–1849)
Fuji in Clear Weather, from the series
Thirty-Six Views of Mount Fuji, ca. 1830–1832
Color woodcut, 9⅞ × 14½ in. (25.1 × 36.8 cm)
Gift of Miss Carlotta Mabury
54755.456

22

Utagawa Toyoharu (1735–1814)
*The Cool of the Evening near Ryōgoku Bridge in
Edo*, from the series *Perspective Pictures*,
ca. 1770–1780
Color woodcut, 10⁷⁄₁₆ × 15¼ in. (26.5 × 38.8 cm)
Gift of Miss Carlotta Mabury
54755.42

23

Katsushika Hokusai (1760–1849)
*Fuji from Onmaya Embankment with Sunset
over Ryōgoku Bridge*, from the series
Thirty-Six Views of Mount Fuji, ca. 1830–1832
Color woodcut, 10⅛ × 14¹³⁄₁₆ in. (25.7 × 37.7 cm)
Gift of Osgood Hooker
1959.124.22

24

Katsushika Hokusai (1760–1849)
Fuji from the Hongan Temple at Asakusa in Edo,
from the series *Thirty-Six Views of Mount Fuji*,
ca. 1830–1832
Color woodcut, 9¹³⁄₁₆ × 14 in. (24.9 × 35.6 cm)
Gift of Patricia Brown McNamara, Jane Brown
Dunaway, and Helen Brown Jarman in
memory of Mary Wattis Brown
64.47.16

25

Katsushika Hokusai (1760–1849)
*Under the Wave off Kanagawa (The Great
Wave)*, from the series *Thirty-Six Views of
Mount Fuji*, ca. 1830–1832
Color woodcut, 9¹³⁄₁₆ × 14½ in. (25 × 36.9 cm)
Museum purchase, Achenbach Foundation
for Graphic Arts Endowment Fund
1969.32.6

26

Katsushika Hokusai (1760–1849)
*Fuji from the Sazai Hall at the Temple of the
Five Hundred Rakan*, from the series
Thirty-Six Views of Mount Fuji, ca. 1830–1832
Color woodcut, 10³⁄₁₆ × 14¹³⁄₁₆ in.
(25.8 × 37.8 cm)
Gift of Patricia Brown McNamara, Jane Brown
Dunaway, and Helen Brown Jarman in
memory of Mary Wattis Brown
64.47.65

27

Utagawa Hiroshige (1797–1858)
*A Daimyō Procession Setting Forth from
Nihonbashi*, from the series *Fifty-Three
Stations of the Tōkaidō*, ca. 1831–1834
Color woodcut, 8¹¹⁄₁₆ × 13⁹⁄₁₆ in. (22 × 34.4 cm)
Achenbach Foundation for Graphic Arts
1963.30.5155

28

Utagawa Hiroshige (1797–1858)
*Cherry Blossoms at Night at Nakanochō in the
Yoshiwara*, from the series *Famous Places in
the Eastern Capital*, ca. 1834–1835
Color woodcut, 10⅛ × 14¹⁵⁄₁₆ in. (25.7 × 37.9 cm)
Gift of Patricia Brown McNamara, Jane Brown
Dunaway, and Helen Brown Jarman in
memory of Mary Wattis Brown
64.47.49

29

Utagawa Hiroshige (1797–1858)
Gion Shrine in the Snow, from the series
Famous Places in Kyoto, ca. 1834
Color woodcut, 9⁷⁄₁₆ × 14⁵⁄₁₆ in. (23.9 × 36.4 cm)
Gift of Miss Carlotta Mabury
54755.691

30

Utagawa Kuniyoshi (1798–1861)
*Pleasure Boat and Fireworks on the Sumida
River*, from the book *The Pillowed Boudoir*,
1839
Color woodcut, 7⅜ × 10⅜ in. (18.7 × 26.4 cm)
Museum purchase, Achenbach Foundation
for Graphic Arts Art Trust Fund
1984.1.91

31

Utagawa Hiroshige (1797–1858)
Night View of Saruwaka Street, from the series
One Hundred Views of Famous Places in Edo,
1856
Color woodcut, 14³⁄₁₆ × 9½ in. (36 × 24.2 cm)
Gift of Miss Carlotta Mabury
54755.766

32

Utagawa Hiroshige (1797–1858)
Kinryūzan Temple in Asakusa, from the series
One Hundred Views of Famous Places in Edo,
1856
Color woodcut with "lacquer" and embossing,
14³⁄₁₆ × 9½ in. (36 × 24.2 cm)
Gift of Miss Carlotta Mabury
54755.764

33

Utagawa Hiroshige (1797–1858)

Edo Bridge from Nihon Bridge, from the series
One Hundred Views of Famous Places in Edo,
1857
Color woodcut with mica and "lacquer,"
13¾ × 9⅛ in. (35 × 23.2 cm)
Museum purchase, Achenbach Foundation
for Graphic Arts Endowment Fund
1981.1.58

34

Utagawa Hiroshige (1797–1858)

Naitō, New Station at Yotsuya, from the series
One Hundred Views of Famous Places in Edo,
1857
Color woodcut, 14⅝ × 9¹⁵⁄₁₆ in. (37.1 × 25.3 cm)
Achenbach Foundation for Graphic Arts
1963.30.5152

35

Utagawa Hiroshige (1797–1858)

Evening Rain at Atake on the Great Bridge,
from the series *One Hundred Views of Famous
Places in Edo*, 1857
Color woodcut with mica, 14⅜ × 9⅝ in.
(33.7 × 22 cm)
Gift of Patricia Brown McNamara, Jane Brown
Dunaway, and Helen Brown Jarman in
memory of Mary Wattis Brown
64.47.53

36

Utagawa Hiroshige II (1826–1869)

Kintai Bridge at Iwakuni in Suō Province, from
the series *One Hundred Famous Places in the
Provinces*, 1859
Color woodcut with mica, 13¼ × 8¹³⁄₁₆ in.
(33.7× 22 cm)
Museum purchase, Achenbach Foundation
for Graphic Arts Art Trust Fund
1983.1.148

37

Utagawa Hiroshige (1797–1858)

No. 11 Hakone: Holding Pine Torches at Night,
from the series *Fifty-Three Stations of the
Tōkaidō*, ca. 1851–1852
Color woodcut, 8⁷⁄₁₆ × 13⅜ in. (21.4 × 34 cm)
Gift of Patricia Brown McNamara, Jane Brown
Dunaway, and Helen Brown Jarman in
memory of Mary Wattis Brown
64.47.91

WARRIORS, MYTHS, AND LEGENDS

38

Utagawa Hiroshige (1797–1858)

Act 11, Gathering before the Night Attack, from
the series *The Treasury of Loyal Retainers
(Chūshingura)*, ca. 1835–1836
Color woodcut, 9⁵⁄₁₆ × 14³⁄₁₆ in. (23.6 × 36 cm)
Gift of Patricia Brown McNamara, Jane Brown
Dunaway, and Helen Brown Jarman in
memory of Mary Wattis Brown
64.47.94

39

Utagawa Kunikiyo II (1850–1887)

Act 11, from the series *The Treasury of Loyal
Retainers (Chūshingura)*, 1857
Color woodcut with embossing,
9⁵⁄₁₆ × 13¹¹⁄₁₆ in. (23.6 × 34.7 cm)
Achenbach Foundation for Graphic Arts
1963.30.5535

40

Utagawa Kuniyoshi (1798–1861)

At the Bottom of the Sea in Daimotsu Bay,
ca. 1851–1852
Color woodcut triptych, 14⅛ × 30 in.
(35.9 × 76.2 cm)
Museum purchase, gift of the Achenbach
Graphic Arts Council
2008.52.1

41

**Utagawa Hiroshige (1797–1858) and
Utagawa Kunisada (1786–1864)**

The Plum Orchard, from the series *Elegant
Prince Genji*, 1853
Color woodcut triptych with embossing,
14⁷⁄₁₆ × 29¾ in. (36.6 × 75.6 cm)
Katherine Ball Collection
41.42.22a–c

**YOSHITOSHI: LAST OF THE
UKIYO-E MASTERS**

42

Tsukioka Yoshitoshi (1839–1892)

A Moonlight Scouting Patrol, from the series
One Hundred Aspects of the Moon, 1885
Color woodcut, 12¹⁵⁄₁₆ in. × 8⅞ in.
(32.9 × 22.5 cm)
Gift of Ronald E. Bornstein
1987.1.115

43

Tsukioka Yoshitoshi (1839–1892)

Sangoku the Monkey King and the Jade Rabbit,
from the series *One Hundred Aspects of the
Moon*, 1889
Color woodcut, 12¹⁵⁄₁₆ × 8¹³⁄₁₆ in.
(32.8 × 22.4 cm)
Museum purchase, Achenbach Foundation
for Graphic Arts Endowment Fund
1984.1.115

44

Tsukioka Yoshitoshi (1839–1892)

Black Monster Attacking a Carpenter's Wife,
from *The Postal News*, 1875
Color woodcut, 14½ × 10 in. (37 × 25 cm)
Museum purchase, Prints and Drawings
Art Trust Fund
2000.63.1

45
Tsukioka Yoshitoshi (1839–1892)
*Memories of Kikugorō (Memorial Portrait
of the Actor Onoe Kikugorō IV)*, 1860
Color woodcut diptych, 14 × 19½ in.
(35.5 × 49.5 cm)
Museum purchase, gift of the Achenbach
Graphic Arts Council
2002.13.2a–b

46
Tsukioka Yoshitoshi (1839–1892)
*Inada Kyūzō Shinsuke Murders the Kitchen
Maid Suspended from a Rope*, from the series
Twenty-Eight Famous Murders with Verse, 1867
Color woodcut, 13¾ × 9½ in. (34.9 × 24.1 cm)
Museum purchase, Achenbach Foundation
for Graphic Arts Endowment Fund
1986.1.86

47
Tsukioka Yoshitoshi (1839–1892)
*Ichigawa Danjurō IX as Musahibō Bankei
in "Kanjinchō,"* 1890
Color woodcut triptych, 14 × 28⅛ in.
(35.5 × 71.5 cm)
Museum purchase, Achenbach Foundation
for Graphic Arts Endowment Fund
1981.1.85a–c

48
Tsukioka Yoshitoshi (1839–1892)
*Fujiwara no Yasumasa Playing a Flute
by Moonlight*, 1883
Color woodcut triptych, 14¾ × 29⅛ in.
(37.5 × 74 cm)
Museum purchase, Achenbach Foundation
for Graphic Arts Endowment Fund
1982.1.32a–c

SIGHT UNSEEN: ARTISTS ENCOUNTER THE WEST AND WESTERNERS

49
Tsukioka Yoshitoshi (1839–1892)
Chronicle of the Imperial Restoration, 1876
Color woodcut, 9¼ × 13⁹⁄₁₆ in. (23.5 × 34.5 cm)
Museum purchase, William and Martha
Steen Fund
1999.119

50
Utagawa Sadahide (1807–1873)
*Parade of People from Five Countries (United
States, Great Britain, France, Russia, Holland)*,
1861
Color woodcut triptych, 14¹⁵⁄₁₆ × 29⅛ in.
(36.4 × 740 cm)
Museum purchase, Achenbach Foundation
for Graphic Arts Endowment Fund
1979.1.37a–c

51
Utagawa Kuniyoshi (1798–1861)
Min Ziqian (Ben Shiken), from the series
24 Paragons of Filial Piety, 1847–1848
Color woodcut, 9⁵⁄₁₆ × 5¹³⁄₁₆ (23.7 × 14.8 cm)
Museum purchase, Achenbach Foundation
for Graphic Arts Endowment Fund
1986.1.87

52
Utagawa Hiroshige II (1826–1869)
Holland America England, 1860
Color woodcut, 14³⁄₁₆ × 9⅝ in. (36 × 24.4 cm)
Gift of Mr. and Mrs. R.E. Lewis in memory
of Lewis MacRitchie
1972.66

53
Utagawa Yoshitora (active 1850–1880)
Americans, from the series *A Collection of
Various Countries*, 1860
Color woodcut, 14⅜ × 9¹³⁄₁₆ in. (36.5 × 25 cm)
Museum purchase, Achenbach Foundation
for Graphic Arts Endowment Fund
1968.13.21

54
Utagawa Yoshikazu (active 1850–1870)
Banquet and Musicale in a Foreigner's Home,
1860
Color woodcut triptych, 14½ × 28¹⁵⁄₁₆ in.
(36.9 × 73.5 cm)
Museum purchase, Achenbach Foundation
for Graphic Arts Endowment Fund
1969.32.27

55
Utagawa Yoshiiku (1853–1904)
An Englishman and a Russian Woman, 1860
Color woodcut, 14 × 9¹³⁄₁₆ in. (35.5 × 25 cm)
Museum purchase, Achenbach Foundation
for Graphic Arts Endowment Fund
1987.1.111

56
Utagawa Yoshikazu (active 1850–1870)
Interior of an American Steamship, 1861
Color woodcut triptych, 14⅝ × 29¾in.
(37.2 × 75.4 cm)
Museum purchase, Achenbach Foundation
for Graphic Arts Endowment Fund
1968.13.22

57
Utagawa Yoshitora (active 1850–1880)
Balloon Ascension in America, 1865
Color woodcut triptych, 14⅛ × 28⁹⁄₁₆ in.
(35.9 × 72.5 cm)
Achenbach Foundation for Graphic Arts
1963.30.5661

58

Utagawa Yoshitora (active 1850–1880)
Balloons in Flight in the United States of North America, from the series *People of Foreign Lands*, 1861
Color woodcut, 8⅝ × 6¾ in. (20.8 × 15.7 cm)
Achenbach Foundation for Graphic Arts
1963.30.5621

59

Utagawa Yoshitora (active 1850–1880)
The Country of America, 1867
Color woodcut triptych, 14⅜ × 28⅜ in.
(36.5 × 72.1 cm)
Museum purchase, Achenbach Foundation
for Graphic Arts Endowment Fund
1969.32.28

60

Utagawa Yoshitora (active 1850–1880)
Acrobats from Central India Performing at Yokohama, 1864
Color woodcut, 14⅜ × 9¾ in. (36.5 × 24.7 cm)
Gift of John Gutmann
1986.1.207

61

Utagawa Yoshitora (active 1850–1880)
Acrobats from Central India Performing at Yokohama, 1864
Color woodcut, 14¼ × 9¹¹⁄₁₆ in. (36.2 × 24.6 cm)
Gift of John Gutmann
1986.1.209

AN UNSETTLED TRANSITION

62

Tsukioka Yoshitoshi (1839–1892)
Battle of the Sannō Shrine, 1874
Color woodcut triptych, 13⅝ × 27⅜ in.
(34.8 × 69.4 cm)
Museum purchase, Achenbach Foundation
for Graphic Arts Endowment Fund
1987.1.101a–c

63

Tsukioka Yoshitoshi (1839–1892)
The Eastern Wind Clears Away the Clouds in the South West, 1878
Color woodcut triptych, 13⅝ × 28¼ in.
(34.61 × 71.76 cm)
Gift of William Eddelman
2022.13a–c

64

Yōshū Chikanobu (1838–1912)
The Women's Brigade of the Kagoshima Rebels in Brave Battle, 1877
Color woodcut triptych, 14⅛ × 28¹⁵⁄₁₆ in.
(35.9 × 73.5 cm)
Achenbach Foundation for Graphic Arts
1963.30.5039

THE EMPEROR SETS THE STYLE

65

Yōshū Chikanobu (1838–1912)
Imperial Party Visits the Park at Asuka, 1888
Color woodcut triptych, 14⅝ × 28⅝ in.
(37 × 72.8 cm)
Museum purchase, Achenbach Foundation
for Graphic Arts Endowment Fund
1987.1.43a–c

66

Yōshū Chikanobu (1838–1912)
Plum Trees in Full Bloom, the Meiji Emperor, Empress, and Women of Nobility, 1888
Color woodcut triptych, 14 × 27⁹⁄₁₆ in.
(35.5 × 70 cm)
Museum purchase, Achenbach Foundation
for Graphic Arts Endowment Fund
1984.1.51

67

Yōshū Chikanobu (1838–1912)
The Meiji Emperor and His Officers Reviewing the Troops, 1887
Color woodcut triptych, 14³⁄₁₆ × 28¹¹⁄₁₆ in.
(36.1 × 72.8 cm)
Achenbach Foundation for Graphic Arts
1963.30.5690

68

Yōshū Chikanobu (1838–1912)
A Military Parade at Aoyama, 1887
Color woodcut triptych, 14³⁄₁₆ × 28⅞ in.
(36 × 72.2 cm)
Achenbach Foundation for Graphic Arts
1963.30.5691a–c

FEATURING WESTERN WAYS

69

Yōshū Chikanobu (1838–1912)
The Hall of Machinery at the Exhibition for the Promotion of Domestic Industry, 1877
Color woodcut triptych, 14³⁄₁₆ × 28¹³⁄₁₆ in.
(37 × 74 cm)
Achenbach Foundation for Graphic Arts
1963.30.5038a–c

70

Kobayashi Kiyochika (1847–1915)
The Journalist Fukuchi Gen'ichirō, from the series *Instruction in the Fundamentals of Success*, 1885
Color woodcut, 14³⁄₁₆ × 9⁹⁄₁₆ in. (36.1 × 24.3 cm)
Achenbach Foundation for Graphic Arts
1963.30.5310

71
Tsukioka Yoshitoshi (1839–1892)
*The Appearance of an Upper-Class Wife of the
Meiji Era*, from the series *Thirty-Two Customs
and Manners*, 1888
Color woodcut, 14¹⁄₁₆ × 9⁷⁄₁₆ in. (35.7 × 24 cm)
Museum purchase, Achenbach Foundation
for Graphic Arts Endowment Fund and gift in
memory of Michael Kent Sandgren from his
friends and colleagues
1996.43

72
Toyohara Kunichika (1835–1900)
Song Composed by the Empress, 1887
Color woodcut triptych, 14½ × 19³⁄₁₆ in.
(36.8 × 48.8 cm)
Gift of Roger Keyes in memory of Keiko
Mizushima Keyes
1991.1.236

73
Toyohara Kunichika (1835–1900)
A Depiction of Mount Asama through Sounds,
1888
Color woodcut triptych, 15½ × 28⅜ in.
(39.5 × 71.9 cm)
Gift of William Eddelman
2020.67.8a–c

74
Utagawa Kunisada III (1848–1920)
*Marionettes Imitating the Sound of a Bell
Playing at Ichimura Theater*, 1893
Color woodcut triptych, 14⅞ × 28⅞ in.
(37.7 × 73.3 cm)
Museum purchase, Achenbach Foundation
for Graphic Arts Endowment Fund
1996.42a–c

A LANDSCAPE TRANSFORMED: TOKYO AND BEYOND

75
Shōsai Ikkei (active 1870s)
Steam Train at Takanawa in Tokyo, ca. 1872
Color woodcut triptych, 14¼ × 29 in.
(36.2 × 73.4 cm)
Museum purchase, Achenbach Foundation
for Graphic Arts Endowment Fund
1968.13.24

76
Utagawa Hiroshige III (1843–1894)
Steam Train at Yatsunoyama in Tokyo, ca. 1875
Color woodcut triptych, 14 × 28 in.
(35.6 × 71.4 cm)
Museum purchase, Achenbach Foundation
for Graphic Arts Endowment Fund
1968.13.25

77
Utagawa Hiroshige III (1843–1894)
Railroad Along the Coast of Yokohama, 1874
Color woodcut triptych, 13¹⁵⁄₁₆ × 28¼ in.
(35.4 × 71.8 cm)
Museum purchase, Achenbach Foundation
for Graphic Arts Endowment Fund
1969.32.25

78
Utagawa Hiroshige III (1843–1894)
*View of Tokyo with a Picture of the Railroad
at Takanawa*, ca. 1875
Color woodcut triptych, 13¾ × 28¼ in.
(35 × 71.8 cm)
Museum purchase, Achenbach Foundation
for Graphic Arts Endowment Fund
1969.32.23

79
Utagawa Kunitoshi (active 1860–1890)
*The National Diet Building of the Empire of
Great Japan*, 1889
Color woodcut triptych, 14⅜ × 28¼ in.
(36.5 × 71.5 cm)
Achenbach Foundation for Graphic Arts
1963.30.5657

80
Utagawa Hiroshige III (1843–1894)
Yanagi Bridge from Asakusa Bridge, from the
series *Thirty-Six Views of Modern Tokyo*, 1874
Color woodcut triptych, 6½ × 8¹³⁄₁₆ in.
(16.5 × 22 cm)
Achenbach Foundation for Graphic Arts
1963.30.5139

81
Utagawa Hiroshige III (1843–1894)
Night View of the Railroad at Yatsuyama, from
the series *Thirty-Six Views of Modern Tokyo*,
1874
Color woodcut, 6⅜ × 8¹³⁄₁₆ in. (16.2 × 22 cm)
Achenbach Foundation for Graphic Arts
1963.30.5142

82
Kobayashi Kiyochika (1847–1915)
Fireworks at Ryōgoku, 1880
Color woodcut, 8¹⁄₁₆ × 12⅝ in. (20.5 × 32.1 cm)
Museum purchase, Achenbach Foundation for
Graphic Arts Endowment Fund
1969.32.59

83
Kobayashi Kiyochika (1847–1915)
Hazy Moon at Ushimachi, Takanawa, 1879
Color woodcut, 8⅞ × 13⅛ in. (22.5 × 33.3 cm)
Museum purchase, Achenbach Foundation
for Graphic Arts Endowment Fund
1988.1.33

WAR AND PROPAGANDA

84

Yōshū Chikanobu (1838–1912)

An Enemy Troop Train Falling through the Ice of Lake Baikal, from *Telegraphed Reports of the Russo-Japanese War*, 1904
Color woodcut triptych, 14³⁄₁₆ × 28⁹⁄₁₆ in. (36 × 72.5 cm)
Achenbach Foundation for Graphic Arts
1963.30.5655

85

Migita Toshihide (1863–1925)

Japanese Sailor Leaps on Onboard a Russian Warship and Kicks Its Captain Overboard, from *Records of the Russo-Japanese War*, 1904
Color woodcut triptych, 14³⁄₁₆ × 28¼ in. (36.1 × 71.8 cm)
Achenbach Foundation for Graphic Arts
1963.30.5662

86

Kobayashi Kiyochika (1847–1915)

A Torpedo Hitting a Russian Warship at Port Arthur, February 1904, 1904
Color woodcut triptych, 14 × 27½ in. (35.6 × 70 cm)
Achenbach Foundation for Graphic Arts
1963.30.5659

87

Kobayashi Kiyochika (1847–1915)

Our Elite Forces Occupying the Pescadores Islands of Taiwan, 1894
Color woodcut triptych, 14⅝ × 28¾ in. (37 × 73 cm)
Museum purchase, Achenbach Foundation for Graphic Arts Art Trust Fund
1984.1.85

88

Utagawa Kokunimasa (1874–1944)

Red Cross Field Hospital of Great Japan Treating the Wounded during the Russo-Japanese War, with inset vignette *Barbarian Russian Soldiers*, 1904
Color woodcut triptych, 28⅝ × 14⅝ in. (37 × 72.8 cm)
Achenbach Foundation for Graphic Arts
1963.30.5716

MASAMI TERAOKA: UKIYO-E POP

89

Masami Teraoka (American, b. Japan 1936)

Tattooed Woman and Geisha III, from the series *McDonald's Hamburgers Invading Japan*, 2018
Color woodcut, 12¼ × 18½ in. (31.1 × 47 cm)
Museum purchase, gift of the Achenbach Graphic Arts Council
2021.74

90

Masami Teraoka (American, b. Japan 1936)

Chochin-Me, from the series *McDonald's Hamburgers Invading Japan*, 1982
Color screenprint, 21⁵⁄₁₆ × 14⁵⁄₁₆ in. (54.1 × 36.4 cm)
Museum purchase, Martha and William Steen Fund and Achenbach Foundation for Graphic Arts Endowment Fund
1989.1.82

91

Masami Teraoka (American, b. Japan 1936)

Geisha with Ice-Cream Cone (Cherry), from the series *31 Flavors Invading Japan*, 1977
Relief print and watercolor (hand coloring), mounted on a scroll, 10¹³⁄₁₆ × 7⅜ in. (27.4 × 18.7 cm)
Museum purchase, Hamilton-Wells Fund
1977.1.344

92

Masami Teraoka (American, b. Japan 1936)

Today's Special, from the series *31 Flavors Invading Japan*, 1977
Color woodcut, 10⅜ × 15¾ in. (26.4 × 40 cm)
Gift of Edward Den Lau
1996.92.3

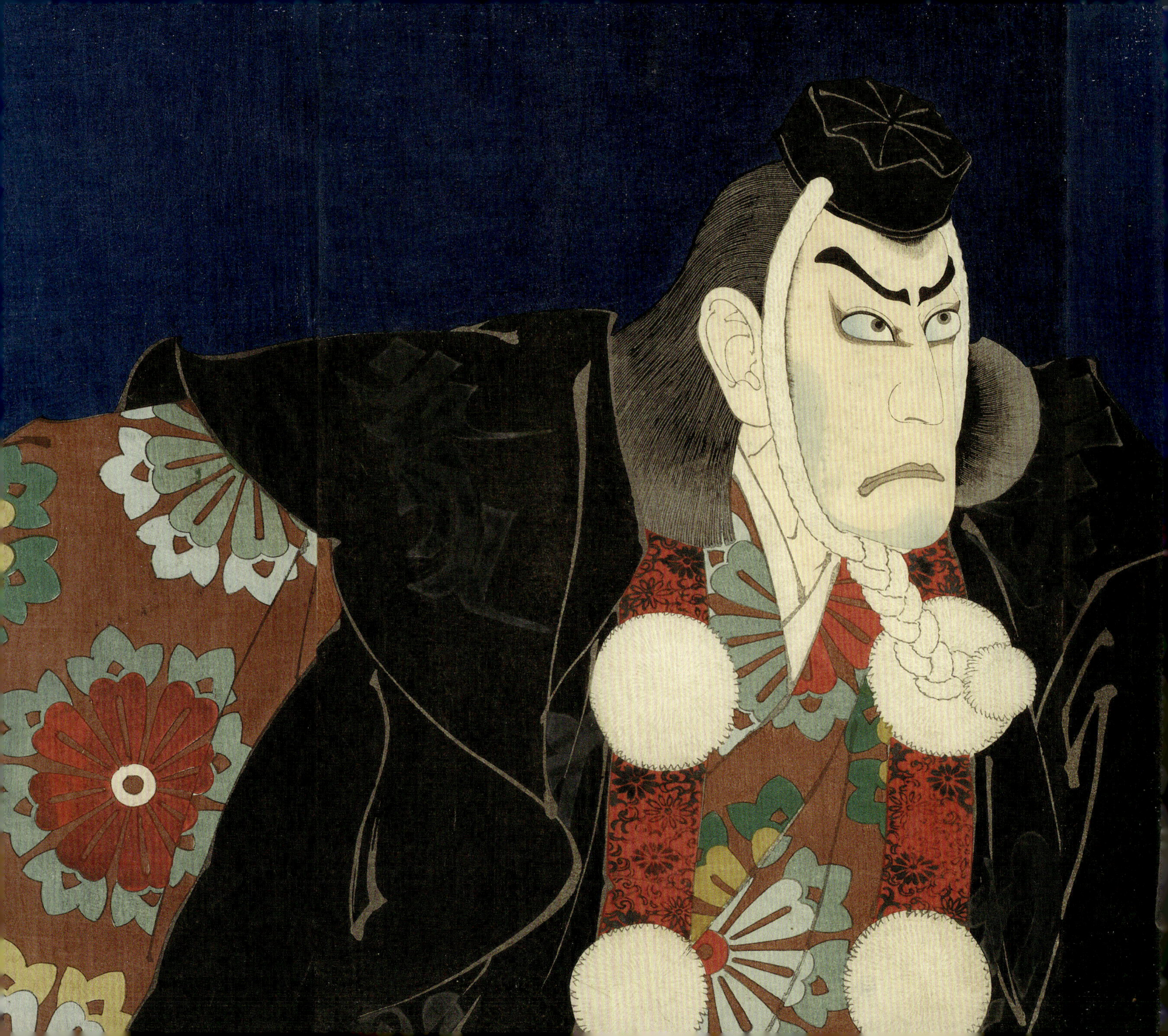

ACKNOWLEDGMENTS

It is a pleasure to acknowledge the many individuals who generously contributed their time and assistance to make the preparation of this endeavor a memorable and enjoyable experience. First among these is Rhiannon Paget, curator of Asian art at the John and Mable Ringling Museum of Art, for contributing an engaging essay that masterfully covers the history of Japanese prints as exemplified by the selections in this volume. A similar debt of thanks is owed to Victoria Binder, head of paper conservation, and her talented staff: Allison Brewer, assistant paper conservator, and Tamia Anaya, Andrew W. Mellon Fellow in Paper Conservation.

I also thank Amy Andersson, museum registrar, whose early organization of the evolving checklist carried this project through its many stages of development. Assistant registrar Egle Mendoza ably tracked the locations of the Japanese prints over many months of project planning. I particularly thank Anna Wu, the Achenbach's curatorial projects coordinator, who proved invaluable in discovering and keeping track of changes to the checklist. Her enthusiasm for the subject infused her myriad contributions, which included extensive research and writing informative labels and didactics.

Leslie Dutcher, director of publications, oversaw every aspect of this volume's production. Her professionalism and leadership in managing the concept and overall conceptualization of this book is especially appreciated. I thank Lesley Bruynesteyn, the book's editor and project manager, for her thoughtful review of this volume, and José Jovel, publications associate, who organized the book's many images. Under the guidance of Sue Grinols, director of photo services and imaging, Randy Dodson, head photographer, created fresh photography, with help from photographer Jorge Bachmann. I am grateful to Abigail Dansiger, former head of library and archives, for adding new titles on the subject of Japanese prints to our library. This beautiful volume was designed by Leslie Dutcher and Matt Mayerchak, with prepress work created by Tony Manzella at Echelon. The fine printing was done by Conti Tipocolor, under the guidance of Marta Conti, Roberto Conti, Laura Cuccoli, and Alfredo Zanellato. I thank Cameron and Company, especially Chris Gruener and Jan Hughes, for their partnership and their work to distribute this title in the trade.

This project was originally endorsed by Thomas P. Campbell, our director and CEO, who has been a tremendous support in its creation. I am further grateful to our Board of Trustees, led by Jason Moment, president, and Diane B. Wilsey, chair emerita, along with Jason Seifer, chief financial officer; Megan Bourne, chief of staff; Krista Brugnara, chief exhibitions and collections officer; and Melissa E. Buron, director of curatorial affairs, for their advocacy. I extend thanks to Linda Butler, director of marketing, communications, and visitor experience, and her talented staff, including Helena Nordstrom, director of communications, and her team; Sheila Pressley, director of education, as well as her team, including Emily Jennings, director of school and family programs; Amanda Riley, former director of development, and her staff; and Stuart Hata, director of retail operations, and Tim Niedert, book and media manager.

Finally, I thank the project's sponsors who provided generous financial support, including significant support from Carrick and Andy McLaughlin and generous support from Paul A. Violich, with additional support from Alexandria and Dwight Ashdown and Sandra and Paul Bessières.

KARIN BREUER
Curator in Charge
Achenbach Foundation for Graphic Arts

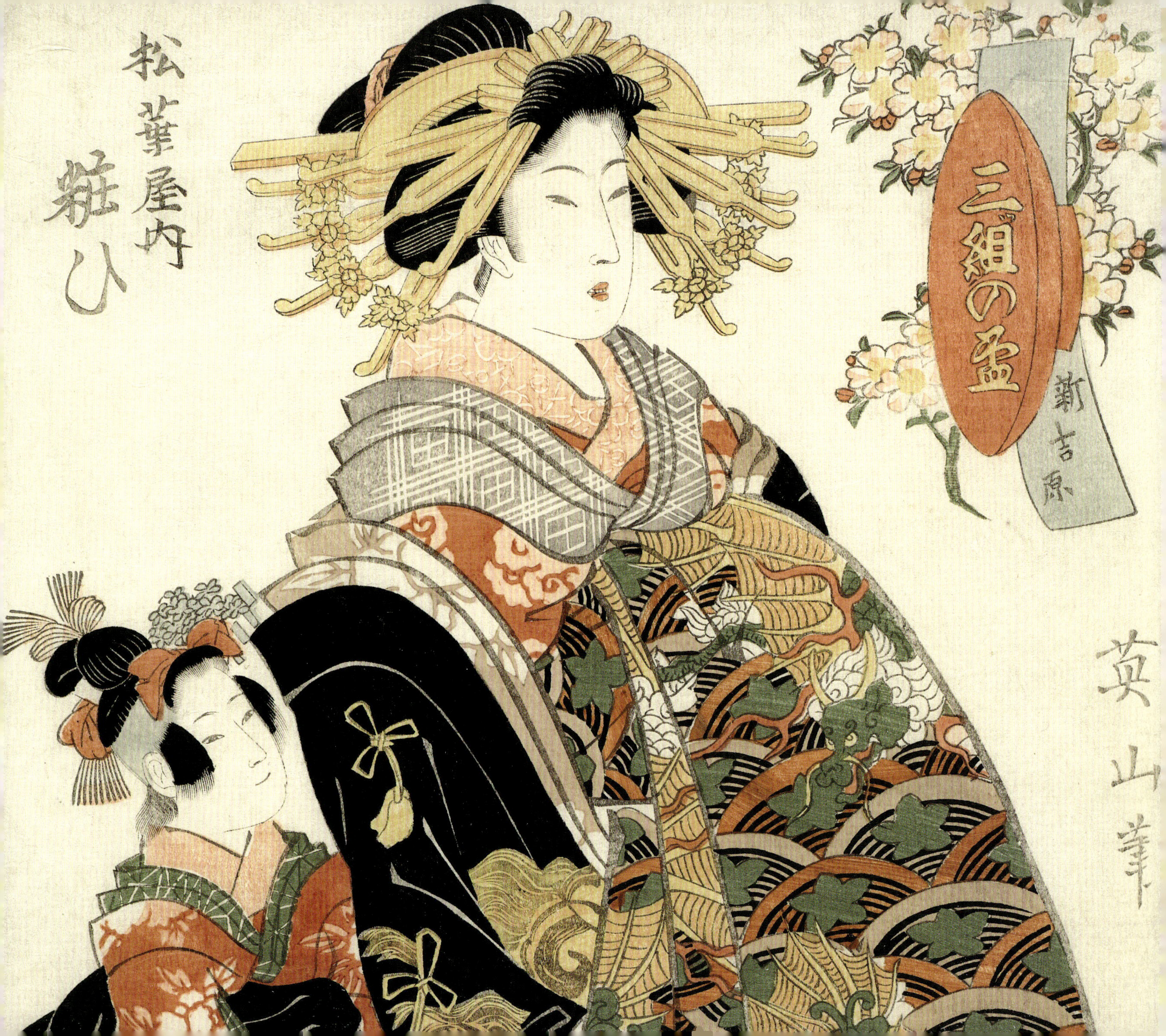
松葉屋内
粧ひ
三組の盃
新吉原
英山筆

PICTURE CREDITS

FIGURE ILLUSTRATIONS

1: Courtesy of the Minneapolis Institute of Art. 2: Courtesy of the Art Institute of Chicago. 3: Photograph copyright © Museum of Fine Arts, Boston. 4: Image copyright © Fine Arts Museums of San Francisco. Photograph by Jorge Bachmann. 5: Image copyright © Fine Arts Museums of San Francisco. Photograph by Randy Dodson. 6: Image copyright © Fine Arts Museums of San Francisco. Photograph by Joseph McDonald. 7: Courtesy of the Lincoln Financial Foundation Collection via archive.org. 8: Courtesy of the John and Mable Ringling Museum of Art, Sarasota, Florida. 9: Copyright © The Metropolitan Museum of Art, New York. Image source: Art Resource, NY. 10: Courtesy of the Smithsonian Institution, Washington, DC. 11: Courtesy of the Saint Louis Art Museum

PLATE ILLUSTRATIONS

1, 6, 19, 21, 22, 23, 24, 27, 28, 38, 39, 42, 43, 44, 45, 46, 47, 48, 49, 50, 51, 52, 53, 54, 55, 56, 57, 58, 61, 62, 64, 65, 66, 67, 69, 70, 71, 72, 74, 75, 76, 77, 78, 79, 80, 81, 82, 83, 84, 85, 86, 87: Image copyright © Fine Arts Museums of San Francisco. Photograph by Randy Dodson. 3, 4, 5, 7, 8, 9, 10, 11, 12, 13, 14, 15, 16, 17, 18, 20, 25, 26, 29, 30, 31, 32, 33, 34, 35, 36, 37, 40, 41: Image copyright © Fine Arts Museums of San Francisco. Photograph by Joseph McDonald. 2, 59, 60, 63, 68, 73, 88: Image copyright © Fine Arts Museums of San Francisco. Photograph by Jorge Bachmann. 89, 90, 91: Courtesy of the artist and Catharine Clark Gallery, San Francisco. Image copyright © Fine Arts Museums of San Francisco. Photograph by Randy Dodson. 92: Courtesy of the artist and Catharine Clark Gallery, San Francisco. Image copyright © Fine Arts Museums of San Francisco. Photograph by Jorge Bachmann

DECORATIVE ILLUSTRATIONS

Frontispiece: detail of Utagawa Hiroshige (1797–1858), *Evening Rain at Atake on the Great Bridge*, from the series *One Hundred Views of Famous Places in Edo*, 1857 (pl. 35). Table of contents: detail of Yōshū Chikanobu (1838–1912), *The Hall of Machinery at the Exhibition for the Promotion of Domestic Industry*, 1877 (pl. 69). Essay frontispiece: detail of Utagawa Hiroshige (1797–1858), *Night View of Saruwaka Street*, from the series *One Hundred Views of Famous Places in Edo*, 1856 (pl. 31). pp. 18–19: detail of Shunkōsai Hokushū (active 1808–1832), *The Actor Nakamura Utaemon III as Ishikawa Goemon, Disguised as the Farmer Gosaku*, 1830 (pl. 5). pp. 26–27: detail of Kitagawa Tsukimaro (active ca. 1800–1818, d. 1830), *The Courtesan Takao Entertaining the Actors Sawamura Gennosuke and Iwai Kiyotarō at the Miuraya*, ca. 1805 (pl. 13). pp. 42–43: detail of Katsushika Hokusai (1760–1849), *Fuji from the Sazai Hall at the Temple of the Five Hundred Rakan*, from the series *Thirty-Six Views of Mount Fuji*, ca. 1830–1832 (pl. 26). pp. 66–67: detail of Utagawa Kuniyoshi (1798–1861), *At the Bottom of the Sea in Daimotsu Bay*, ca. 1851–1852 (pl. 40). pp. 72–73: detail of Tsukioka Yoshitoshi (1839–1892), *Fujiwara no Yasumasa Playing a Flute by Moonlight*, 1883 (pl. 48). pp. 82–83: detail of Tsukioka Yoshitoshi (1839–1892), *Chronicle of the Imperial Restoration*, 1876 (pl. 49). pp. 98–99: detail of Yōshū Chikanobu (1838–1912), *The Women's Brigade of the Kagoshima Rebels in Brave Battle*, 1877 (pl. 64). pp. 104–105: detail of Yōshū Chikanobu (1838–1912), *Imperial Party Visits the Park at Asuka*, 1888 (pl. 65). pp. 110–111: detail of Toyohara Kunichika (1835–1900), *Song Composed by the Empress*, 1887 (pl. 72). pp. 118–119: detail of Utagawa Hiroshige III (1843–1894), *View of Tokyo with a Picture of the Railroad at Takanawa*, ca. 1875 (pl. 78). pp. 130–131: detail of Kobayashi Kiyochika (1847–1915), *Our Elite Forces Occupying the Pescadores Islands of Taiwan*, 1894 (pl. 87). pp. 138–139: detail of Masami Teraoka (American, b. Japan 1936), *Today's Special*, from the series *31 Flavors Invading Japan*, 1977 (pl. 92). p. 154: detail of Tsukioka Yoshitoshi (1839–1892), *Ichigawa Danjurō IX as Musahibō Bankei in "Kanjinchō,"* 1890 (pl. 47). p. 156: detail of Kikukawa Eizan (1787–1867), *Yosooi of the Matsubaya*, from the series *Three Wine Cups in the New Yoshiwara*, ca. 1815–1825 (pl. 19)

JAPANESE PRINTS IN TRANSITION
From the Floating World to the Modern World

This catalogue is published by the Fine Arts Museums of San Francisco to document and celebrate the Japanese prints collection at the Achenbach Foundation for Graphic Arts.

The project is organized by the Fine Arts Museums of San Francisco and made possible by our donors.

SIGNIFICANT SUPPORT

Carrick and Andy McLaughlin

GENEROUS SUPPORT

Paul A. Violich

Additional support is provided by Alexandria and Dwight Ashdown and Sandra and Paul Bessières

Library of Congress control number: 2022937128
ISBN: 978-1-951836-98-6

Cover illustration: detail of Yōshū Chikanobu (1838–1912), *Plum Trees in Full Bloom, the Meiji Emperor, Empress, and Women of Nobility*, 1888 (pl. 66). Image copyright © Fine Arts Museums of San Francisco. Photograph by Randy Dodson

Jacket illustration: detail of Utagawa Hiroshige (1797–1858) and Utagawa Kunisada (1786–1864), *The Plum Orchard*, from the series *Elegant Prince Genji*, 1853 (pl. 41). Image copyright © Fine Arts Museums of San Francisco. Photograph by Joseph McDonald

**de Young **
\\ Legion of Honor
fine arts museums of san francisco

Fine Arts Museums of San Francisco
de Young, Golden Gate Park
50 Hagiwara Tea Garden Drive
San Francisco, CA 94118-4502
www.famsf.org

Leslie Dutcher, director of publications
Trina Enriquez, senior editor
Victoria Gannon, senior editor
Lesley Bruynesteyn, editor
José Jovel, publications associate

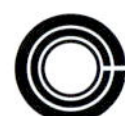

CAMERON + COMPANY
a division of ABRAMS
149 Kentucky Street, Suite 7
Petaluma, CA 94952
www.cameronbooks.com

Project management and editing by Lesley Bruynesteyn
Proofread by Trina Enriquez and Victoria Gannon
Picture research by José Jovel
Designed by Leslie Dutcher and Matt Mayerchak
Color separations by Tony Manzella, Echelon, LA
Printing and binding by Conti Tipocolor, Italy